Death Watch: A Death Penalty Anthology

DISCARD

Lane Nelson

Burk Foster

Prentice
Hall

Upper Saddle River, New Jersey 07458

Library of Congress Cataloging-in-Publication Data

Library of Congress Cataloging-in-Publication Data
Nelson, Lane.
   Death watch : a death penalty anthology / Lane Nelson ; Burk Foster.
     p. cm.
   Includes bibliographical references and index.
   ISBN 0-13-085201-5
   1. Capital punishment—United States. 2. Death row inmates—United States. 3. Death
row—United States. I. Foster, Burk. II. Title.

HV8699.U5 N45 2000
364.66′0973—dc21   00-040083

Publisher: Dave Garza
Senior Acquisitions Editor: Kim Davies
Assistant Editor: Marion Gottlieb
Managing Editor: Mary Carnis
Production Editor: Cindy Miller
Interior Design: Clarinda Publication Services
Production Liaison: Adele M. Kupchik
Director of Manufacturing and Production: Bruce Johnson
Manufacturing Buyer: Ed O'Dougherty/Cathleen Petersen
Creative Director: Marianne Frasco
Cover Design Coordinator: Miguel Ortiz
Editorial Assistant: Lisa Schwartz
Marketing Manager: Chris Ruel
Marketing Assistant: Joe Toohey
Marketing Coordinator: Adam Kloza
Printer/Binder: R.R. Donnelley and Sons, Inc.
Cover Design: Marianne Frasco
Cover Illustration: Kevin Seward
Cover Printer: Phoenix Color

Prentice-Hall International (UK) Limited, *London*
Prentice-Hall of Australia Pty. Limited, *Sydney*
Prentice-Hall Canada Inc., *Toronto*
Prentice-Hall Hispanoamericana, S.A., *Mexico*
Prentice-Hall of India Private Limited, *New Delhi*
Prentice-Hall of Japan, Inc., *Tokyo*
Prentice-Hall Singapore Pte. Ltd.
Editora Prentice-Hall do Brasil, Ltda., *Rio de Janeiro*

C10 9 8 7 6 5 4 3 2 1
ISBN 0-13-085201-5

Contents

Acknowledgments

This book grew out of two different perspectives on the death penalty—one the perspective of a man who has lived the experience of death row, the other the perspective of a university professor who teaches capital punishment as a legal and public policy issue. Lane Nelson, a former death row inmate whose conviction and sentence for robbery and murder were later modified by an appellate court that determined he possessed no intent to kill the victim, worked as a prison paralegal on death row for four years. In 1993 he became a staff writer for *The Angolite,* the newsmagazine of the Louisiana State Prison at Angola. His "Death Watch" columns feature inmates sentenced to death and issues related to capital punishment.

Burk Foster, a former police officer and long-time criminal justice professor at the University of Louisiana at Lafayette (which was until last year the University of Southwestern Louisiana), teaches a senior-level college course on the death penalty and works across Louisiana as a consultant to criminal defense attorneys in capital cases. He has worked with inmates and staff at Angola for more than 20 years.

In 1997, at a day-long spiritual gathering of death row inmates, their families, and attorneys, Nelson and Foster first discussed collecting enough of their shorter articles on the death penalty to produce a book. Two years later, after much editing and rewriting, and with the addition of several new articles, including five articles by other writers—two by death row inmates and three by outsiders—here it is.

The authors would like to thank the reviewers of this text for their helpful comments: Charles Crawford, Western Michigan University; William E. Kelly, Auburn University; and James E. Newman, Rio Hondo Community College.

Lane Nelson and Burk Foster

The following articles were possible only through the sufferings of the condemned men and women this book is about. I hope their anguish and pain not in vain, and that the book will help educate everyone about the truths and fallacies of capital punishment.

The people I should thank are many and, because I don't want to accidentally omit someone, I won't list their names. There have been at least 100 during my 18 years in prison, of all backgrounds and opinions, who have contributed to the way I think, see, and feel. While most have sprinted through my life, others have pulled up a chair and stayed. I thank them all, especially my "big sister," who crossed my path a few years ago, chair in hand.

Lane Nelson

Many people have helped me learn about the application of the death penalty in America, both historically and currently. I would like to acknowledge the support of these people who directly contributed to the work contained in this book:

> Warden Burl Cain of the Louisiana State Penitentiary at Angola, the publisher of *The Angolite* magazine in which most of the articles in this book originally appeared; I would like to thank Warden Cain for his permission to reprint these articles, and I would like to acknowledge his support and the assistance of Cathy Jett, Angola's Director of Classification, throughout this project.

> Father Wayne Richard

> Linda Anson, for her research help in documenting executions for rape in Louisiana

> Mary Ann Baker and Mariette Hebert, especially for their research on the "Toni Jo" Henry case

> Rajko Jelen, for his research on recent executions in Louisiana

> Professor Clifford Dorne, of Saginaw Valley State University

> Kathy Lynn Cook

> The staff of *The Angolite* magazine of the Louisiana State Penitentiary, with which I have been associated since 1987, including editor Wilbert Rideau and writers Douglas Dennis, Kerry Myers, and Clarence Goodlow. I would also like to mention the work of the following *Angolite* writers who have died since I began working with the magazine: Ron Wikberg, Michael Glover, Keith Elliott, and Tommy Mason

> Professor Craig Forsyth

> Watt Espy, execution archivist *extraordinaire*

> Leslie D. Schilling, of UL-Lafayette's Humanities Resource Center, for her expert computer assistance

> Victor L. Streib, for his work in preparing the foreward to this volume, and for his continuing research that is frequently cited here.

> Juliet, wherever she may be.

I would also like to acknowledge the support of advocates for life on both sides of this controversial issue. To be against the death penalty does not mean that you are in favor of murder; to express concern for victims of violent crime does not mean that you are in favor of killing criminals in return. I pray that all of us—victims and offenders—can move toward reconciliation.

Finally, I would like to thank my parents, Dean and Neta Foster, for teaching me to think for myself.

Burk Foster

Foreword

Victor L. Streib

The continuing debate over the death penalty stretches from arguments in our legislatures and courts to catchy slogans on T-shirts and bumper stickers. Everyone seems to have a strong opinion about the death penalty, but very few have any solid information about it. Perhaps it is just a life-and-death example of "My mind is made up! Don't confuse me with the facts!" If this is your approach, prepare to be confused.

Global history from the earliest recorded times reveals the use of the death penalty for a wide variety of major and minor offenses in nearly every corner of the world from the earliest recorded times. School children everywhere study the burning of Joan D'Arc at the stake and the beheading of various English citizens. And the most famous execution of a condemned criminal offender is the crucifixion of Jesus, the impact of which still dominates the Western world. The consistency of this human history makes it all the more surprising to be witnessing the disappearance of the death penalty in our time. Only in a handful of countries is this age-old punishment still inflicted. Among these holdouts is the United States, though it seems only a matter of time before we join the rest of the civilized world in putting this practice behind us.

Governmental executions of human beings are often thought of as punishment reserved for particularly horrible crimes, such as demonic Nazi government officials or mass killers. In this vein, the United States has reduced the formerly long list of capital crimes essentially to only murder at the close of this century. At the same time, nonetheless, the current trend is to extend the list of murder variations that count (murder after kidnapping, murder during robbery, murder after rape, etc.). Despite this lengthening list of capital murders, a person who commits murder today has about a 98% chance of never being sentenced to death and a 99.5% chance of never being executed for that murder. Capital punishment is something we talk about all the time but almost never carry out.

If actual executions are such rare occurrences, why the enormous amount of political discussion, media coverage, and social angst over the death penalty? For urban areas seeing hundreds of (often) innocent victims of homicide each year, why should we care about a few (usually) guilty murderers being executed each year? The reasons for the continuing commentary and debate include its usefulness to our media-fed hysteria about crime, our changing social order, and our need to "send a message" to all of the real and imagined sources of our fears.

This leads us to the obvious questions about whether the death penalty "works" or not. No, it clearly doesn't work, if this means reducing our homicide rate. Research findings over generations of studies have made it clear that the death penalty is not a greater general deterrent to homicide than is its alternative, long-term imprisonment. Particularly troubling findings of this research are that the death penalty may actually result in a higher homicide rate than imprisonment would. This is true at least in part because government-approved killing of undesirables encourages reluctant homicidal individuals to kill people they find undesirable.

If the death penalty doesn't reduce homicide, what other societal goals might it accomplish? The commonly promoted goals of criminal sentencing also include reformation and/or rehabilitation of criminal offenders, but no one suggests that executing the offender will achieve these goals. Perhaps the one criminal sentencing goal best served is making the offender unable to repeat the offense: An executed murderer will never repeat his crime. This most certainly is true, but other sentencing alternatives exist that also achieve this goal to a nearly perfect degree. We are then left with what criminologists call "retribution" as our only remaining reason for the death penalty. Some supporters call it "justice." Opponents call it "legal revenge." The death penalty for murderers has a nice symmetry: an eye for an eye, a life for a life. However, no legal system follows this symmetry for any other crimes. We do not rape the rapist, steal from the thief, or trespass against the trespasser. And remember, 99.5% of murderers never get executed but get something other than death for the life they took.

But what of the real world of the death penalty, which this collection of articles so well reveals to us? What lies beyond the holier-than-thou rhetoric from both sides of the debate over the jurisprudential principle of capital punishment? Confronting the stench of this real world system causes even the strongest death penalty proponent to gag. Even if certain offenders "deserve to die," can we continue a governmental system of death so terribly biased along unacceptable lines? Knowing that government programs often make mistakes, how many executions of innocent persons can we tolerate in order to maintain this system? Yes, what actually happens is considerably messier than the lofty, scholarly debate over death penalty jurisprudence.

From the earliest executions in our colonial period, these same truths have plagued the death penalty. Completely separate from the crime, additional key factors determining who lives and who dies have always included the race, class, religion, and sex of the offender and victim. Despite all of our efforts to remove these biases from the system, they remain today much as they always have been. Consider the economically disadvantaged Black Muslim male who kills the middle-class white Christian female and is represented by a poorly paid, ill-prepared defense attorney. He is the defendant most likely to be executed.

While undoubtedly there are those who think the real-world death penalty system discriminates in ways that are acceptable, most people, even among its strongest advocates, don't want it to continue to be so biased. Our courts, and to a lesser degree our legislatures, have made a variety of changes to reduce these flaws but to no avail. The bottom line is that the real-world death penalty system, in the light of day, discriminates grossly, based on the race, class, and sex of the offender and victim. It always has been so, in the United States and every other country in which it has been used.

Recent developments may have provided the last straw. Given our experience with government-run programs, we just know that mistakes will be fairly common. The mistake we fear most in the death penalty system is executing an innocent person. Research during the last decade has uncovered an ever-growing list of such fatal errors. As of this writing, the state of Illinois is suffering shock waves from its discovery of several innocent death row inmates. The American Bar Association has called for a moratorium on executions until some of these major defects in the real-world operation of the death penalty can be fully diagnosed and corrected. Internationally, the United States is being abandoned as every other country joins international agreements to end the death penalty. We remain the only advanced nation in the world still using the death penalty—and literally the only nation of any kind continuing to execute child offenders. As we engage in international human rights discussions to urge other nations to provide for the basic needs of all of their citizens, we carry the stench of a death penalty nation.

This collection of articles examining so many of the problems with our operating death penalty system could help bring it to an end. So where would we go from there? Our violent-crime problem, while diminishing in recent years, remains much too high. What do we do about the problem of crime? As we begin to abandon harsh punishment as its solution, we naturally turn more to prevention instead of reaction. But crime is to be prevented, we must know more about why it happens. Discovering the answers to our questions will take us back to our communities, our schools, and our families. These will not be easy inquiries, and we often will not like what we find out about ourselves. However, prevention, not punishment, is the only rational path to follow. We have given capital punishment ample opportunity to prove whether or not it can reduce violent crime. It has made us only more violent and less sensitive to human suffering. We now must put this barbaric practice behind us and confess our shame at having used it for so many centuries before seeing the light.

1

Why Death Is Different: Capital Punishment in the Legal System

BURK FOSTER

This especial concern is a natural consequence of the knowledge that execution is the most irremediable and unfathomable of penalties; that death is different.

Justice Thurgood Marshall

"Death is different," Supreme Court Justice Thurgood Marshall is often quoted as saying. Justice Marshall's quotation above, from his 1986 opinion in *Ford v. Wainwright* (citing earlier language in the 1976 case of *Woodson v. North Carolina*), came toward the end of a distinguished legal career more than half a century long—a career as a litigator and judge that many times brought him face to face with the issues of capital punishment as practiced in twentieth-century America.

One such encounter happened early and made a lasting impact. As a young defense attorney in Maryland, Marshall lost a death penalty case in which the defendant was a high-school classmate. The man was hanged in Baltimore on August 8, 1936. Marshall had planned to attend the execution but backed out, saying later the experience profoundly affected his views.

Early in Thurgood Marshall's legal career, the death penalty was frequently used, not only legally but also often extralegally as well. Lynchings were popular public events in the South through the 1930s. The number of legal executions in America reached a peak in the 1930s, averaging almost 170 per year. In the 1940s it declined to 130, and in the 1950s, as public support for the death penalty began to wane, it declined even more sharply, averaging only 70 executions per year for the decade.

Executions ceased altogether after 1967 as we awaited a definitive Supreme Court case that would decide whether or not the death penalty per se constituted "cruel and unusual punishment" under the Eighth Amendment. When that decision finally came, in 1972's *Furman v. Georgia,* the answer was a resoundingly equivocal "maybe," leading to the follow-up decision of *Gregg v. Georgia* four years later, which said the death penalty was all right after all, provided certain procedural standards were followed.

The timing of this decision was critical. It gave the Supreme Court's stamp of approval to the death penalty just as America's high rate of violent crime was generating political heat for tougher anticrime measures. Rehabilitation was out; punishment was in. And so it would remain through the rest of Thurgood Marshall's tenure on the Supreme Court.

For two decades, from his 60-page concurring opinion in *Furman* until his sharply worded dissent in *Payne v. Tennessee* (decided on June 27, 1991, the day before he announced his retirement), Justice Marshall adamantly opposed the death penalty. His position can be summed up in four main points:

1. The death penalty is not a deterrent.
2. As retribution, the death penalty is inappropriate to a civilized society.
3. Innocent people will invariably be executed.
4. The death penalty cannot be consistently applied.

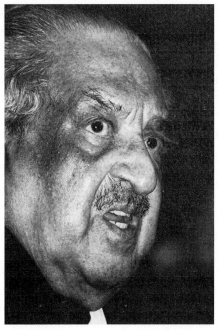

Thurgood Marshall, U.S. Supreme Court, at the home of his retirement, June 29, 1991.

Justice Marshall was also mindful that the defendants most likely to be sentenced to death were both socially and legally disadvantaged. "Cast aside today are those condemned to face society's ultimate penalty," he wrote in *Payne,* which overruled an earlier decision disallowing prosecutors' use of victim-impact evidence.

"Death is different," Justice Marshall persisted until the end, and anyone who has worked on either side of a death penalty case would likely agree. But, aside from arguments against capital punishment, how is the death penalty different in practice? Why do capital cases stand out so conspicuously in the American legal system of today?

1. To start with, someone was killed. When Justice Marshall began his legal career as an attorney in 1933, several nonfatal crimes, including most often kidnapping, treason, rape and carnal knowledge, and robbery, could also result in death sentences. This practice ended with the Supreme Court decision in *Coker v. Georgia* (1977), in which the court ruled that the death penalty was inappropriate in the nonfatal rape of an adult woman. Some states have kept the death penalty on the books for non-homicide offenses, and Louisiana recently brought back the death penalty for the aggravated rape of a child under the age of 12, but in fact everyone on death row in the United States today is there for murder.

All death sentences result from criminal events in which at least one human being was killed. And not just any homicide will qualify. The crime, labeled a first-degree, or capital, or aggravated murder, most often involves a felony against the person, such as robbery or rape, though the 38 death penalty states may define the death-deserving circumstances in various ways—often covering certain classes of victims, such as children, the elderly, police officers and prison guards, killings for hire, and those involving multiple victims with special provisions.

No two states have exactly the same laws defining the death penalty offense. The general perception is that the death penalty is the right punishment for the "worst" murders, which means in practice the highly visible, often shocking offenses in which extreme violence is used by strangers against innocent victims. They are the crimes that attract public attention and stir public sentiment against the offender.

Most homicides, as crimes of passion between relatives and friends, do not fit into this category. Even in the South, where the death penalty is pursued most vigorously, no more than about 20–25% of homicides are actively prosecuted as capital cases. In other states, typically fewer than 5–10% of homicides pass muster to enter the courts as capital cases. Applying to no more than 2,500–3,000 possible cases a year nationwide, then, the death penalty is different from the start in its narrow applicability.

2. The death penalty involves defendants who almost universally have the deck stacked against them—they are poor, mentally slow or disturbed, prior felons, victims of extreme physical and sexual abuse, transients, the outcasts of society. Studies of death row inmates have found that these people have lived tough lives. As a group, they have suffered an unusually high incidence of head injuries, drug overdoses, seizures, psychiatric disturbances, and difficulties at birth. They generally have below-normal IQs. They have often been victims of severe parental violence long before their own history of violence directed at others began.

To these personal problems in their background, capital defendants add a serious legal problem in that being almost universally poor has enormous impact on the quality of their legal defense. Bob Egelko, who writes for the Associated Press in San Francisco, reported that every one of the 384 men and 4 women awaiting execution on California's death row as of July 1, 1994, had been represented by a public defender at state expense. Although this is not to say that defenders of the indigent generally do a bad job on capital cases, it is certainly more likely to find incompetent or "no-care" counsel in such cases. Moreover, even competent counsel are often handicapped by lack of investigative assistance, mitigation experts, and other resources available to defendants with money. And capital defendants, not placing much trust in their state-appointed attorneys, can be very uncooperative clients, further aggravating their disadvantaged legal status. The capital trial of an indigent is very different from the capital trial of a middle- or high-income defendant, and the results are consequently completely different in many cases.

3. Death penalty cases are the most visible illustration of the role of discretion within the legal system. In other cases, decisions about charges and penalties deal with options to prosecution, the amount of the fine, the choice between probation and imprisonment or between jail time and prison time, and the length of the prison term. In capital cases, the decisions determine life or death.

The "gatekeeper" function of the prosecutor is well-known. The popularly elected district attorney determines if a death penalty will be sought. Relying on a combination of personal belief and political advantage, some prosecutors seek the death penalty just as adamantly as Justice Marshall opposed it. Others seek it rarely or not at all.

Trial court judges and appellate judges make critical decisions about evidence, venue, jury selection, and other issues. A trial judge who is determined to bring in a death penalty (as defense counsel, you know you are in trouble when the judge refers to the prosecution as "we") can do a lot to make this happen, even knowing he or she may be overturned years down the road.

The jury's role is obviously critical. In most death penalty states, the choice between life and death is theirs alone. Locale, culture, gender, and race are important background variables, and the jury dynamics during deliberation will make the difference between life and death in many cases.

Combining prosecutorial, judicial, and jury discretion, a mixed-up pattern emerges. The *Furman* formula for achieving valid death sentences stresses proportionality within each state, but in practice some jurisdictions within a state will have a disproportionately high number of death sentences, whereas others will have a disproportionately low number.

Using Louisiana as an example, Orleans Parish has about five times as many homicides annually as each of the three next largest parishes—Jefferson, East Baton Rouge, and Caddo. But in the 1990s, Orleans gave 12 death sentences, while East Baton Rouge gave 17, Jefferson 12, and Caddo 6. Fewer than half the parishes in the state have given anyone a death sentence in the past two decades; only 14 parishes (of 64) have given more than 2.

James Liebman, a law professor at Columbia University, said in a 1995 *New York Times* article, "Lots of states have death belts. In southern Georgia, there are lots of death sentences; in northern Georgia, there aren't. In Tennessee, there are tons of death sentences in Memphis and East

Knoxville, but not in Nashville." The same article points out that of 254 counties in Texas, only 42 sent any inmates to Texas's death row, and half of those sent only one. Almost a third of Texas's death row came from one jurisdiction, Harris County, where prosecutor Johnny B. Holmes is known as "the deadliest prosecutor in America."

4. Death penalty cases are a lot of trouble for attorneys to take to court. Whole separate legal specialties have been developed to prosecute and defend death penalty cases. Attorneys on both sides attend seminars to share the tricks of their trade, seminars at which opposing counsel are not welcome. Inches-thick manuals prescribe the case law, the procedures, the legal forms, and the maneuvers to prosecute and defend death penalty cases.

One North Louisiana prosecutor, recognized as an able and experienced death penalty attorney, now hires out as a "special assistant district attorney" in other parishes where prosecutorial expertise or enthusiasm is lacking. Traveling from parish to parish to prosecute capital murder cases, he has become a sort of roving ambassador for the death penalty in North Louisiana.

Death penalty procedural law has become so highly technical that most attorneys lacking extensive criminal law experience cannot hope to do a competent job as either a prosecutor or defense counsel in a capital case. An American Bar Association report concluded that "put simply, there are relatively few attorneys who are competent to try capital cases." The report was addressing defense counsel, who are often "underskilled, unprepared, and underpaid," but the work is no easier on prosecutors.

Death penalty work requires a mass of technical knowledge, several years of adversarial apprenticeship, and the capacity to put in hundreds or even thousands of hours. Common estimates of the attorney's time required to prepare one capital case for trial range from 500 to 2,000 hours or more. Death penalty work also requires accepting the moral responsibility that, whether prosecuting or defending, someone's life is in your hands. Many attorneys, especially defense counsel, do not want to work under this kind of pressure. Small wonder that most defense attorneys who do much death penalty work tend to do primarily (or almost exclusively) death penalty work: their practice does not allow them time for another field of legal expertise.

5. The death penalty trial itself, when it finally arrives, is long, complicated, expensive, and fraught with possibilities of reversible error. The legal complications are the continuation of the pretrial preparation already described, aggravated by the pressure of courtroom give-and-take, where a

brief mental lapse or a slip of the tongue may cause a mistrial or a whole new trial on appeal.

Jury selection, which most defense counsel prefer be done in small panels or in individual sequestered voir dire, is the longest part of the trial—a week in many routine capital cases, two weeks or more in the most highly publicized cases. Judges are called upon to discharge or retain particular prospective jurors. The ideal capital juror must be willing to impose a death sentence, but only if it is deserved.

The positions seem clear-cut, but jurors' responses are often anything but clear, ranging back and forth across the spectrum of positions depending on the direction of the leading questions they are asked by prosecution and defense counsel. It is also a truism of capital voir dire that some jurors may lie to get off the jury or, less often, to get on. Judges may retain jurors whom the defense wants excluded, or exclude jurors the defense wants retained: either action can be the cause of reversible error and frequently is.

Picking the jury is expensive. In the Alvin Scott Loyd retrial that will be discussed here, selecting and sequestering the jury for the three-and-a-half week trial cost an estimated $29,000 (equivalent to the cost of keeping an inmate 18 months in the state penitentiary). Other expenses include fees for two defense attorneys, fees for prosecution and defense expert witnesses (which in cases involving issues such as DNA, mental illness, retardation, brain damage, and substance abuse can be considerable), expenses for the lay witnesses for both sides, and overtime pay for court and security personnel.

How much does a death penalty trial cost? An ordinary trial in the South, where twothirds of all capital trials occur, may cost $100,000 to $250,000. Margaret Garey calculated a minimum of $500,000 to complete a capital case in California in the 1980s. At about the same time, New York, which was then considering adopting the death penalty, estimated the cost would be $1,828,000 per capital trial.

And the trial is, as they say, just the tip of the iceberg. The appeal through state and federal courts is likely to be several times more expensive, with more attorneys' fees and the costs of lots of copying of legal documents, more expert witnesses, extra hearings, travel, and ultimately the execution itself, which is actually the cheapest part of the process.

A life sentence of 30 to 40 years in prison is estimated to cost $1 million (according to the National Council on Crime and Delinquency). Recent estimates of the cost of a death sentence range from twice to seven times that figure, depending primarily on the estimated costs of attorneys' fees within the state.

Phillip J. Cook and Donna Slawson, who studied the total costs of every death penalty case in North Carolina over a two-year period, concluded that taking a death penalty case to execution cost $2.16 million more than imposing a 20-years-to-life sentence. The state of Florida estimated that it cost about $3.17 million for each of the 18 men it executed in the 1980s. And one of them, serial killer Ted Bundy, was estimated to have cost $6 to $7 million.

Between 1973 and 1996 exactly one third of all death sentences were overturned on appeal, sending those cases back for fresh trials, and incurring the extra expense of re-prosecution. When Kansas was considering re-instating the death penalty a decade ago, political officials agreed it was cheaper not to have the death penalty, but this economic decision was later outweighed by the political decision to reinstate it. The sentiment in the legislature was that it ought not be used too much, because of the expense, but that the extra expense was worth it in some instances.

6. Death penalty cases provide the only two-part criminal trial commonly seen in our legal system today. The trial is divided into separate guilt and penalty phases. This almost always means two defense attorneys, one for each part, and two separate campaigns, one involving issues of guilt or innocence, the other mitigation of sentence. The campaigns may be connected by theme or theory, or they may not, but jury unanimity is required in both parts for a death sentence.

The *guilt phase* is a conventional criminal trial. If the jury returns a verdict of guilty to capital murder, then the penalty phase begins. The *penalty phase* is essentially a sentencing hearing, in which the prosecutor provides evidence that the defendant deserves a death sentence and the defense counsel counters with evidence showing the defendant deserves life in prison.

The penalty phase presents aggravating and mitigating circumstances for the jury's consideration. The prosecution's aggravating circumstances might typically include such elements as:

a. The heinousness of the crime, which might focus on torture, suffering, special cruelty, or other evidence of meanness.

b. The offender's prior criminal record and other nonadjudicated "bad acts."

c. Victim-impact evidence, which is usually directed at allowing relatives and friends to testify (without showing excessive emotion) that the victim was loved and will be missed.

d. Future dangerousness, which goes into the defendant's personalty and past history, leading to a prediction of future violent behavior.

The defense presentation of mitigating circumstances is often more wide-ranging. Indeed, "there is an almost unlimited right to present evidence in mitigation," the *Louisiana Death Penalty Defense Manual* says. The controlling U.S. Supreme Court case here is *Lockett v. Ohio* (1978), which said the jury must consider "any aspect of the defendant's character or record . . . that the defendant professes as a basis for a sentence less than death."

Article 905.5 of the Louisiana *Code of Criminal Procedure* lists eight mitigating circumstances:

a. No significant prior criminal history.

b. An extreme mental or emotional condition at the time of the crime.

c. Being under the domination of another person.

d. The existence of moral extenuation for the defendant's act (which should be sufficient to make you wonder how the jury could have found him or her guilty of first-degree murder in the first place).

e. Mental disease or defect or intoxication.

f. Young age.

g. Lesser participation in the act than another defendant.

h. Any other relevant mitigating circumstance.

It is the last general criterion that allows the defense to bring in the broadest possible mitigation evidence, including the defendant's family history, school and work records, jail and prison records, religious activities, suitability for life imprisonment, capacity for rehabilitation—practically anything bearing on the defendant's past or future life that might influence the jury's decision.

Because many capital trials involve defendants who are obviously guilty of capital murder, the penalty phase is often the more important part of the trial. Here the defense's whole effort is directed toward convincing the jury that a life sentence is appropriate. The critical nature of the penalty phase has led some death penalty defense counsel to take specialization one step further: they become experts in penalty-phase mitigation.

7. The moral condemnation attached to a death sentence marks the offender for life. The meanest thing human beings can say to another human being is, "We've decided you ought to die."

Craig Forsyth and Burk Foster discussed the moral position of the death-sentenced inmate in an article a few years ago:

If the crime must be an affront to whatever is left of universal human values, the offenders singled out for the death penalty, in our perspective, have by definition excluded themselves from the pale of humanity. Their lives are ordered forfeited to the state not only because of the gravity of their offenses and their own blameworthiness, for what they have done and for who they are, but also for what they represent. They are held in public as the worst humanity has to offer. . . . They are given death sentences as examples to the rest of us of the absolute worst the system may do to a deserving criminal offender.

Their eventual deaths, years down the road, are intended to have salutary effects on us, by showing us their offenses are "off limits." The result is not cause-and-effect deterrence, but rather disavowal. They have, in effect, taken the scale of equivalency into a different plane, one in which normal human concerns do not apply. What they represent, symbolically, is the ultimate evil, a level of meanness to which only one in a million might aspire. They are killed to make the rest of us feel better.

Other writers have described at greater length the symbolic meaning of the death penalty. Rather than deterrence, rather than retribution, rather than incapacitation or any other possible objective, the death penalty thrives in America today as a symbol. It is the political sign of a public willingness, a public urge in many instances, to take a tough stand in fighting crime. A juror in a recent death penalty case in Louisiana summed up the jury's attitude: "I felt like I had to do it as a service to the families and the community." A death sentence as a public service? Why? To show that they had the guts to tell the murderer not just, "We think you are a bad person," or, "We think you have done a terrible crime," but rather, "Our sense of community demands that we kill you."

Political officials latch on to the death penalty as one more weapon in their arsenal of practical tools to enhance their own political power. The message they sell to the public is, "I promise you I will see someone pays for this heinous crime." If the evidence is not strong enough to support a death sentence in that particular case, the public can be mollified by some other offender paying the ultimate price. To a society terrified of violent crime and determined to get even with violent criminals, what matters is not that all murderers be executed, or even that the worst murderers be executed; what matters is that *some* murderers be executed.

Death-sentenced inmates are symbols in a larger struggle; the whole capital punishment controversy exists on a symbolic plane. Society reserves the right to almost randomly select a few scapegoats from a vast pool of murderers and eventually put some of them to death, just to show we have not lost our will in the war on criminal violence. These selected deaths have no real impact on crime; they only show that we still mean business. We like capital punishment because it is tough, direct, and easy to understand. In the search for simple solutions to crime, the death penalty leads the way.

8. It's not over when it's over. People who expect closure at the end of the trial are mistaken. The appellate process through state and federal courts currently averages about 10 to 12 years, but it can go on indefinitely. The most recent Bureau of Justice Statistics annual bulletin, "Capital Punishment 1996," identifies three men sentenced to death in 1974 who were still on death row at the end of 1996, 22 years later, and 133 people who spent more than 15 years on death row.

When Alvin Scott Loyd was tried for the third time in Louisiana's Vermilion Parish in July 1998 (for the rape/murder of a three-year-old girl in St. John the Baptist Parish in 1981), he had already been on death row for 15 years. The third time the jury deadlocked, and he was given a life sentence. If he had been given another death sentence, he would have gone back to death row, with a new appeals clock ticking, to wait another 10 to 15 years before he was executed. Having committed the crime at age 26, Loyd would have been pushing 60 before his life on death row came to an end.

Contrast this with the case of William Hamilton, an 18-year-old black youth from Shreveport. He raped (but did not kill) a nine-year-old white girl in a Shreveport park on September 29, 1942. Sixty-five days later, on December 3, he was electrocuted in the Caddo Parish Jail. Not everything moved slower in the old days.

Delays take their toll on the members of the legal system and families and supporters of both victims and defendants. Both sides have to wait out an emotionally draining, seemingly interminable process. The trial ending in the death sentence is merely "the end of the beginning," as Winston Churchill said. "We're glad this is over," victims' families often say when the death verdict is brought in. "We're looking forward to the execution."

But the execution is a long time coming, and it is difficult to sustain that level of emotional intensity through the appellate process. Research suggests that victims' families feel very ambivalent about the execution when it does finally arrive. The execution often does not bring the sense of peace or relief—the closure—that they seek or expect. Many victims' families, becoming locked in on the legal process and the series of set-back execution dates, seem stuck in a perverse existence: their satisfaction is tied to achieving the death of another person, which is not, when you think of it, a very happy way to live.

Shannon Brownlee, Dan McGraw, and Jason Vest had this observation in a recent article on vengeance in *U.S. News and World Report:*

> Grief counselors suspect that some people focus on their hatred of the killer to keep the more painful feelings of sorrow at bay. Since an appeals process can take years, survivors who nurse their rage may go more than a decade without really grieving. For some survivors, the anger is intensified by guilt. A parent fails to protect a child from a pedophile; a wife feels remorse that the last words she exchanged with her husband before his death were spoken in anger.
>
> More often than not, families of murder victims do not experience the relief they expected to feel at the execution, says Lula Redmond, a Florida therapist who works with such families. "Taking a life doesn't fill that void, but it's generally not until after the execution that the families realize this. Not too many people will honestly say publicly that it didn't do much, though, because they've spent most of their lives trying to get someone to the death chamber."

Survivors who manage to avoid this state of mind, who retain their good memories of their loved one and get on with their own lives, often seem much healthier and more balanced, years after the crime, than the ones stuck in the past. "If I'm filled with hatred and revenge," one murder victim's grandmother said, "then (the murderer) won. He would have succeeded in totally ruining my life."

9. Preparations for the execution bring on a final review. Most crimes are strictly downhill after sentencing: the offender moves on into the correctional system and disappears, never to be heard from by the trial participants again.

The death penalty case is more like a long cross-country ski race, with up and down hills, parts of the course where the racer disappears from public view, other parts where he falls, makes wrong turns, and has misadventures along the way, until the finish line comes in sight. Then there is that final dash to cross the line, the crowd cheering, waiting to see how he will finish.

The race is long enough to allow the defendant the opportunity to change. She is, for a start, 10 or 15 years older by the time of execution. And she is far removed from the drugs and alcohol that were instrumental in her earlier life. She has had a lot of time to think. Even given the generally lower intelligence level of death row inmates (though there are notable exceptions), she is probably better read, more reflective, and more articulate than when she arrived. She may well have turned to religion: you can do a lot of Bible study in 10 years.

The inmate may, in short, become a very different person while awaiting death. The attorneys and supporters of many death row inmates in the post–Gary Gilmore era have made this very point, most often to state pardon boards with the power to commute death sentences to life: "This is not the same person sentenced to death years ago. He (or she) is changed." He's found God, he's found literature, he's found humanity. Consider Karla Faye Tucker, Willie Otey, Antonio James. Don't kill this person for what he used to be.

Wait a minute, the victims' families and legal officials protest in dismay. It doesn't matter what the murderers are now; what matters is what they were, and what they did. The defendants should be thankful they had the extra time to accomplish these positive changes, changes they denied their victims by cutting their lives short in beginning their own "journey of change." One Texas inmate, executed last year, used his last words to thank the state for giving him the time to become a better human being on death row. The dead victims are forever frozen in time while their killers may have moved forward into a new life.

10. Finally, there is the drama of the execution as an event. As other traditional forms of state-sanctioned violence—war, taming the frontier, and putting down rebellion—recede from memory, the execution endures as a demonstration of the ultimate power of the state.

With the number of executions increasing over time, to a 40-year high of 74 last year, executions may be in danger of becoming routinized, but individually they retain their elements of interest. The media report the condemned's last hours. Last-minute legal maneuvers are nerve-wracking. Will someone intervene to stop the process? What might go wrong?

As the pace of executions has accelerated, journalists have struggled with the problem of distinguishing one execution from all the others—yesterday's, last week's, next week's. More than one capital punishment observer has suggested that we have entered an era in which executions are so ordinary, especially in the states that do very many of them, like Texas, Virginia, and Florida, that the only ones to attract much attention are those where something goes wrong—someone's head shoots flames in Florida, or the Mexican government protests the execution of one of its citizens in Texas. Less distinctive executions are simply lost in the numbers.

Although we continue to focus on the act of execution (even to the point of discussing televising executions live to enhance their deterrent effect), perhaps the time has come for shifting our concentration from the end to the beginning. An execution is, after all, merely a sanitized, methodical extermination; there ought not be anything really interesting about the process of using any instrumentation to kill a human being, even if it is legally sanctioned.

What we should look at is not the trial, or the appellate process, or how the criminal changes, or what the victim's family thinks, or how the execution was carried out, but rather at the lives of both offenders and victims before the act that brought them together. Why? To perhaps discover ways of preventing similar acts. In focusing on the legal process and the mechanics of execution, we often forget that the most important question to ask about a homicide is, "Why did this happen?" If we sought the answer to this question more seriously, we might begin to see that our persistent use of the death penalty really creates more problems than it solves.

If we could answer the "why" of the crime, then perhaps we could better understand the "why" of our need to seek the ultimate penalty for the crime. And if we understood that, would we still pursue its application? Justice Thurgood Marshall thought not. In his long *Furman* opinion, he wrote the following, which the Death Penalty Information Center continues to use as the slogan on its web site today:

> [T]he question with which we must deal is not whether a substantial proportion of American citizens would today, if polled, opine that capital punishment is barbarously cruel, but whether they would find it to be so in the light of all information presently available.

Justice Marshall goes on to say this, later in the same opinion:
> I cannot believe that at this stage in our history, the American people would ever knowingly support purposeless vengeance. Thus, I believe that the great mass of citizens would conclude on the bases of the material already considered that the death penalty is immoral, and therefore unconstitutional.

By the time of *Payne v. Tennessee,* in June 1991, Justice Marshall was very discouraged at the conservative turn of the Supreme Court. The Court, which at one time had seemed so close to abolishing capital punishment altogether, was moving back to an earlier, noninterventionist mode of thought. In this last death penalty dissent, Justice Marshall wrote,

> Power, not reason, is the new currency of this Court's decision making. . . . In dispatching *Booth* and *Gathers* [cases establishing the principle that victim-impact evidence was not to be presented in the penalty phase of a capital trial] to their graves, today's majority ominously suggests that an even more extensive upheaval of this Court's precedents may be in store.

Justice Marshall died less than two years later. His predictions, in regard to both the Court and the practice of capital punishment, have been borne out after his death. In their most significant decision of the 1997–98 term, the justices of the Supreme Court expressed impatience with the slow pace of executions, warning the federal courts not to delay executions for frivolous reasons.

The death penalty, as a peculiarly American legal practice, is now back to where it was 40 years ago; if current trends continue, by early next century we will have moved all the way back to the 1930s. If Justice Marshall were fresh out of law school today, ready to start his legal career over again, he would feel right at home.

2

How the Death Penalty Really Works: Selecting Death Penalty Offenders in America

Burk Foster

Adapted from *The Angolite,* September/October 1995, Angola, La: Louisiana State Penitentiary.

In *Gregg v. Georgia* (1975), the United States Supreme Court defined a legal process to impose the death penalty in America. The process approved by the Court requires a separate sentencing hearing, after a conviction of capital murder, at which aggravating and mitigating circumstances are considered. The aggravating circumstances must be prescribed by statute; the mitigating factors, as redefined in subsequent cases, can be anything the judge or jury thinks is relevant and important. So the process of imposing a death sentence, as it has evolved over 20 years, requires, first, proof that the defendant has committed a homicide falling within certain narrow circumstances, and, second, a much more wide-open consideration of aggravating and mitigating evidence to determine if the death penalty is appropriate.

The question we take up here is this: From the vast pool of potential death penalty cases, how do we select the few who actually end up sentenced to death? How do we get from 20,000 homicides to 300 death-sentenced inmates each year? Table 2.1 traces the levels of the funnel through which offenders pass on their way to the chair—or the table, as lethal injection has replaced electrocution as the most prevalent means of execution in the United States.

The selection process, can be said to involve two types of variables: those within the system, or *systemic variables,* and those involving the intersection of the offender and the offense, or *crime/criminal variables.* The major systemic variables are as follows:

1. *Whether the state has a death penalty law on the books.* Thirty-eight states, the federal government, and the military have death penalty statutes. Six northern states, North Dakota, Minnesota, Wisconsin, Michigan, Maine, and Rhode Island, have no death penalty and have not executed anyone since at least 1930. Alaska and Hawaii have not executed anyone since statehood. Wisconsin, which has not held a legal execution since 1830, is seriously discussing a death penalty statute: some people there express regret that Jeffrey Dahmer had to be murdered in prison to "get what he deserved." Three states, Texas, California, and Florida, continue to lead the way with death penalty convictions, accounting for almost 40% of the total death row population, which now numbers well over 3,000 inmates.

2. *The breadth of the state's death penalty statute.* Some are very narrow, and others are increasingly broader. Louisiana started with four qualifying circumstances: felony murders, multiple murders (including attempts), contract murders, and killings of law enforcement officers. Recent years have seen the addition of five more: killing a child under 12, an elderly person over 65, or someone during drug deals, drive-by shootings, or Satanic rituals. Some will certainly view it as unfair that in middle age a person's life

TABLE 2.1

From Murder to Death Row: Tracking the Processing of Criminal Homicides

20,000 criminal homicides; clearance rate 70–75%

15,000 homicides cleared by arrest; prosecution rate 80–85%

12,000 homicides prosecuted

For first-degree murder:

Delete:

 Crimes of passion/single victim

 Spontaneous disputes

 Ordinary drug killings

 Juvenile gang killings

Retain:

 Felony murders (robbery, rape)

 Multiple victims (including attempts)

 Child abuse

 Contract killings

 Killings of police officers

10,000 ± convicted of some crime (65–70% of arrests):

 Negligent homicide 5%

 Manslaughter 30%+

 Second-degree murder 30%+

 First-degree murder 20%+

 Other/conspiracy/attempts 10%+

5,000 possible first-degree murder cases:

 1,500 First-degree murder guilty pleas

 1,200 First-degree murder trials

 1,100+ trial convictions (1st, 2nd, manslaughter)

About 2,000–2,500 first-degree murder convictions total

About 300 death sentences

is deemed to be worth less than in childhood or old age, so that a murderer might get the death penalty on the basis of the victim's age alone.

3. *The prosecutor's attitude toward death penalty cases.* "The seriousness of his intentions" is the way this variable is phrased. The prosecutor must be willing to take the time to prosecute death penalty cases for whatever political benefits he or she may reap. DA John Holmes, of Harris County, Texas, who now wears the mantle of "deadliest prosecutor in America" because of the number of people sent to death row, has made it clear he will go to whatever trouble necessary to prosecute those offenders he believes ought to get the death penalty. In September 1994 Holmes's office was conducting six death penalty trials at the same time, trying to stick to his promise: "I say without apology that if you murder someone here, the state of Texas is going to kill you."

4. *The availability of competent defense counsel with supporting resources, including investigators, expert witnesses, and supporting staff.* A defense attorney with skills and resources equal to those of the prosecutor can make it very difficult to get a death penalty case to trial and can reduce at least a portion of the prosecutor's built-in advantage.

5. *The attitude of the victim's family.* Many prosecutors will not pursue a death penalty verdict if the victim's family does not want them to.

6. *The cultural cross section assembled as the jury.* Jurors must be willing to impose a death sentence if justified. The system plays to the jury as audience: thumbs up or down? There are sharp differences in jurors' attitudes in different locales, such as South versus North and big cities versus suburbs versus small towns. But even in large cities like Houston, the prosecutor always seems able to keep drawing from the jury pool enough death-prone jurors to keep percentages high for death penalty convictions, at least in some states.

The preceding are variables within the legal system itself. Other variables focus on the criminal event and the two people at its center—the victim and the offender. The most important of these crime/criminal variables follow:

1. *The victim's race (and class).* The defendant is much more likely to get a death sentence if the victim was white and middle-class. About 85% of the post–Gilmore executions involve white victims. In only a handful of instances have whites been executed for killing blacks.

2. *The innocence of the victim—children and the elderly preferred.* The victim's noninvolvement in the circumstances leading up to the homicide is a definite plus for the prosecutor. If he or she "had it coming," as in the cases of drug dealers or gang members (see Table 2.1), it will likely not be a death penalty case.

3. *The number of victims.* The more victims, the more likely the offender is to get a death sentence.

4. *The heinousness of the crime, demonstrating unusual cruelty or depravity.* If a victim was tortured or mistreated before being murdered, this perversity may well come back to haunt the defendant when the jury is deciding his or her fate.

5. *The offender's prior criminal history, particularly felony convictions and prior homicides.* Two thirds of all death-sentenced inmates have prior felony convictions; 10% have a prior homicide conviction.

6. *The absence of mitigating factors in the criminal's background.* Mitigating factors include mental retardation, mental illness, documented history of drug or alcohol abuse, dysfunctional family history, physical or sexual abuse. The factors not only have to be there, they have to be brought out in court and explained in a way that persuades the jury that the defendant deserves a mitigated sentence.

7. *Clarity of the evidence pinpointing guilt.* Obviously, strong evidence of absolute guilt will work to the defendant's disadvantage. Uncertain evidence may make it impossible for any defendant to receive a death sentence, even if the crime seems to deserve it.

8. *In cases involving multiple offenders, which one is most to blame, and is he or she willing to take the fall for the others?* Since most people are on death row for felony murders, typically robbery and rape, all participants can legally be given death sentences, but many times co-participants who were less involved will be spared if one defendant acknowledges greater guilt.

9. *Remorse (or the lack thereof).* Jurors often remark, "He (or she) looked cold." This notion considers the defendant's demeanor after the crime, while in custody and during the trial, including whatever is said on the stand. A defendant who adamantly maintains that he didn't do it, that he is the victim of a frame-up, in the face of incontrovertible evidence to the contrary, may convince his fellow convicts that he is a real man. He will also probably convince a jury that he really belongs with the other sub-humans on death row.

10. *Where the defendant is from.* Transients do not do well in capital trials, particularly when they kill locals who are well thought of. Death rows are full of people who were "just passing through." Of course, being a local boy is not always an asset. A bad local reputation can get a defendant a "get even" death sentence, one in which the sentence is based more on deserved punishment for past offenses he has gotten away with than on the instant offense.

All of these variables, systemic and crime/criminal-based, combine to influence the probability of whether a death sentence will be given to a particular defendant in a first-degree murder trial. If we calculate a "meanness ratio" (the rate of death sentences per 100 homicides) by state, we find that the "meanest" states are not the populous ones of Texas, California, and Florida, but instead Oklahoma, Idaho, Nevada, Delaware, and Arizona. These states are most likely to impose death sentences for murder.

What makes some states so much meaner than others (Oklahoma and Idaho are four times more likely to give a death sentence for murder than Texas and Louisiana)? Although that question cannot be answered completely here, an inverse ratio seems to exist between population and meanness. Perhaps it is "the fewer, the meaner." The more small-town and rural the state's population (which is to say how strongly people identify with small-town values and oppose the conditions of big-city life), the greater appears the likelihood of a death sentence.

For use in analyzing the application of the death penalty in America today, we offer a difficult-to-quantify but fundamentally simple legal equation: $PS \times PE = PDS$. PS is public sentiment, PE is prosecutorial enthusiasm, and PDS is the probability of a death sentence. If public sentiment and prosecutorial enthusiasm are present to high degrees, and other variables (systemic and crime/criminal) are supportive, over time there will be plenty of cases to offer a reasonable chance of getting a death penalty verdict from a sympathetic jury. Legal equations are not the same as mathematical equations: mathematical equations should always yield the same result; legal equations, even in cases of life and death, remain imprecise.

3

Who Is the Meanest of Them All?

Burk Foster and Craig J. Forsyth

From *The Angolite,* July/August 1994, Angola, La: Louisiana State Penitentiary.

One perspective on the death penalty holds that it is a largely symbolic punishment as it is used here in the United States at the end of the twentieth century. It is applied only when the political culture finds the act and the actor so heinous and condemnable that no other form of punishment, including a natural life prison term, satisfies the popular and political imagination.

Since the crime, to be considered worthy of a death sentence, must be an affront to whatever is left of universal human values, the offenders singled out for the death penalty, have by definition excluded themselves from the pale of humanity. Their lives are ordered forfeited to the state not only because of the gravity of their offenses and their own blameworthiness, for what they have done and for who they are, but also for what they represent. They are held up in public as the worst humanity has to offer.

When it comes to the death penalty, "many are called, but few are chosen." Even the most dedicated death penalty opponent will admit that from the vast pool of terrible murders, those which by their features are worse than ordinary murders among friends and relations, only a handful of even the worst cases actually get the death penalty. The rest, because they have committed their crimes in states that do not use the death penalty, or in jurisdictions where the district attorney does not aggressively pursue the death penalty, or because the victim's family does not seek the death penalty, or because no one really cares about this particular victim (as is the case with many impoverished or deviant murder victims), or because of evidentiary problems, or for many other reasons, are never put on trial for their lives.

The ones who do end up going through the now familiar ritual of the first-degree murder trial, post *Furman,* are testing our standards of public indecency. They have demanded public scrutiny of their conduct, and in the end they have met with our most profound disapproval: they are absolutely guilty. They are given death sentences as examples to the rest of us of the absolute worst the system may do to a deserving criminal offender.

Their eventual deaths, years down the road, are intended to have salutary effects on us by showing us that certain offenses are "off limits." The result is not cause-and-effect deterrence, but rather disavowal. Death-sentenced murderers have, in effect, taken the scale of equivalency into a different plane, one in which normal humane concerns do not apply. What they represent, symbolically, is the ultimate evil, a level of meanness to which only one in a million might aspire.

One in a million is the approximate odds of any American getting a death sentence in a recent year. With an estimated population of more than 250 million, the United States gave death sentences to an average of about

280 inmates each year from 1983 through 1992; the low was 1983, with 256, the high was 1986, with 311.

Of the total 4,702 state inmates (two federal inmates are not counted here) sentenced to death in the 20 years post *Furman,* only 188 had been executed by the end of 1992. Over a third of all death-sentenced state inmates (1,697), have had their sentence or conviction overturned on appeal; 117 had their death sentence commuted; 100 died in prison, most of natural causes; and another 26 were removed for other reasons. These dispositions left a total of 2,574 inmates on death rows in 34 states at the end of 1992.

We ask our central question, "Who is the meanest of them all?" in looking at how the states impose death sentences. We explain our choice of the term "meanest," in this application, as being a measure of the state's response to criminal homicides. If criminals are mean in the ways they kill their victims, then states can also be mean, or determined to exact maximum punishment, as they seek to kill the killers in return.

The three states that we tend to think of as being the meanest, in conventional terms, are Texas, California, and Florida, because these states have the largest death row populations: 344, 332, and 312, respectively, as of December 31, 1992. Together these states housed almost 1,000 of the 2,574 inmates awaiting execution.

Another way of looking at meanness is to look at how many death row inmates are actually executed. Here it is not much of a contest. At the time of this writing, Texas has executed 54 of the 188 persons executed post *Furman* (the new era that began with the firing squad execution of Gary Gilmore in Utah in January 1977), Florida executed 29 and Louisiana 20 by the end of 1992. More than half of the executions have occurred in just these three states, though 17 other states executed at least one offender during the same period.

Yet another way of considering meanness is to look at the efficiency with which states dispose of their death row inmates. At the time of this writing, Texas has executed 54 but still has a death row population of 344, so its efficiency rating is only about 13.6%. California has only executed one man, with 332 others remaining on death row, so its efficiency rating is a paltry 0.3%. Utah has done much better, executing four, with another 10 remaining, for an efficiency mark of 28.6%, and Louisiana has done even better, executing 20 and leaving 44 more on death row, for an efficiency rating of 31.3%. Tops in this category, though, has to be Wyoming. It executed one man in 1992, leaving no one else on death row (of Wyoming's other eight capital inmates over the past 20 years, one died in prison and the other seven had their sentences overturned on appeal). Wyoming thus

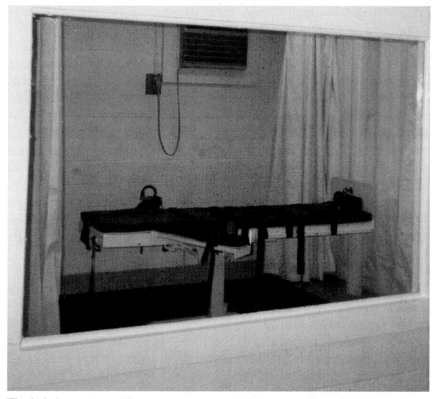

The lethal injection table currently in use at the Louisiana State Penitentiary. (Copyright: Chris De Lay.)

achieves perfection, a startling efficiency rating of 100%: one execution, and death row is closed, until the next candidate comes along.

Given options A, (death row population), B, (number of executions), and C, (percentage of death row inmates actually executed, or "efficiency rate" of executions), which would one choose as the best indicator of meanness? Our answer is D, none of the above. If the death penalty serves primarily as a symbolic punishment, it does not really matter whether the sentence is ever carried out or not. Of course, it matters to the person being executed, and to his or her family, and to the homicide victim's family, and to some of the members of the legal system involved in the case, all of whom are often emotionally strung out by the time the execution is carried out, eight or ten years down the road. But in terms of the death sentence as symbolic punishment for extreme evil, it is the pronouncement that matters, not the execution itself. No matter how many people stack up on death row, nor how many sentences state supreme courts overturn or governors commute, the importance of the death penalty is in its labeling. The return of the death sentence verdict is telling the defendants that society is washing its hands of them; they have been weighed in the balance and found wanting. Too few redeeming or mitigating factors exist to allow them to live. The sentence says, "You deserve to die." Symbolically, what could be more conclusive? No matter what track these defendants follow afterward, this judgment of their fellow human beings will stay with them for the rest of their life. If they live to be 90, they will always be "ex–death row inmates."

Recall that one measure of meanness is the extent to which a state uses the death sentence as a response to criminal homicide. Since the *Gregg* and *Coker* decisions of the 1970s clarified *Furman* and said that the death penalty is an acceptable punishment, but only for murder, practically everyone sent to death row has been convicted of killing another person; in the states, the crime is usually called first-degree or aggravated murder, with a list of circumstances that define the crime.

The trend in the states in recent years has been to expand the circumstances that make up first-degree or aggravated murder. Louisiana, for instance, started with four situations: murder for hire, felony murder, murder of a peace officer, and murder while attempting to kill more than one person at a time. In the last 10 years, Louisiana has added to the first-degree category the murder of a child under 12, the murder of a person 65 or older, murders during drug deals, murders while engaged in Satanic rituals, and drive-by shootings.

Several states continue to carry non-homicide capital offenses on the books, including treason in California, Georgia, and Louisiana; capital rape in Mississippi; aircraft hijacking in Georgia; and train wrecking in California. Occasionally other states, refusing to take the Supreme Court as the final authority, invoke new death penalty statutes for other noncapital crimes, but these statutes have not withstood legal challenges: no one has been executed for any crime except murder in the post-*Furman* era.

Table 3.1 is based on the idea that the best indicator of meanness is the proportionality of death sentences to criminal homicides. First the population, criminal homicide, and death sentence statistics are presented for all 50 states from 1973 through 1992. An average population is calculated for each state for the 20-year period. All the criminal homicides, which would include all forms of murder and voluntary manslaughter as tabulated in the FBI's *Crime in the United States* annual reports have been totaled and then averaged over the 20-year period in order to rank the states according to their homicide rates. This is the first "Rank" column. Next, from "Capital Punishment 1992," prepared by Lawrence A. Greenfeld and James J. Stephan of the Bureau of Justice Statistics, the number of death sentences pronounced

TABLE 3.1

Who's the Meanest of Them All?

State	Population in Millions			Homicides (Murder/Manslaughter) 1973–1992	Average Homicides per Year	Twenty-year Homicide Rate (per 100,000)	Rank	Death Sentences 1973–1992	Meanness ratio (DS/ homicides)	Rank
	1973	1992	Av.							
Oklahoma	2.66	3.21	2.94	4,939	247.0	8.40	21	216	.0437	1
Idaho	0.77	1.07	0.92	690	34.5	3.75	38	30	.0434	2
Nevada	0.55	1.33	0.94	2,181	109.1	11.61	7	84	.0385	3
Delaware	0.57	0.69	0.63	705	35.3	5.60	31	25	.0355	4
Arizona	2.08	3.83	2.96	4,823	241.2	8.15	23	164	.0340	5
N. Carolina	5.31	6.84	6.08	11,969	598.5	9.84	16	314	.0262	6
Florida	7.75	13.49	10.62	24,771	1,238.6	11.66	6	629	.0254	7
Utah	1.15	1.81	1.48	989	49.5	3.34	42	22	.0222	8
Alabama	3.54	4.14	3.84	9,187	459.4	11.96	5	198	.0216	9
Mississippi	2.32	2.61	2.47	6,101	305.1	12.35	4	117	.0192	10
Nebraska	1.53	1.61	1.57	1,064	53.2	3.39	41	20	.0188	11
Wyoming	0.35	0.47	0.41	495	24.8	6.05	28	9	.0182	12
Ohio	10.75	11.02	10.89	14,525	726.3	6.67	25	253	.0174	13
Tennessee	4.09	5.02	4.56	9,336	466.8	10.24	14	156	.0167	14

Continued

TABLE 3.1 – (CONTINUED)

Who's the Meanest of Them All?

State	Population in Millions			Homicides (Murder/Manslaughter) 1973–1992	Average Homicides per Year	Twenty-year Homicide Rate (per 100,000)	Rank	Death Sentences 1973–1992	Meanness ratio (DS/homicides)	Rank
	1973	1992	Av.							
S. Carolina	2.72	3.60	3.16	7,011	350.6	11.09	10	115	.0164	15
Georgia	4.82	6.75	5.79	14,717	735.9	12.71	3	234	.0159	16
Arkansas	2.03	2.40	2.22	4,120	206.0	9.28	19	62	.0150	17
Pennsylvania	11.85	12.00	11.93	14,077	703.9	5.90	29	207	.0147	18
S. Dakota	0.68	0.71	0.70	297	14.9	2.13	49	1	.0034	19
Texas	11.83	17.66	14.75	41,414	2,070.7	14.04	2	542	.0131	20
Missouri	4.77	5.20	4.99	9,308	465.4	9.33	18	104	.0112	21
Oregon	2.22	2.98	2.60	2,554	127.7	4.91	34	28	.0110	22
Louisiana	3.75	4.29	4.02	12,234	611.7	15.22	1	131	.0107	23
Indiana	5.30	5.66	5.48	7,518	375.9	6.86	24	76	.0101	24
Illinois	11.17	11.63	11.40	22,565	1,128.3	9.90	15	201	.0089	25
Kentucky	3.32	3.76	3.54	6,008	300.4	8.49	20	53	.0088	26
Virginia	4.85	6.38	5.62	9,278	463.9	8.25	22	80	.0086	27
California	20.64	30.87	25.76	57,202	2,860.1	11.10	9	478	.0083	28
New Mexico	1.10	1.58	1.34	2,863	143.2	10.69	11	22	.0077	29

Washington	3.44	5.14	4.29	4,120	206.0	4.80	35	21	.0051	30
Maryland	4.07	4.91	4.49	8,675	433.8	9.66	17	36	.0041	31
New Jersey	7.32	7.79	7.56	8,739	437.0	5.78	30	34	.0039	32
Colorado	2.48	3.47	2.98	3,732	186.6	6.26	26	14	.0038	33
Rhode Island	0.97	1.01	0.99	711	35.6	3.60	40	2	.0028	34
Montana	0.73	0.82	0.78	651	32.6	4.18	37	13	.0015	35
Connecticutt	3.08	3.28	3.18	2,848	142.4	4.48	36	4	.0014	36
Massachusetts	5.81	6.00	5.91	4,380	219.0	3.71	39	4	.0009	37
New York	18.21	18.12	18.17	41,563	2,078.2	11.44	8	3	.0001	38
Alaska	0.33	0.59	0.46	967	48.4	10.52	13	0	.NR	
Hawaii	0.84	1.16	1.00	1,053	52.7	5.27	33	0	.NR	
Iowa	2.86	2.81	2.84	1,215	60.8	2.14	48	0	.NR	
Kansas	2.27	2.52	2.40	2,578	128.9	5.37	32	0	.NR	
Maine	1.04	1.24	1.14	557	27.9	2.45	47	0	.NR	
Michigan	9.08	9.44	9.26	19,552	977.6	10.56	12	0	.NR	
Minnesota	3.89	4.48	4.19	2,093	104.7	2.50	45	0	.NR	
New Hampshire	0.80	1.11	0.96	472	23.6	2.46	46	0	.NR	
N. Dakota	0.63	0.64	0.64	166	8.3	1.30	50	0	.NR	
Vermont	0.47	0.57	0.52	271	13.6	2.62	44	0	.NR	
W. Virginia	1.78	1.81	1.80	2,194	109.7	6.09	27	0	.NR	
Wisconsin	4.54	5.01	4.78	3,102	155.1	3.24	43	0	.NR	

since 1973 was obtained for each state and divided by the number of criminal homicides in that state during the same 20-year period. this gives what we consider to be the most accurate "meanness ratio." It represents the probability that a homicide will result in a death sentence. The last column ranks the states from highest to lowest according to these ratios.

What do all these statistical manipulations tell us? First, the 20-year homicide rates were generally higher in the South. Seven of the ten states with the highest homicide rates over this period were Southern states. Louisiana was first, Texas a close second, Georgia third, Mississippi fourth, Alabama fifth, Florida sixth, Nevada seventh, New York eighth, California ninth, and South Carolina tenth. All of these had homicide rates above 11 per 100,000. (As a subnote, we would like to point out that five of the top six touch the Gulf of Mexico, and Georgia almost does, giving rise to a whole new set of subcultural and hydromantic hypotheses for further inquiry.)

Notice, too, that 38 of the 50 states gave at least one death sentence during this 20-year period, even if it was later invalidated or the death penalty done away with altogether, as was the case in New York for a time. Of the top ten states in giving death sentences, ranging from Florida with 629, down through Texas with 542, to California with 478, to North Carolina with 314, to Ohio with 253, to Georgia with 234, to Oklahoma with 216, to Pennsylvania with 207, to Illinois with 201 and Alabama with 198, five (or six if you count Oklahoma) are in the South.

The meanness ratio varies substantially among those states that have the death penalty on the books. The states that use the death penalty most, in proportion to the number of criminal homicides occurring, are Oklahoma (4.37 death sentences for every 100 homicides), Idaho (4.34), Nevada (3.85), Delaware (3.55), Arizona (3.40), North Carolina (2.62), Florida (2.54), Utah (2.22), Alabama (2.16) and Mississippi (1.92).

These are states more geographically diverse—four, or five with Oklahoma, in the South—and generally smaller in population than most other states. Seven of the ten meanest states rank in the lower half of the states in population, with average populations of less than 3 million residents each, giving rise to a hint of an inverse ratio between population and meanness: can it be that victims are symbolically missed more (or offenders symbolically despised more) where there are fewer people? Other research has tended to show that victims are more important to the imposition of the death sentence than offenders are.

The states that ranked high on the meanness scale were much more likely to give death sentences than the more populous states that have much larger death row populations. Texas, California, and Florida may think that they are tough, but Oklahoma and Idaho give three-and-a-half times as many death sentences proportionally as Texas does, over five times as many as California, and almost twice as many as Florida. If Texas gave death sentences at the same rate Oklahoma does, Texas would have 1,200 inmates on death row, enough for an entire prison of people awaiting execution.

We noted, furthermore, that there is no strong correlation between a state's homicide rate and its meanness ratio. Only four states—Alabama, Florida, Mississippi and Nevada—made both top-10 lists, and four of the five meanest states were not even in the top 20 with their homicide rates. Supporters of deterrence might proclaim that this is what they have been saying all along: kill more murderers, and the murder rate will drop. But abolition advocates could respond in kind: abolish the death penalty, and the homicide rate declines, as proved by the homicide rankings of the 12 states with no death sentences: 12, 13, 27, 32, 33, 43, 44, 45, 46, 47, 48, and 50. Seven of the ten states with the lowest homicide rates did not even have the death penalty in their arsenal of weapons against crime.

We tend to think that both homicide rates and death sentences are culture-driven, and that neither of them has any direct bearing on the other. In one last calculation not included in the table, we noted that 412,580 criminal homicides were counted in the United States from 1973 through 1992. With 4,704 death sentences meted out in return (state and federal), this gives us a national "meanness index" of .0114, or 1.14 death sentences per 100 criminal homicides. If the criminal were rationally evaluating her chances of getting a death sentence as she contemplated pulling the trigger, she might decide to risk it, since her odds nationally would only be about 1 in 88.

As we have established here, however, the national odds do not distribute evenly. The criminal contemplating the murder of a convenience store clerk in Ardmore, Oklahoma, would do much better to drive south on I-35 a few miles to Gainesville, Texas. He would do even better to drive north instead, to Wichita, in Kansas, a state that had no death penalty at the time this research was conducted, though it does now.

But criminals probably do not think that way, and citizens may not think that way either in continuing to support a punishment that is so infrequently pronounced and even less frequently carried out. The entire issue of the death penalty is in the realm of the symbolic, and Americans are apparently most willing to leave it there, even as another 300 people take up residence on death row this year and almost 20,000 more become victims of criminal homicides for reasons that have nothing to do with the use or non-use of the death penalty.

Is There a Doctor in the Chamber?

LANE NELSON

I will give no deadly medicine to anyone if asked nor suggest any such counsel . . .

Hippocratic Oath

From *The Angolite,* July/August 1994, Angola, La: Louisiana State Penitentiary.

National medical and human rights organizations are stepping up their efforts to persuade states to prohibit involvement of medical personnel in the execution of criminals. Of the 37 capital punishment states in the country, 29 require the presence of a physician at executions. Opponents charge that such involvement violates the medical Hippocratic Oath.

In the 1994 report, *Breach of Trust: Physician Participation in Executions in the United States,* four organizations criticize state laws that require medical personnel to participate in executions. The report expresses scorn for doctors who willingly lend a hand in the killing ritual. "Execution is not a medical procedure, and is not within the scope of medical practice. Physicians are clearly out of place in the execution chamber, and their participation subverts the core of their professional ethics."

This report, which takes no position on capital punishment itself, was prepared in part by the American College of Physicians, the nation's largest medical specialty society, with more than 80,000 internists who focus on ensuring top quality patient care. Other contributors were the Human Rights Watch, a worldwide organization that strives to resolve abuses of internationally recognized human rights; the National Coalition to Abolish the Death Penalty; and Physicians for Human Rights, a large group of physicians and other professionals concerned with the consequences of human rights abuses internationally.

The posture of the new report parallels the ethical stance reemphasized by the American Medical Association (AMA) in 1992: "An individual's opinion on capital punishment is the personal moral decision of the individual. A physician, as a member of a profession dedicated to preserving life when there is hope of doing so, should not be a participant in a legally authorized execution." Disturbed by the similarities between the lethal injection gurney and an operating table, the AMA first announced its position in 1980, when lethal injection was catching on as the "new and improved" killing method. The American Nurses' Association followed suit in 1983 when they declared that such participation was "a breach of the ethical tradition of nursing."

The participation of doctors in state-sanctioned executions is nothing new. The guillotine, introduced during the French Revolution, is associated with Dr. Joseph Guillotin, a liberal humanist of the late 1700s. He came up with the idea of a head-cutting machine, believing it a more advanced form of execution than other methods used at the time. The machine named after Dr. Guillotin was later redesigned and perfected by the French surgeon Dr. Antoine Louis, who created a blade that made a cleaner cut and other refinements. Use of the guillotine was widespread and frequent in France from the time of the Revolution until the abolition of the death penalty in the 1970s; the guillotine was also widely used in Germany under the Nazis in the 1930s and 1940s.

It was also in quest of a more humane way of executing prisoners that the first electric chair replaced hanging in New York. Although the machine was not designed by a member of the medical profession, the initial skepticism surrounding it was put to rest by two doctors who were present at the first electrocution in 1890. The positive assistance and advice of Dr. Carlos MacDonald and Dr. E. C. Spitzka were crucial in establishing the chair as the primary means of execution for many decades to follow.

At the 1982 Texas execution of Charles Brooks, the first death by lethal injection in the United States, Dr. Ralph Gray was on hand. Gray was medical director of the Texas Department of Corrections. He made sure Brooks's veins would accept the lethal drugs and monitored Brooks's heartbeat during the execution. Shaking his head five minutes into the process, he commented, "A couple more minutes."

The biggest difficulty in unifying support to distance the medical profession from executions has been the interpretation of "participation." According to the report, and drawing from the suggestions of 1991 guidelines offered by the AMA Council in Ethical and Judicial Affairs (CEJA), participation is defined as

> Selecting lethal injection sites.
>
> Starting intravenous lines to serve as ports for lethal injections.
>
> Prescribing or administering pre-execution tranquilizers or other psychotropic agents.
>
> Inspecting, testing, or maintaining lethal injection devices.
>
> Consulting with, or supervising, lethal injection personnel.
>
> Monitoring vital signs on site or remotely (including monitoring electrocardiograms).
>
> Attending, observing, or witnessing executions as a physician.
>
> Providing psychiatric information to certify competence to be executed.
>
> Providing psychiatric treatment to establish competence to be executed.
>
> Soliciting or harvesting organs for donation by condemned prisoners.

The report also clarifies the murky waters between "determining/pronouncing" and "certifying" the cause of death: "Determining death includes monitoring the condition of the condemned during the execution and determining the point at which the individual has actually died.

"Certifying death includes confirming that the individual is dead after another person has pronounced or determined that the individual is dead."

The distinction is important. In some executions the condemned person does not die when he is supposed to. If the physician checks and determines the prisoner's heart is still beating, as in the case of Brooks and other documented cases, the doctor will notify the rest of the execution team. At this point, a doctor's ethical and moral obligation would require him to perform *life-saving* procedures. Instead, his professional opinion acknowledging that the prisoner is still alive prompts the executioner to do whatever more it takes to send the condemned to his grave.

Some doctors disagree with the report and the AMA. "I've never experienced any difficulty with the physicians or staff performing their function in pronouncing death," said Dr. Frank Kilgo, retired physician from the Florida prison system. "It may be contrary to what the AMA wants them to do, but they all realize that's part of the job when they apply." Kilgo participated in five Florida executions. "All [the doctor] has done is announce a situation or status," continued Kilgo. "It's not like he's turning the valves and letting the poison seep into the man's system or anything like that."

Angola Warden John Whitley agrees with Kilgo. "The execution has taken place; it's happened," he explained. "The doctor is simply pronouncing the man dead. I don't see that as part of the execution process. I understand the argument both ways. I'm just saying that I don't feel that a doctor pronouncing the man dead is part of the execution."

In the *Breach of Trust* report, participation of medical personnel is discouraged even when the purpose is to assure a painless and flawless execution.

> Although physician participation in some instances may arguably reduce pain, there are many countervailing arguments. First, the purpose of medical involvement may not be to reduce harm of suffering, but to give the surface appearance of humanity. Second, the physician's presence also serves to give an aura of medical legitimacy to the procedure. Third, in the larger picture, the physician is taking over some of the responsibility for carrying out the punishment and in this context, becomes the handmaiden of the state as executioner. In return for possible reduction of pain, the physician, in effect, acts under the control of the state, doing harm.

The report makes reference to the "egregious violations of medical ethics perpetrated by physicians during the Nazi regime." Hitler used doctors to conduct horrible experiments on humans, experiments that included testing to see how much torture they could endure. Doctors performed the tests under authority of Nazi law. These brutal acts are burned into the conscience of the medical community. Dr. Roy Schwar, vice president of the AMA, recently told a reporter, "I guess everyone is so sensitive to history and what has happened at times when doctors lost their moral anchors, that many people are overprotective and say no, stay away, the slope's too slippery, and even a millimeter of movement over the top of the hill and you could slide so quickly."

Society's trust is crippled when doctors assist in killing people. As AMA executive vice president James Todd, M.D., explains, "When the healing hand becomes the hand inflicting the wound, the world is turned inside out." The report agrees: "Physicians are committed to humanity and the relief of suffering; they are entrusted by society to work for the benefit of their patients. This trust is shattered when medical skills are used to facilitate state executions."

The Louisiana State Medical Society (LSMS) is unofficially against physician participation in executions, and they do not interpret the law as requiring physician involvement. LSMS also states that it has no intention of initiating legislation regarding the participation of medical assistants in executions.

Louisiana Department of Corrections Regulation No. 10-25, Section G(2) requires that a physician be present at each execution. State law offers somewhat of a safeguard to the attending medical personnel in that no licensed health care professional "shall be compelled to administer a lethal injection" (La. R.S. 15:569.C). Even so, a doctor's presence is required by the regulation; otherwise an execution cannot be performed.

"I would never ask anybody to have any part in an execution that they didn't feel comfortable with," said Warden Whitley. He explained that no reprisal would be taken against any employee—doctor or otherwise—who requested not to be part of the execution staff. Whitley, who has overseen Angola's last three executions, also verified the physician's role: "A doctor pronounces the man dead, that's it." Whitley added that although the persons who hook up the IV are qualified to do so, they are not doctors. Asked who sticks the needle in, he responded, "That's nobody's business."

No state requires a physician to be the actual executioner, but New Jersey is the only state in the nation that specifically excludes physicians from that role.

The report notes that "the National Commission on Corrections Health Care (NCCHC) (regulated through the Department of Justice) has set standards for the accreditation of correctional health systems. In the U.S., these standards prohibit the participation of correctional health professionals in all forms of punishment, which includes executions. Unfortunately, accreditation is voluntary, and less than 15% of all state prison systems have gone through the NCCHC process." The Louisiana prison system has not. Instead, it is under the more lenient accreditation of the American Correctional Association (ACA), which has no provision for medical participation in executions.

In 1992 the U.S. Department of Justice began requiring a doctor's presence at federal executions to pronounce the death of the condemned. The federal mandate triggered harsh protest by the medical profession and other human rights organizations. As a result, the Justice Department changed its policy, and physicians are no longer required to attend a federal execution.

States, on the other hand, are not as easily persuaded. The 1990 execution of Charles Walker in Illinois is a good example. Prior to Walker's execution, medical organizations appealed to then governor James Thompson, urging him not to require a doctor's presence inside the death chamber. The plea was unsuccessful, and three physicians participated in Walker's death. A few months later, Illinois lawmakers passed a law that conceals the identity of any doctor participating in an execution.

But there are encouraging signs for keeping the medical profession out of executions. In April 1994, Timothy Spencer was executed in Virginia. The chief doctor for the Virginia Department of Corrections, who usually attends the executions, took an unexpected vacation on the day Spencer was scheduled to die. Concerned that he might suffer sanctions or retaliation, the AMA offered the doctor whatever assistance he needed.

The *Breach of Trust* report calls for a concerted national effort by medical personnel to eliminate all participation in the execution process, to place their Hippocratic Oath above state law:

> "Many physicians will continue to participate in executions (some perhaps without enthusiasm) unless there is strong professional pressure combined with state acknowledgment of the professional ethics against medical involvement. Professional pressure is usually exerted through the influence of state medical societies and the regulatory power of state licensing boards."

The report concludes with the following recommendations:

The laws and regulations of all death penalty states should incorporate AMA guidelines on physician participation. In particular, laws mandating physician presence and pronouncement of death should be changed to specifically exclude physician participation.

Laws should not be enacted that facilitate violations of medical ethical standards (such as anonymity clauses). The medical profession cannot regulate and police itself properly if laws protect violators from scrutiny and review.

All state medical societies should adopt the AMA guidelines on physician participation in executions. Medical societies should inform state medical boards on the seriousness of this violation of medical ethics, and urge that prompt action be taken against violators.

State medical boards, which are responsible for licensure and discipline, should define physician participation as unethical conduct, and take appropriate action against physicians who violate ethical standards.

Postscript: The push by the AMA and other medical organizations to exclude medical participation in executions has lost momentum over the past four years. The number of states with the death penalty has increased to 38 as of October 1, 1998. Prison doctors and other medical personnel in most of those 38 states have no qualms about assisting in carrying out the ultimate sentence. Table 4.1 presents the positions of state medical societies for all states on this issue.

TABLE 4.1

State Medical Society Positions on Physician Participation in Executions

State	Oppose[1]	AMA[2]	Refuse[3]	Sanction[4]
AL	NO	YES	NO	NO
AR	YES	NO	N/A	NO
AZ	NO	N/A	NO	NO
CA	YES	NO	YES	YES
CO	NO	N/A	NO	NO
CT	NO	NO	NO	NO
DE	NO	YES	NO	YES
FL	NO	YES	NO	NO
GA	NO	YES	YES	N/A
ID	NO	YES	NO	NO
IL	YES	NO	YES	N/A
IN	NO	YES	NO	NO
KY	NO	YES	YES	NO
LA	NO	NO	NO	NO
MD	NO	YES	YES	YES
MS	NO	YES	YES	NO
MO	NO	YES	YES	YES
MT	NO	NO	N/A	N/A
NB	NO	NO	N/A	N/A
NV	NO	YES	NO	NO
NH	YES	NO	YES	YES
NJ	YES	NO	YES	YES
NM	NO	YES	YES	N/A
NC	YES	NO	NO	NO

Continued

TABLE 4.1 (CONTINUED)

State	Oppose[1]	AMA[2]	Refuse[3]	Sanction[4]
OH	NO	YES	NO	NO
OK	NO	YES	YES	YES
OR	YES	NO	YES	YES
PA	NO	YES	YES	YES
SC	NO	YES	N/A	N/A
SD	NO	NO	N/A	N/A
TN	NO	NO	N/A	N/A
TX	YES	NO	NO	NO
UT	YES	NO	YES	YES
VA	NO	YES	YES	YES
WA	YES	NO	YES	YES
WY	NO	YES	N/A	N/A

[1]State society's written policy specifically opposes physician participation in executions.

[2]Society has no policy and defers to the AMA.

[3]Society actively supports physicians who refuse to participate in executions.

[4]Society sanctions physicians who participate in executions.

5

Women on the Row

LANE NELSON

From *The Angolite,* September/October 1995, Angola, La: Louisiana State Penitentiary.

On a cool night in March 1995 New Orleans police officer Antoinette Frank walked into the Kim Anh restaurant in the eastern part of the "Crescent City." The restaurant's employees, well aware of the city's national reputation for violent crime, welcomed her presence. Frank's was a familiar face. In her off time she moonlighted as a security guard for the Vietnamese family-run eatery.

But on this night Chau Vu, the cook and adult child of the restaurant owners, was a bit troubled by Frank's appearance. Frank had already stopped by twice earlier that evening, and called several times. Vu was uneasy enough about the officer's uncharacteristic behavior to take $10,000 from the safe and hide it in the microwave.

Frank and her cousin, 18-year-old Rogers Lacaze, entered the restaurant, pulled out their pistols, and subdued off-duty police officer Ronald Williams II. Williams, working part time as a security guard for the Vus, was Frank's former partner on the police force. He was forced to his knees, then shot in the head.

When Chau Vu heard the gunshot, she hid in the walk-in cooler. She heard more shots ring out, then silence. She stayed in the cooler until she heard Frank and Lacaze leave the building. When she came out she discovered Williams lying dead in a pool of blood. In another area she found her brother and sister. They, too, had been shot while on their knees. Three murdered and the $10,000 taken from the microwave.

Police were notified of the robbery/murders and raced to the restaurant. Frank was one of the officers responding to the call. When she saw Chau Vu, she asked her what happened. "You were there. Why you ask me that question?" Vu responded.

Vu's accusation led to an interrogation in which the 23-year-old Frank broke down and confessed to the crime. According to police, in her first taped statement Frank blamed all the killings on Lacaze, but changed her story in a second statement, saying Lacaze killed Williams, then held a gun to her head and forced her to kill the other two as they prayed on their knees. Lacaze was apprehended the following day, and both were indicted for first-degree murder. Prosecutors quickly decided to seek the death penalty.

Lacaze went to trial first and told jurors he was never in the restaurant and that Frank had "set him up." The prosecution, however, presented his confession, made hours after his arrest, in which he admitted being on the scene but blamed the killings on Frank. In response, Lacaze said the confession was forced: "Every time I said I wasn't there, that I didn't have anything to do with it, [the police] would slap me in the back of the head with the phone book," he testified. The jury sided with the prosecution and found Lacaze guilty, then sentenced him to die for the triple murder.

Frank went on trial in September. After the prosecution presented a strong case, her attorney, Robert Jenkins, decided not to offer a defense. Instead he reminded the jury it was not the defendant's obligation to prove her innocence but the state's duty to prove her guilt. It took only 22 minutes for the jury to find Frank guilty as charged, and 35 minutes to decide her fate—death by lethal injection. Antoinette Frank is the first woman in Louisiana to be sentenced to death in 20 years.

As the only death-sentenced female in the state, she will be confined at the Louisiana Correctional Institute for Women (LCIW) in St. Gabriel. LCIW has no death row unit, but Warden Johnny Jones foresees no problem housing Frank. She will be held in a specially modified cell, referred to as *Cell 6,* and will have her own enclosed exercise yard she will use only in the early morning hours when other prisoners are still asleep. Installation of a camera surveillance system to monitor Frank's cell is being discussed. Prison officials will keep her separated from the rest of the inmate population—not only because she is sentenced to death, but because she is an ex–police officer. When her death date draws near, she will be transported to Angola, which has the only death chamber in the state.

Frank's journey to the death chamber is just beginning. She has rounds of appeals to pursue and years of isolation to endure. Pamela Lynn Perillo, who is nearing the end of the journey, knows about isolated years, living the day-to-day burden of impending execution. Her journey began in 1980, when a Texas jury sentenced her to die. She is the longest confined female death row inmate in the nation.

Perillo, James Briddle, and his wife, Linda Fletcher, left California to avoid arrest for an aggravated robbery they committed to support their heroin habit. Hitchhiking through Texas, they were picked up in Houston by Robert Banks. Banks was moving furniture from an apartment into his new house and offered to put them up for a couple of days in exchange for their help. They accepted. The following day Banks's friend from Louisiana, Bob Skeens, arrived at the house. That night they had a drug and alcohol party. The following morning Briddle and Perillo took Banks's M-1 rifle and .45 caliber pistol. They subdued the two men by tying their ankles and hands with nylon rope. With Banks first and Skeens second, Briddle and Perillo wrapped a rope around their throats and each pulled one end until the men were dead. The trio then fled Texas with Skeens's car and other stolen property.

When Perillo's drug-induced state wore off, she found herself in Colorado, alone. She flagged down a Denver police officer and confessed to the killings. "I want to stop running and get my son back," she told Denver detectives. Once back in Texas she was tried, convicted, and given the death

Pamela Perillo, Texas death row inmate. (Copyright: Texas Department of Criminal Justice.)

sentence. James Briddle also received the death sentence and awaits execution. Fletcher, for her cooperation with prosecutors, received five years' probation.

Until recently Perillo desperately tried to avoid the media. "Everyone wants exclusive rights to my story," she told the Associated Press this past July. "I'm beginning to feel like my name is 'Money' instead of Pam." She explained that the media usually burns people on death row by pounding away at the gruesome facts of their crimes. "Mostly, the main thing is I don't think it's fair to the victims' families to rehash, rehash, rehash," she told the reporter while giving him a guided tour through the female death row unit. "I don't think it's fair to my family. I don't want to make people relive it, and I don't like reliving it over and over and over. And I don't want to hurt the victims anymore than I already have."

Perillo has been on death row in Gatesville, Texas, for over 15 years. She has lived an isolated yet transforming life. Her once hard, drug-distorted personality has changed to that of a soft, caring woman. But that transformation doesn't amount to a hill of beans to the state of Texas. Texas wants her dead.

Perillo told *The Angolite* that she grew up in a poor family in Lynwood, California, under the care of an abusive father. She began using drugs at the age of 10, and quickly found heroin to be her drug of choice.

When she was old enough to pass for 21, she tended and danced in bars. She is the mother of a 17-year-old-son who she says is the happiest part of her life.

Apart from her family, some friends, her lawyers, and God, she feels that the world is against her. Yet, she stands strong in the face of death. The 42-year-old woman is quick to claim Jesus as her source of strength. Perillo has become a devout Christian over the years and a spiritual beacon for the women who have come to death row after her.

One of those women is Karla Faye Tucker, sentenced to die for a 1984 double murder. She was 23 at the time of her crime. Now 35, Tucker has spent her eleven years on death row trying to redeem herself for the pickax murders she and her boyfriend Danny Garrett committed. (Garrett received the death penalty, won a new trial in 1993, and died in state custody awaiting retrial.)

When Houston police discovered the bodies of Jerry Dean and Deborah Thornton in Dean's apartment, a pickax was embedded in Thornton's chest. Tucker and Garrett were arrested after their siblings heard them bragging about the murders and called authorities. According to court records, Garrett's brother claimed Tucker expressed sexual gratification every time she swung the axe. "Doug, I came at every stroke," he said she told him.

That was Karla Faye Tucker then: a young and beautiful woman who latched onto hard drugs at the age of 10 and ran the fast life of rock and roll, hanging out with headline bands and partying until she dropped. Shortly after her arrest, Tucker turned to Christianity. She viewed her years on the row as salvation. "It's been better for me," she told Houston journalist Leah Karotkin in 1993, "because I was taken out of an environment where drugs and violence were the norm, and put in here and given a chance to really kind of stop and realize what's right and good. It's been great for me."

During the years in prison Tucker tried to help troubled kids: "My message is not 'Karla shouldn't die.' My message is, 'You're accountable for what you do . . . . When you fill your mind with altering substances, you lose all your inhibitions . . . .[I want to] let them know, from my perspective, what I think would have kept me out of here."

Although Tucker's Christian motives gained her support from various Christian groups, human rights organizations, and even some of the victim's relatives, prosecutors and skeptics took a different view regarding her redemption. They saw it as irrelevant. They pushed four execution dates in their efforts to have her killed.

One of Tucker's biggest supporters was Dallas-based prison ministry worker Dana Brown, who has been carrying the message of the Gospel into the female death row unit for years. Tucker and Brown began exchanging

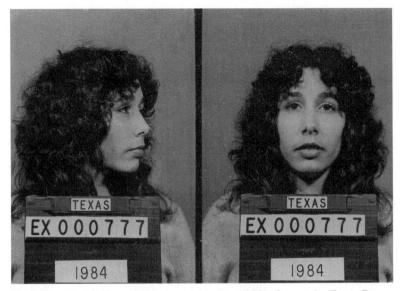

Karla Faye Tucker, Texas inmate executed in 1998. (Copyright: Texas Department of Criminal Justice.)

letters and eventually fell in love. The two were married by proxy this past summer. Because his new bride was a death row inmate, Brown had to relinquish his role as death row minister and lose the special privilege of contact visits (physical touching) that had been extended while he was holding church services. The death row unit has a policy of noncontact visits with friends or family members, so Brown and Tucker were forbidden to touch after their marriage.

Pamela Perillo tops the list of 45 women (as of September 30, 1995) presently awaiting execution in this country. On November 2, 1984, North Carolina killed Margie Velma Barfield by lethal injection. Since the 1977 execution of Gary Gilmore in Utah, to the August 31, 1995, execution of Barry Fairchild in Virginia, 295 males and only two females have been executed. Still, this country does have a bloody history of executing women (see Table 5.1).

That history began with the hanging of Jane Champion, in James County, Virginia, in 1632. Other than the fact Champion was legally hanged under English Code Law, no information exists about her crime or her age. According to Watt Espy, director of the Capital Punishment Research Project, in Headland, Alabama, and the leading authority on the history of executions in America, Champion's death marked the first of the 511 known legal executions of women in this country.

TABLE 5.1

Death Sentences of Females by State and Race (1973-1995)

State	White	Black	Latino	N. Amer.	Total
Florida	11	2	1	0	14
North Carolina	8	3	0	1	12
Ohio	3	6	0	0	9
Texas	6	2	0	0	8
California	4	3	1	0	8
Alabama	5	2	0	0	7
Mississippi	4	2	0	0	6
Oklahoma	4	1	0	1	6
Georgia	4	1	0	0	5
Illinois	1	3	1	0	5
Missouri	4	0	1	0	5
Indiana	2	2	0	0	4
Pennsylvania	1	3	0	0	4
Maryland	1	0	0	2	3
Idaho	2	0	0	0	2
Kentucky	2	0	0	0	2
Nevada	1	1	0	0	2
Louisiana	1	1	0	0	2
Arizona	1	0	0	0	1
Arkansas	1	0	0	0	1
New Jersey	1	0	0	0	1
South Carolina	1	0	0	0	1
Tennessee	1	0	0	0	1
Totals	69	32	4	4	109

Source: Victor Streib, *Capital Punishment of Females.*

The oldest woman ever executed was a slave known only by her surname Greene. She was hanged on February 13, 1857, at the age of 65 for murder in Prince William County, Virginia. The youngest put to death was 12-year-old Hannah Ocuish, a Native American hanged in New London County, Connecticut, on December 20, 1786. Hannah was convicted of the murder of a six-year-old white girl.

Executions of the 1600s, 1700s, and early 1800s were not carried out the way they are today. They were performed almost immediately after sentencing, and were public carnivals held in the center of town. Although women could be executed, they were not expected to attend the spectacle. In effect, a condemned woman was not allowed the comfort of female family members and friends in her last moments of life. Rather, she was forced to stand on the scaffold humiliated before a crowd of cavorting men cheering the executioner.

The over 3,000 men presently on death row far outnumber the 44 women. Yet, according to Victor L. Streib, professor of law at Cleveland-Marshall College of Law at Cleveland State University, women are sentenced to death more often as first offenders. Streib has monitored the death sentencing of females since 1988, and periodically publishes updated research on the information he generates. In *Capital Punishment of Females: Present Female Death Row Inmates and Death Sentences and Executions of Female Offenders, January 1, 1973 to June 30, 1995,* he states that "female executions constitute less than 3% . . . of approximately 19,000 confirmed executions since 1608." Streib's historical information is based in large part on Espy's findings.

Streib found that out of the 5,434 death sentences handed out nationally since 1973, 109 have been given to women. Excluding the 44 women presently on death row, 64 death sentences have been reversed, while only two women have been executed, creating a reversal-to-execution rate among death-sentenced females greater than 98%. The reason for so many reversals may simply be that these are *women* the country is trying to put to death.

There has been and remains a serious shortage of capable death penalty attorneys to handle the influx of death-sentenced prisoners. Federally funded capital punishment resource centers, which offer pro bono legal services to death row inmates, have been understaffed, underfunded, and head-high in appeal cases for years. Texas houses over 300 condemned people, six of whom are women. Some of these men have no attorney to appeal their case in federal court, but all of the women do. Just being a woman can hit a soft spot, even in a lawyer's heart.

Of course this is not the case at trial. Like men who receive the death sentence, the women are also usually poor and undereducated. They must rely on overburdened public defenders who are financially strapped. No person on death row has ever come close to having an O.J. Simpson "Dream Team" representation.

In a 1992 study conducted by the National Coalition to Abolish the Death Penalty, research showed female death row prisoners are (1) mostly poor and therefore must rely on court-appointed attorneys, many of whom have never before handled a capital case; (2) sometimes mentally retarded; (3) often mothers; and (4) usually from abusive families that abandoned them and as a result easily fall prey to other abusive relationships.

Professor Streib's study points out that several female death row inmates now waiting to be executed "were battered women who killed their batterers," or were persuaded to kill by their batterers. In the book *Women Prisoners—A Forgotten Population*, Kathleen A. O'Shea shows almost half of the women presently on death row "have a history of abuse and are there for the murder of an abusive spouse or lover." O'Shea points out that evidence of abuse is admissible at trial and is especially helpful in the sentencing phase when a jury has to decide whether the woman should be given life or death. However, investigating a client's past is time-consuming and expensive. It is something that "poorly funded public defenders cannot afford."

According to a 1991 U.S. Surgeon General's report, domestic violence is the leading cause of injury to women. In a 1992 study by the Georgia Department of Corrections, 44% of the 235 women serving time for murder or manslaughter killed a husband or lover. Out of that 44 %, 102 were classified as domestic killings. Half of that 102 claimed they were regularly beaten by their partner. How many beatings will a woman take before she strikes back? According to O'Shea, when they do strike back and kill their intimate partner, "they are given longer and more severe prison sentences than men."

O'Shea visited and interviewed the five women on Oklahoma's death row—three white, one black, and one Native American. (Since then one of the women had her death sentence reversed and is now serving life). She found that the five women combined were the mothers of 11 children and the grandmothers of several more. It was the loss of physical contact with their children, noted O'Shea, that was hardest for them to deal with in their day-to-day life on death row.

These women are locked in small cells 23 hours a day and not allowed contact visits. They cannot mingle among themselves, and, as one condemned woman put it, "It's loneliness, it's cruel, it's hell."

But as with the male death rows across the country, conditions vary from state to state. In Texas, the six condemned women eat together, share a dayroom where they can talk or watch TV, and they have a workshop where they make Cabbage Patch–like dolls. (There is a four-month backlog for orders on these extremely popular dolls.) They are allowed some modifications to their cells, and most of them try to add a soft, personal touch to their hard environment—such as in Perillo's cell, which has a handmade throwrug, pink crocheted bedspread, and small electric fan.

Still, no amount of decorating dispels the weight of impending execution. Apart from the Bible, the most visible book in Perillo's cell is titled *Facing Death and the Life After.* For the first years of her life on the row Perillo had immense faith that she would not be executed. She saw and heard of woman after woman getting their death sentences reversed. But after 15 years, and with nearly every legal avenue exhausted, Perillo's hope is dissipating. "With Karla [Tucker] and myself having close execution dates set, the reality of execution is causing tension and worry among the women here," Perillo told *The Angolite* before Tucker's execution. "It seems to me that a female execution is overdue in this country. Do I still believe my sentence will be reversed? I'm really not sure any more."

The United States houses more women condemned to die than any other country in the world. Other than when their crimes occur or when a serious execution date is upon one of them, they remain invisible to the public. Perhaps that is how society wants it. It does not want to be reminded that mothers and grandmothers are destined to die at the hands of the state. And when people are reminded, they ease their conscience by picturing these women as the worst of the worst, women too dangerous to even be around other prisoners, women who have committed unspeakable crimes.

But the fact is that most of these women are no different than the thousands of others serving life sentences or a long stretch of years in prison for murder. These few condemned women—.01% of the female prison population—are simply the unluckiest ones.

◆ "KITTY"

Catherine "Kitty" Dodds was convicted and sentenced to death in 1975 for the murder of her husband, Charles Dodds. At trial, the prosecution convinced the jury that Dodds hired her next door neighbor, Rodney Blackwell, to carry out the killing. Blackwell also received the death penalty. Both Dodds and Blackwell were released from death row in 1976 through a

U.S. Supreme Court ruling that held Louisiana's mandatory death penalty statute unconstitutional.

In 1980, while on a trip to the hospital, Dodds escaped and ended up in Missouri. She took the name of Linda D. Winter, married, and became a model citizen. She was arrested two years later by the FBI and brought back to Louisiana to serve out her life sentence. Four and a half years later she was granted clemency by the pardon board and governor. She served two more years for the escape and was released; she has been a free woman ever since.

Dodds and Blackwell have always contended that Charles Dodds, a New Orleans police officer who retired under a stress disability pension, was physically abusive to his wife and that the abuse drove Dodds to have him killed. It was "either him or me," she explained in later interviews. A made-for-TV movie portrayed this same account of the killing. Blackwell was aware of the abuse and felt that Dodds would be killed by her husband if something wasn't done. He remains in prison serving his life sentence.

◆ "TONI JO"

The last woman put to death by the state of Louisiana was Annie Beatrice "Toni Jo" Henry, on November 28, 1942. She was electrocuted for the murder of Joseph P. Calloway, who was shot in the head while kneeling in prayer in a rice field in Calcasieu Parish. According to historical documents, Henry wanted Calloway's car so she could rob a bank and get enough money to hire a lawyer to spring her husband from a Texas prison.

◆ "THE DUCHESS"

Clinton Duffy supervised 90 executions during his 11 years as warden of San Quentin (1940–1951). In his book, *88 Men and 2 Women,* he provides accounts of the men and women he walked to the gas chamber. One person was Juanita Spinelli, a.k.a. "The Duchess," a gang leader sentenced to die for the murder of one of her mob members. Spinelli ordered the murder of 19-year-old Robert Sherrard after she believed Sherrard was going to talk about a previous murder the gang had committed. She was convicted on the testimony of one of the three men who assisted her in the killing. Gang member Albert Ives cooperated with the prosecution and was later found to be insane and sent to the state mental hospital. The two other gang members who participated in Sherrard's murder, Gordon Hawkins and Spinelli's common-law husband, Mike Simeone, were also sentenced to death.

Duffy recounts his impression of Spinelli: "She was the coldest, hardest character, male or female, I have ever known. . . . I was amazed at her utter lack of feminine appeal. At 52, she was a homely, scrawny, near-sighted, sharp-featured scarecrow, with thin lips, beady eyes, and scraggly black hair flecked with gray. It had hardly seemed possible that even young punks with neither brains nor character would take orders from her."

Because she was a woman, Spinelli's pending execution generated heavy publicity. That publicity earned her three different stays of execution, which was uncommon among death-sentenced prisoners in the 1940s. "She was receiving special consideration because of her sex . . . if she [had been] a man, she would have died on schedule," wrote Duffy. While some at that time cried out to spare the woman's life, others cried just as loud for her death. "There was increasing opposition to her cause on the part of law enforcement authorities and the press."

Inside San Quentin a small group of male prisoners petitioned Duffy and the governor of California to spare Spinelli's life. According to Duffy, that petition asked for special consideration because Spinelli was a woman and a mother. The prisoners also offered to take her place in the gas chamber by drawing straws to see who would be executed. Duffy points out that the petition, signed by about 30 prisoners, came from a small fragment of the prison population, and that "the vast majority didn't care what happened to the Duchess or anyone else."

The San Quentin warden recounts taking that final walk with Spinelli. Once they approached the gas chamber, Duffy realized the witnesses had not been seated. He told Spinelli there would be a short wait and apologized. Standing there, just outside the death chamber, Duffy describes those last moments:

> "Would you prefer to return to your cell [to wait]?"
> "No," she said. "We'll just stand here."
> She looked toward the open door where the witnesses were still filing in. "The sun's out, isn't it, Warden?" she remarked.
> "Yes."
> "It's a beautiful day."
> "Yes," I said. Bright and sunshiny."
> "It sometimes gets so damp and foggy here."
> The witnesses were all inside and the door closed behind them.

"All right, Mrs. Spinelli," I said. "It's time. Keep your chin up."

"O.K.," she said shortly.

Then she walked quickly into the gas chamber and sat down as casual as if it were a chair in a beauty parlor. She was the only person I knew who could stand and talk about the weather while waiting to die.[1]

Postscript: Texas executed James Briddle, Perillo's codefendant, on December 12, 1995. As of January 1, 1999, Perillo remained the longest-confined female on death row.

Amidst heavy media coverage and emotional debates, Karla Faye Tucker, a white, Christian convert with a magnetic personality, was executed on February 3, 1998, becoming the second woman put to death since the moratorium on executions was lifted in 1976. Less than two months later, on March 30, 1998, the state of Florida executed Judy Buenoano, without a media carnival and lacking the hard-hitting support for her life that Tucker had enjoyed. But, then, Buenoano, convicted of poisoning her husband, did not profess Christianity, was an ethnic minority, and did not have the beautiful flowing hair and smiling persona of Karla Faye Tucker.

In 1996 Rodney Blackwell, Kitty Dodds's codefendant, received a commutation of his life sentence to 60 years, which made him immediately eligible for parole. Blackwell remains in a medium security prison, unable to convince the parole board to grant his freedom.

Table 5.2 presents statistics on females on death row.

T A B L E 5.2

Females on Death Row: 1995

State	Name	Age Race	Age (crime)	(now)	Crime and Victim	Date Sentenced
Alabama*	Haney, Judy	White	32	44	paid to have her husband killed	11/18/88
Alabama	Harris, Louise	Black	34	42	paid to have her husband killed	8/11/89
Alabama	Lyon, Linda	White	45	47	killed white male police officer	12/21/94
Alabama	Neelley, Judith	White	18	31	killed 13-year-old white girl	4/18/83
Arizona	Milke, Debra	White	25	31	killed her 4-year-old son	1/18/91
California	Alfaro, Maria	Latino	18	23	burglary/murder of Hispanic girl	7/14/92
California	Carrington, Celeste	Black	30	32	burglar/murder of Hispanic adult male & adult white female (separate incidents)	11/23/94
California	Coffman, Cynthia	White	24	33	killed adult white female	8/30/89

State	Name	Race				
California	McDermott, Maureen	White	37	48	killed adult white male	6/8/90
California	Samuels, Mary	White	40	46	paid to have her husband killed then murdered her husband's killer	9/16/94
California	Thompson, Catherine	Black	42	47	paid to have her husband killed	6/10/93
California	Dalton, Kerry Lynn	White	28	35	killed white adult female	5/23/95
California	Young, Caroline	Latino	49	51	slashed throats of her two grand kids	9/29/95
Florida**	Buenoana, Judias	White	28	52	poisoned her husband	11/26/85
Florida	Cardona, Ana	Latino	30	35	killed her 3-year-old son	4/1/92
Florida	Larzelere, Virginia	White	38	42	killed her husband	5/11/93
Florida	Wuornos, Aileen	White	33	39	serial killings—7 white males	1/31/92 & 5/15/92
Idaho	Rowe, Robin	White	35	38	killed of husband, son, daughter	2/16/93
Illinois*	Garcia, Guinevere	White	32	36	murdered her Hispanic husband	10/9/92
Illinois*	Mulero, Marilyn	Latino	20	23	killed 2 adult Latino males	11/12/93

Continued

TABLE 5.2 (CONTINUED)

State	Name	Age Race	Age (crime)	(now)	Crime and Victim	Date Sentenced
Illinois	Pulliam, Latasha	Black	19	23	killed neighbor's 6-year-old girl	6/15/94
Illinois*	Geraldine, Smith	Black	39	47	hired someone to kill her lover's wife	2/20/91
Illinois	Williams, Dorothy	Black	35	41	killed 97-year-old black woman	4/18/91
Indiana	Brown, Debra	Black	21	32	murdered 7-year-old black girl	6/23/86
Louisiana	Frank, Antoinette	Black	24	24	killed white male police officer & 2 adult Asians (1 male & 1 female)	9/13/95
Mississippi	Ballenger, Vernice	White	46	58	killed 75-year-old white woman	1/13/93
Missouri	Copeland, Faye	White	67	76	killed 4 white adult males	4/27/91
Missouri*	Phillips, Shirley	White	53	59	murdered elderly white female	4/6/92
Nevada	Ford, Priscilla	Black	51	66	killed 3 white females/ 3 white males	4/29/82

State	Name	Race			Crime	Date
N. Carolina	Jennings, Patricia	White	47	52	killed her 77-year-old husband	11/5/90
N. Carolina	Moore, Blanche	White	56	62	murdered her white boyfriend	11/16/90
Oklahoma	Allen, Wanda	Black	29	35	killed adult black female	4/26/89
Oklahoma*	Jones, Patricia	White	36	43	killed 2 white adults (male/female)	12/14/89
Oklahoma	Plantz, Marilyn	White	27	34	paid to have her husband killed	3/31/89
Oklahoma	Smith, Lois	White	41	54	killed adult white female	12/29/82
Pennsylvania	Hill, Doneta	Black	23	28	killed elderly Asian male and adult black male (2 incidents)	4/9/92
Pennsylvania	King, Carolyn	Black	28	30	robbery/murder	11/30/94
Pennsylvania	O'Donnell, Kelly	White	25	27	killed adult white male	7/1/93
Pennsylvania	Rivers, Delores	Black	34	41	killed elderly female	1/30/88
Tennessee	Owens, Gaile	White	32	42	paid to have her husband killed	1/15/86
Texas	Beets, Betty	White	46	57	killed her husband	10/14/85
Texas	Newton, Francis	Black	21	30	killed husband, son & daughter	11/17/88

Continued

TABLE 5.2 (CONTINUED)

State	Name	Age Race	Age (crime)	(now)	Crime and Victim	Date Sentenced
Texas	Perillo, Pamela	White	24	39	robbery/murder 2 white adult males	9/2/80
Texas	Sheppard, Erica	Black	19	21	killed adult white female	3/3/95
Texas	Tucker, Karla	White	23	35	killed 2 white adults (male/female)	4/25/84

Source: Victor Streib, Capital Punishment of Females.

*Indicates those women, as of February 9, 1998, who have been removed from death row, either through a commutation or court decision.

**Indicates women executed since the date of this article (September 1995). Those two women were Karla Tucker in Texas, executed February 3, 1998, and Judias Buenoana in Florida, executed March 30, 1998.

Some states added women to their death row between September 1995 and February 1998. Among those women are Melanie Anderson, 28, white, sentenced to death on 9/26/97 by North Carolina for killing a two-year-old white child; Christa Pike, 22, white, given the death penalty in Tennessee on 3/29/96 for killing a 19-year-old Latino female; Darla Router, 29, white, sentenced to death by Texas on 2/4/97 for killing her five-year-old son; Cathy Henderson, 42, white, sentenced to death by Texas on 5/25/97 for killing an infant she was baby sitting; and Leslie Nelson, 41, white, given the death penalty by New Jersey on 5/97 for killing two adult males (a state investigator and a policeman)—Nelson was a man who underwent a sex change operation in 1992.

6

Killing Kids

LANE NELSON

From *The Angolite,* November/December 1995, Angola, La: Louisiana State Penitentiary.

In 1974 14-year-old Dalton Prejean of Lafayette, Louisiana, shot and killed a cabdriver in a bungled robbery attempt. He turned himself in to the authorities, and the juvenile court sent him to the Louisiana Training Institute (LTI), a juvenile prison. On the recommendation of an LTI psychiatrist, Prejean was released back into society in 1976, unprepared to tackle the adult responsibilities awaiting him. Seven months later he killed again.

On July 1–2, 1977, Prejean, his brother Joseph, and two friends spent the night drinking at bars in the Lafayette area. They were headed home in the wee hours of the morning when State Trooper Donald Cleveland noticed faulty taillights on Prejean's '66 Chevy. He pulled over the four young blacks.

Cleveland got Joseph out of the Chevy and pushed him hard against the patrol car. Angered over the rough way the trooper handled Joseph, Prejean pulled a .38 caliber revolver from underneath the seat, stepped out of the car, walked toward Cleveland, and shot him twice, killing him. Prejean was arrested, transferred to adult court, convicted, and sentenced to death for the murder. He was 17 years old.

Prejean spent 12 years in a cell on Angola's death row. On May 2, 1990, he was strapped into the state's electric chair and put to death for a crime he committed while a juvenile.

Dalton Prejean, Louisiana death row inmate in 1985. (Copyright: Louisiana State Penitentiary.)

Dalton Prejean with his attorney Thomas Guilbeau at the pardon board hearing of November 27, 1989. (Copyright: Thomas Guilbeau.)

Nine juvenile offenders have been executed in this country (to 1995) since the 1976 reinstatement of capital punishment. Texas, which keeps its death machine well oiled, accounts for five of those executions. Although the nine amount to only about 3% of the total executions during the past 20 years, that ratio is likely to change.

With violent juvenile crime on the rise, the juvenile death row population will grow as well. According to the U.S. Department of Justice, arrests for juveniles increased 14% in 1992–93. During that same period, homicide arrests for kids under the age of 15 increased by 24%. Various studies additionally show that juvenile murders are more vicious than ever. These statistics suggest not only a larger juvenile death row population, in the future, but perhaps future state statute modifications in sentencing kids to death at a younger age.

Legally sanctioned juvenile executions came to this country via English law. Through its long, turbulent history, and until 1908, England legally sanctioned execution of teens and preteens for such crimes as picking pockets, theft, rape, and murder, even though actual executions of juveniles were rare. According to Victor Streib, "Research at Old Bailey revealed that although more than 100 youths had been sentenced to death from 1801 to 1836, none had been executed. While some cases do exist, it appears settled that execution of youths was never at any time common in England." The United Kingdom abolished capital punishment in 1969.

Executing children in the United States has been similarly rare. Although many have been sentenced to death by juries, the commutation rate has been very high. From the 1890s through the 1920s, the number of juvenile offenders executed ranged from 20 to 27 per decade—1.6% to 2.3% of all executions. In the 1930s executions hit an all-time high, 1,670 for the decade. During this same decade, juvenile executions also rose to 41; still, that was only 2.5%.

The historical data reveal that executing a juvenile offender has never been a popular practice; yet, the idea of killing kids is not new in this country. The first documented juvenile execution occurred in Roxbury, Massachusetts, in 1642. Sixteen-year-old Thomas Graunger was hanged for the crime of bestiality. The youth, who sodomized a horse and cow, was convicted by a jury of adult males and sentenced under the Old Testament law described in Leviticus 20:15: "And if a man lie with a beast, he shall surely be put to death: and ye shall slay the beast." Authorities carried out the law to the letter, killing the horse, the cow, and all the calves, then dropping young Graunger from the gallows floor, hanging him until dead.

Hannah Ocuish was the youngest documented female executed in this country. Born to an alcoholic Pequot Indian mother and a white father who abandoned his family, Hannah was a so-called "wild child" with obvious signs of retardation. She was known as a "fierce young savage" by townsfolk. On the morning of July 2, 1786, Hannah attacked and killed Eunice Bolles, a six-year-old white girl and daughter of a well-to-do businessman in New London, Connecticut. According to records, the little girl was first beaten with a heavy stone, then strangled. When arrested and confronted with the dead girl's body, Hannah confessed in tears. Defense attorneys pleaded her guilty and tossed her to the mercy of the court. "The sparing of you on account of your age would, as the law says, be dangerous consequences to the public by holding up the idea that children might commit such atrocious acts with impunity," the judge told her. "[You will] be hanged with a rope by the neck, between heaven and earth, until you are dead, dead, dead." So much for mercy. On December 20, 1786, 12-year-old Hannah was escorted to the gallows platform. Just before the noose was placed around her neck, she thanked the sheriff for the kindness she received in his jail. Then the sheriff gave the order to end her life—before it ever had a chance to begin.

Hannah was one of three documented 12-year-olds executed in American history. The two others were boys. Clem was a black slave child raised on a plantation in Sussex County, Virginia. The plantation owner's two sons treated Clem roughly, and one day Clem decided to "catch back." On a spring afternoon in 1787, 12-year-old Clem ambushed the boys in the woods. He hit them repeatedly with a stick until they were dead, then pushed their bodies into a swamp. The following day Clem confessed to the crime during an interrogation by the county coroner. His conviction and execution were swift. With no appeals in those early days, Clem was hanged in front of the courthouse exactly one month after the day of the crime.

The last executed 12-year-old was a black slave in Alabama known as Godfrey. He was owned by Mrs. Margaret Stuart of Mobile. Stuart also had custody of her four-year-old grandson, Lawrence. In the late morning of April 30, 1857, Stuart left Lawrence in Godfrey's care while she went across the street to visit with neighbors. The two boys went outside to play. When Stuart returned home, she found little Lawrence lying in the yard dying of hatchet wounds. Godfrey denied killing the boy and told authorities that fierce Indians committed the crime. But he had blood on his clothes, and no Indians were in the area at the time. Later that day, Godfrey allegedly confessed to a neighborhood friend and was arrested. He was 11 at the time. A jury found Godfrey guilty, and the judge sentenced him to die. He was hanged in Mobile, Alabama, on July 16, 1858.

Thirteen at the time of her execution, Eliza was 12 when she killed the two-year-old son of a white family she worked for as a servant in Henry County, Kentucky. The little boy's body was found in some brush behind the barn, his head bashed in by a heavy object. Under intense questioning by town officials, Eliza confessed and showed authorities the bloody stone she had used. The black servant girl was arrested, convicted, and sentenced to death. Several hundred men, black and white, gathered on a cold February day in 1868 to witness the hanging. Eliza wore a black gown and cap as deputies and a preacher escorted her up the scaffold. Her body trembled uncontrollably as she stepped toward the noose—perhaps from the icy winter wind, probably from fear. A newspaper account described the 13-year-old girl as she dropped to her death: "She writhed and twisted and jerked many times, but at last she was still—in death." While three black men cut Eliza's body down and carried her to the all-black cemetery, others in the crowd scrambled for pieces of the rope to collect as souvenirs.

The youngest person executed in this century was George Junius Stinney, Jr., a 14-year-old black child. He was executed on June 16, 1944, for the attempted rape and murder of two young white girls—one 11, the other 8 years old. Because of pressure from townspeople and local politicians in Clarendon County, South Carolina, Stinney's trial began exactly one month after his arrest. Fifteen hundred spectators spilled into the street of the courthouse to witness the event. The prosecutor's tight case was helped along by Stinney's court-appointed attorneys, who presented no witnesses or evidence. The all-white male jury took 10 minutes to reach a verdict—guilty with the death sentence. Defense attorneys never advised Stinney nor his family of the right to appeal.

Less than two months later, and with a Bible snuggled close to his chest, Stinney was led to the death chamber. Because the state's electric chair had been built for adults, the guards had difficulty strapping the youngster in. A local newspaper described the execution: "As the current surges through his body, Stinney's wide-eyed face emerges from under the loose-fitting mask on his head. Tears are flowing from his eyes." After three minutes and three jolts of electricity, the child was pronounced dead. To this day, controversy remains over whether Stinney was innocent.

Stinney's execution led to public debate about putting such young people to death. Except on rare occasions, prosecutors in all states began adhering to 15 as the age of accountability in regard to capital punishment. The last offender executed for a crime committed at age 15 was Irvin Mattio of Louisiana.

According to old clippings from the *New Orleans Times-Picayune,* Mattio was in the Dixie movie theater on Rampart Street on May 2, 1945. He got into a fight with an older black youth. Theater manager Paul Brunet rushed to quell the disturbance and hit Mattio over the head with a billy-club. Stunned but not out, Mattio ran for the front door and encountered Sylvian P. Cassagne, a local political leader who was visiting Brunet at the time. A struggle between Mattio and Cassagne carried on to the sidewalk, where a few others attempted to help Cassagne hold the youth down. In the melee Mattio stabbed Cassagne with a pocket knife and fled the scene. Cassagne died of a stab wound to the heart. Mattio was apprehended the next day and confessed, telling authorities he was frightened during the incident and that the blow to the head by Brunet's "billy" dazed him.

Mattio went on trial two months later. He was found guilty of murder and sentenced to death. On January 9, 1948, he was executed.

For the two decades following the Mattio execution, prosecutors nationwide seemed to cool their heels a bit, not racing to put any more kids to death who were below the age of 16 when they committed a capital crime. Most state legislatures were not nearly as amenable. They either set new laws or kept old ones that held the minimum age requirement for capital punishment lower than 15. Thus, and although prosecutors were reluctant to have the executions actually carried out, kids 15 and younger still ended up on death row—but eventually had their sentences commuted to life or to a number of years. All that changed in 1988, with *Thompson v. Oklahoma.*

In *Thompson,* the U.S. Supreme Court ruled that executing children who committed crimes at the age of 15 or younger was unconstitutional. Wayne Thompson was 15 when he and three older persons murdered Charles Keene, Thompson's brother-in-law. According to court records, Thompson wanted to even the score for the abuse his sister suffered at the hands of Keene. On January 22, 1983, Keene was shot twice and stabbed in the throat, chest, and stomach. His body was then chained to a concrete block and thrown into a river, where it was discovered four weeks later. The four defendants were tried separately; each received the death penalty.

Jurors did consider Thompson's young age in recommending the death sentence, but they believed the crime was especially cruel and that the youngster deserved to pay with his life. On appeal to the U.S. Supreme Court, a majority of the justices felt differently. They did not accept the state's argument that some 15-year-olds need to be executed in order to prevent others the same age from committing the same acts. The Court pointed out that the small number of people Thompson's age or younger who have been executed during the twentieth century did not have any viable deterrent effect. "Inexperience, less education, less intelligence make the teenager less able to evaluate the consequences of his or her conduct while at the same time he or she is much more apt to be motivated by mere emotion or peer pressure than is an adult," stated the majority opinion. "The reasons why juveniles are not trusted with the privileges and responsibilities of an adult also explains why their irresponsible conduct is not as morally reprehensible as that of an adult. . . . The road we have traveled during the past four decades—in which thousands of juries have tried murder cases—leads to the unambiguous conclusion that the imposition of the death penalty on a 15-year-old offender is now generally abhorrent to the conscience of the community."

The *Thompson* decision forced an across-the-board minimum age requirement on all states, making it illegal to execute any person who was under the age of 16 when the crime was committed.

A year later another move to completely halt the execution of juvenile offenders failed. In *Stanford v. Kentucky* the Supreme Court held that executing those who commit crimes at the age of 16 and 17 did not violate the Eighth Amendment provision against cruel and unusual punishment.

Presently, 38 states, the U.S. government, and the U.S. military have capital punishment statutes. While 15 of these 40 jurisdictions set the minimum age limit at 18, 13 set the limit at either 16 or 17. The remaining

12 states either have no statutory minimum age requirement or have an old one that sets the age at 15 or lower; therefore, they are controlled by the *Thompson* decision—unable to execute any offender under the age of 16. It is safe to assume that many of the 25 states, if allowed by the U.S. Supreme Court, would execute younger offenders.

Case in point: Natchitoches Parish District Attorney Mike Henry told the Associated Press in August 1993 that he intended to seek the death penalty for Jason Pilcher and Brandy Wiley, two 15-year-olds who shot and killed a 33-year-old woman and her 11-year-old son. According to authorities, the kids knocked on the woman's door requesting some water, then shot her and the boy to death.

Henry had visions of getting death sentences against the two youngsters, then using those sentences to challenge the *Thompson* decision in the courts. That vision did not materialize. Pilcher went on trial and was convicted on April 20, 1994, of two counts of second-degree murder, receiving two consecutive sentences of life without parole. Wiley, who became the chief prosecution witness against Pilcher, cut a deal with Henry for a manslaughter sentence, which was eventually set aside by the courts on appeal.

The current era of capital punishment sentencing began in 1973. As of June 30, 1995, 141 death sentences have been imposed on 129 juvenile offenders (some receiving more than one death sentence). Over the past 22 years the percentage of juvenile death sentences, compared to the total death row population, is just over 2%. The reversal rate (court action that leads to a lesser sentence) among death-sentenced juvenile offenders—excluding those presently awaiting the outcome of their appeals–is 91%. All but four of the 129 condemned juvenile offenders have been males. Three of the four females were sentenced in the deep South—Mississippi, Alabama, and Georgia—and the other in Indiana. They have all had their sentences reversed. No female juvenile offender was confined to death row as of June 30, 1995.

At the beginning of 1984, 33 juvenile offenders were confined to death row. By June 1995, 44 were waiting to die—just over 1.5% of the present total death row population (3,000). Texas confines the most: 17 of the 44. Louisiana has two juvenile offenders on death row. One is black, the other white. Both committed their crime at age 17. The general profile of today's juvenile offender on death row is that of a 17-year-old black or Hispanic male sentenced to die for killing a white adult. Although more black juvenile offenders have been sentenced to death since 1973, more white juvenile offenders have been executed. Tables 6.1, 6.2, and 6.3 present some statistics on juvenile executions.

TABLE 6.1

Juvenile Executions as Percentage of Total Executions by Decade

Decade	Total Executions	Juvenile Executions	Percentage of Total Executions
1890s	1,215	20	1.6%
1900s	1,192	23	1.9%
1910s	1,039	24	2.3%
1920s	1,169	27	2.3%
1930s	1,670	41	2.5%
1940s	1,288	53	4.1%
1950s	716	16	2.2%
1960s	191	3	1.6%
1970s	3	0	0.0%
1980s	117	3	3.5%
1990s*	175	6	3.4%
Total:	8,775	216	2.5%

*As of August 31, 1995 (about 350 juvenile offenders have been executed since 1642).

Source: Victor Streib, *The Death Penalty for Juveniles,* 1995, and *Death Row U.S.A.,* NAACP Legal Defense and Education Fund, Inc., 1999.

The increase in serious crime committed by juveniles, along with the "tougher and tougher" approach to deal with that crime by lawmakers, indicates future challenges to the *Thompson* decision. But how executing younger and younger offenders will reduce violent crime is not clear.

Dalton Prejean's release from LTI prior to killing State Trooper Cleveland was prompted by a state psychiatrist's recommendation. The pretrial psychiatric evaluation Prejean underwent after the Cleveland murder determined the 17-year-old had the mental capacity of a 13½ year-old, with lots of frustration bubbling inside him. Had Prejean stayed in a juvenile facility longer than he did, and during his incarceration received proper

TABLE 6.2

Juvenile Death Sentences as Percentage of Total Sentences: 1973–1997

Year	Total Death Sentences	Juvenile Death Sentences by Age			Juvenile Death Sentences Total	Percent of Total Sentences
		15	16	17		
1973	42	0	0	0	0	0.0%
1974	149	1	0	2	3	1.8%
1975	298	1	5	4	10	3.1%
1976	234	0	0	3	3	1.2%
1977	138	1	3	8	12	7.5%
1978	186	0	1	6	7	3.3%
1979	154	0	1	3	4	2.3%
1980	175	2	0	3	5	2.5%
1981	229	0	2	6	8	3.3%
1982	269	0	1	13	14	5.3%
1983	254	0	4	3	7	2.7%
1984	287	3	0	3	6	2.1%

education and intense counseling, he might have straightened out his life, and Trooper Cleveland would still be alive.

◆ THE YOUNGEST

Louisiana executed the youngest documented offender. In September of 1855 the state hanged a 10-year-old boy. The arrest, trial, and execution took place behind a veil of secrecy. Apart from the age and gender of the child nothing else has been discovered, not even his race or his crime.

TABLE 6.2 (CONTINUED)

Year	Total Death Sentences	Juvenile Death Sentences by Age			Juvenile Death Sentences Total	Percent of Total Sentences
		15	16	17		
1985	271	1	1	5	7	2.5%
1986	305	1	3	6	10	3.4%
1987	290	1	0	1	2	0.7%
1988	295	0	0	5	5	1.7%
1989	264	0	0	1	1	0.4%
1990	252	1	3	4	8	3.3%
1991	271	1	0	4	5	1.9%
1992	293	0	1	5	6	2.2%
1993	295	0	1	5	6	2.1%
1994	319	0	4	6	10	3.9%
1995	310	0	0	2	2	1.5%
1996	300*	0	4	5	9	3.0%
1997	300*	0	3	2	5	1.7%
Totals:	6,180*	13	37	117	167	2.7%

*Estimates

Source: Victor Streib, *The Juvenile Death Penalty Today,* 1997.

◆ NO ESCAPE

Willie Francis was a black 15-year-old who worked at a drugstore in St. Martinville, Louisiana, in 1944. The owner, Andrew Thomas, was a prominent white businessman and brother to the chief of police. On at least one occasion Thomas harshly reprimanded Francis regarding his work performance. Considering the era and location, the reprimand probably took on racial tones. It stuck in Francis's craw.

On the night of November 7, 1944, Thomas was ambushed outside his home, shot three times and stripped of his wallet and watch. Although

TABLE 6.3

Juvenile Death Sentences by State: 1973–97

State	Race			Sex		Age at Crime			Total Death Sentences
	Black	Latino	White	Male	Female	15	16	17	
Texas	20	13	7	40	0	0	0	40	40
Florida	8	1	18	27	0	3	7	17	27
Alabama	7	0	7	13	1	1	7	6	14
Mississippi	6	0	5	10	1	0	5	6	11
Georgia	4	0	6	9	1	1	0	9	10
Louisiana	8	0	0	8	0	2	3	3	8
N. Carolina	4	0	2	6	0	1	0	5	6
Ohio	5	0	1	6	0	0	1	5	6
Oklahoma	0	0	6	6	0	1	2	3	6
S. Carolina	3	0	3	6	0	0	2	4	6

State									
Arizona	5	3	2	0	0	5	2	3	0
Pennsylvania	5	3	1	1	0	5	1	0	4
Missouri	4	2	2	0	0	4	2	0	2
Virginia	4	3	1	0	0	4	2	0	2
Indiana	3	2	0	1	1	2	1	0	2
Arkansas	2	0	1	1	0	2	0	0	2
Kentucky	2	1	0	1	0	2	1	0	1
Maryland	3	3	0	0	0	3	1	0	2
Nevada	2	0	2	0	0	2	0	1	1
Nebraska	1	0	1	0	0	1	0	0	1
New Jersey	1	1	0	0	0	1	0	0	1
Washington	1	1	1	0	0	1	1	0	0
Totals:	167	117	37	13	4	163	67	18	82

Source: Victor Streib, The Juvenile Death Penalty Today, 1997.

Francis was a key suspect in the murder, the case remained unsolved for nine months. Finally, authorities arrested Francis in Port Arthur, Texas, and discovered Thomas's wallet on the youngster. He was returned to St. Martinville, where he allegedly signed a confession and took police to the hidden murder weapon.

His first-degree murder trial lasted a day and a half. The jury found him guilty and sentenced him to die. After an unsuccessful appeal and request for clemency to the governor, the portable electric chair was delivered to the St. Martinville jail. On May 3, 1946, the executioner strapped Francis in. The switch was thrown, sparks were visible . . . but nothing happened. As the executioner and witnesses stood bewildered, Francis yelled to have the hood over his face removed because he was smothering. The switch was turned off and he was unstrapped and taken back to his cell. It appeared that Francis had beaten death. A wire in the electric chair had burned out, sending only a light amount of current into Francis's body. "It tickled a bit, but did not hurt much," he told a reporter.

The malfunction produced a unique issue for a new round of appeals. Defense attorneys now argued that to execute the youngster again would violate the double jeopardy clause and inflict cruel and unusual punishment. His lawyers also added that the delivery from death was an act of God. The appeal made it all the way to the U.S. Supreme Court, where it drew national attention. On January 12, 1947, in a 5-4 decision, the Court ruled Francis could legally be electrocuted a second time. On June 7, 1947, inside the St. Martinville jail, Francis was strapped into the portable electric chair a second time. It worked.

Postscript: In 1996, Louisiana sent Shareef Cousin to death row for a New Orleans robbery/murder he had alledgedly committed at age 16. His age, his cries of innocence, and claims of misconduct by police and prosecutor attracted national media attention. Two years later the Louisiana Supreme Court reversed Cousin's conviction and sent the case back for retrial. On January 8, 1999, three days before the second trial was scheduled to start, New Orleans District Attorney Harry Connick dropped the murder charge, saying there was not enough evidence to get another guilty verdict against the teenager. Cousin remains in prison, serving 20 years on other robbery charges.

Cousin's removal from Louisiana's death row leaves one man awaiting execution for a juvenile murder. Nationally, 73 juvenile offenders were awaiting execution as of October 1, 1998. After two juvenile executions in Texas in the spring of 1998 and one in Virginia in the fall, a total of 12 men, all 17 at the time of their crimes, had been executed since capital punishment resumed in 1977. One man scheduled for lethal injection in early 1999 was Sean Sellers, convicted of three murders in Oklahoma when he was 16.

Tables 6.4 and 6.5 present statistics on juvenile death sentences.

TABLE 6.4

Juvenile Death Sentences in Louisiana: 1974–96

Date*	Name	Age at Crime	Status
1974	Gary Tyler	16	Reversed
1978	Dalton Prejean	17	Executed
1979	Joseph Brown	17	Reversed
1979	Reginald Smith	16	Died on death row
1980	Joseph Marshall	15	Reversed
1986	Adam Comeaux	17	On death row
1987	Troy Dugar	15	Reversed
1994	Dale Craig	17	On death row
1996	Shareef Cousins	16	Reversed

Source: The Angolite

TABLE 6.5

Juvenile Executions Since 1973 Reinstatement of Capital Punishment by State: 1973–98

Name	Execution	State	Race	Age at Crime	Age at Execution
Charles Rumbaugh	9-11-85	Texas	White	17	28
J. Terry Roach	1-10-86	S. Carolina	White	17	25
Jay Pinkerton	5-15-86	Texas	White	17	24
Dalton Prejean	5-18-90	Louisiana	Black	17	30
Johnny Garrett	2-11-92	Texas	White	17	28
Curtis Harris	7-1-93	Texas	Black	17	31
Frederick Lashley	7-28-93	Missouri	Black	17	29
Ruben Cantu	8-24-93	Texas	Latino	17	26
Chris Burger	12-7-93	Georgia	White	17	33
Joseph Cannon	4-22-98	Texas	White	17	38
Robert Carter	0-18-98	Texas	White	17	34
Dwayne Wright	10-14-98	Virginia	Black	17	24

Source: Death Row U.S.A., NAACP Legal Defense and Education Fund, Inc., 1998.

7

Enlarging the Circle

LANE NELSON

From *The Angolite,* September/October 1996, Angola, La: Louisiana State Penitentiary.

Death was common punishment for the crime of rape in this country for two centuries, especially when the victim was white and the rapist black. Capital punishment authority Hugo Bedau reports that between 1930 and 1972, when the U.S. Supreme Court temporarily outlawed the death penalty, 455 people were executed for the crime of rape. Of that number, 405 of the condemned were black, the vast majority convicted of raping white women. From 1941 to 1957 Louisiana executed 14 rapists; all were black, and 13 had committed their crimes against white women.

In 1977, after the death penalty had been restored for first-degree murder, death for rapists became obsolete. That year, the U.S. Supreme Court ruled in *Coker v. Georgia,* "Rape is without a doubt deserving of serious punishment; but in terms of moral depravity and of the injury of the person and to the public, it does not compare with murder. . . . The murderer kills; the rapist, if no more than that, does not. . . . We have the abiding conviction that the death penalty, which is unique in its severity and irrevocability . . . is an excessive penalty for the rapist who, as such, does not take human life."

In the 1990s, however, Louisiana began spearheading an effort to resurrect the death penalty for rapists and enlarge the small circle of death-eligible crimes. In 1995 Louisiana lawmakers amended the state's aggravated rape statute (La. R.S. 14:42) to include the death penalty for a person who rapes a child under the age of 12. The thrust of the state's legal argument to execute those convicted of child rape comes from the very decision that propelled states to abolish death for rapists in the first place. In *Coker,* the justices stopped short of announcing a blanket ruling that would have qualified death for all rapists unconstitutional. Instead, the Court decided it was cruel and unusual punishment to execute a person for the rape of an *adult* woman, leaving open the question of whether it was cruel and unusual when the victim was a child.

"We thought it was over, states wanting to execute people convicted of rape," defense attorney John Holdridge told *The Angolite.* Holdridge, working for the Louisiana Capital Assistance Project in New Orleans, is representing a case being prosecuted under the new death penalty statute. "This has to do with Louisiana politics. If other states felt strongly about this issue of executing those who rape children, then those states would have statutes like the one Louisiana now has."

One other state does. Mississippi had a child-rape death penalty statute long before *Coker* was decided and kept it on the books thereafter. It is active today. "Prosecutors use it as a bargaining chip," said attorney Clive Stafford-Smith. "When you threaten a person with the death chamber, even somebody who is innocent will consider cutting a deal and take a life sentence. It makes for an easy day at the office for the prosecutor."

Only one person in recent history has been sentenced to death under the Mississippi rape statute—Alfred Dale Leatherwood, who was convicted of raping an 11-year-old girl. Leatherwood, who is black, was 18 at the time of the crime and mentally retarded. He was convicted and sentenced to death by an all-white jury. Stafford-Smith represented him on appeal in 1989. When the Mississippi Supreme Court decided the appeal, it sidestepped the issue of whether execution for child rapists is unconstitutional and instead threw out Leatherwood's conviction on other grounds. Avoiding further confrontation with the statute, prosecutors allowed Leatherwood to plead guilty to credit-for-time-served. "They don't want the statute struck down because that would end the plea-bargaining power it gives prosecutors," Stafford-Smith explained.

Although the court refused to rule whether execution for a child rapist is unconstitutional, a concurring opinion by Mississippi Supreme Court Justice James L. Robertson clearly said it is:

> The punishment simply does not fit the crime. Rape is a vile deed deserving of damnation but short of death. However heinous or offensive child rape may be—and is—the victim's life is not taken. Though the victim may hardly forget the nightmarish experience, sensitive response by the family, friends and competent professionals may often assure recovery so that in time the victim comes to lead a quite scarred, though quite livable, life. In this sense the harshness of the death penalty is qualitatively greater than the gravity of the offense. . . . I find not without relevance that one may search the feminist literature on the subject of rape and find not the first argument that our society ought to execute rapists.

In Louisiana's move to execute child rapists, it has picked two guinea pigs—Patrick Dewayne Bethley, from Ouachita Parish, and Anthony Wilson, from Orleans Parish. Holdridge represents Bethley, who is accused of raping three girls under the age of 12. Prosecutors allege that he was HIV-positive and knew it when he committed the rapes. Whether Bethley is really HIV-positive, now or at the time of the rapes, has yet to be proved. Wilson is accused of aggravated rape of a five-year-old girl.

In Bethley's case, the trial judge ruled the new capital punishment rape statute unconstitutional. In Wilson's case, the trial court ruled the statute permissible. The two cases have been consolidated and appealed to the Louisiana Supreme Court. In his writ to the court, Holdridge noted that death for raping a child is out of sync with the rest of the country. "No one

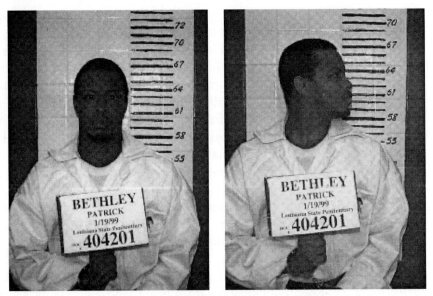

Prison mug shots of Patrick Bethley, originally charged with the capital rape of a child, now serving life at Angola. (Copyright: Louisiana State Penitentiary.)

is housed today on a death row for any other crime not involving a homicide. No one has been executed in the United States for rape in 32 years."

Holdridge further argued that death for child rapists "makes no measurable contribution to the acceptable goals of punishment" and suggested that the capital rape statute may even have the opposite effect. "Death as a penalty for statutory rape will have a chilling effect on the already inadequate reporting of the crime." He cited judicial, social, and criminal justice authorities to prove the point that most child rapes are committed by family members and that a child, as well as the mother, will be more hesitant to report the crime when they know the family member may be executed. He backed his argument with FBI statistics that show sex crimes against children are already greatly unreported. The consequences of death to the offender, he declared, will only magnify the problem.

The Louisiana Foundation Against Sexual Assault agreed, and has filed a friend-of-the-court brief in support of Holdridge's argument. This victims' rights organization opposes death for child rapists on the principle that the extreme sentence will not only lead to less reporting of the crime, but will also provide incentive for the rapist to kill his small victim to avoid arrest. Hugo Bedau, in *The Death Penalty in America,* surmises that "the criminal has every reason to kill his victim, since in this way he removes at a stroke the best possible witness against him without appreciably increasing the severity of his punishment if he is caught."

A wide variety of other friend-of-the-court briefs have been submitted to the state supreme court in support of Holdridge's argument, including those from the National Association of Social Workers, the Louisiana Chapter of Social Workers, and the Louisiana Chapter of NOW.

Constitutionality of the new death penalty statute will be argued before the state supreme court in mid-October. Whatever the ruling is, chances are it will be contested in the federal courts. The U.S. Supreme Court will ultimately decide the question of whether it is acceptable to execute a child rapist who has not killed his victim. It is worth noting that only last year the federal government expanded its circle of death-eligible crimes to include 50 additional offenses. In that long list, the crime of raping a child is nowhere to be found.

Postscript: The Louisiana Supreme Court reviewed the consolidated cases of Bethley and Wilson and upheld the validity of the death penalty statute for the aggravated rape of a child under 12. Defense attorneys appealed that decision to the U.S. Supreme Court but were denied a review. In essence, the Court refused to entertain the matter because neither Bethley nor Wilson had yet received a death sentence (both were on pre-trial motions). This leaves the door open for a future appeal lodged by a person who has been sentenced to death under the rape statute.

The time for that review may not be far off. As of January 1, 1999, Louisiana prosecutors were seeking the death penalty in more than 40 cases of aggravated child rape. While Wilson remains among these cases, Bethley is not. He pleaded guilty in 1998 for a sentence intended to keep him in prison for the rest of his life.

8

Tossing in the Towel

LANE NELSON

From *The Angolite,* January/February 1994, Angola, La: Louisiana State Penitentiary.

From the time the moratorium on capital punishment lifted, in 1976, to November 10, 1993, 29 death row prisoners abandoned their appeals and walked willingly into the hands of executioners. Seven of the 29 "volunteers" (as they are known in prison argot) did so in 1993. These were consensual executions, in which death row prisoners terminate available legal remedies and pursue a quick death at the hand of the state. While consensual executions are acceptable, if not encouraged, by a society that overwhelmingly supports the death penalty, they are a bewildering and exasperating problem for death penalty opponents, who charge that the nation's death chambers are being used as suicide vehicles for the condemned, and the so-called volunteers are actually victims of state-assisted homicides.

Gary Gilmore broke the moratorium on capital punishment. This three-time loser, sentenced to death for the murder of a college student gas station attendant in Provo, Utah, refused to file any appeal that would prolong his life. As a repeat offender, he knew the misery of prison life. From his death row cell he wrote a letter to his girlfriend saying, "What do I do, rot in prison, growing old and bitter? Hope that the state executes me? That's more acceptable and easier than suicide." Gilmore stepped in front of a firing squad on January 17, 1977, and became the first of the 29 volunteers to be executed. His last words were, "Let's do it." For Gilmore, immediate death was preferable to decades of life in prison.

Thomas Grasso, another volunteer, likewise screams, "Let's do it! Let's do it!" as he sits in his cell at Attica, New York. Grasso wants to be executed now, not 20 years from now.

On Christmas Eve 1990 a lonely Grasso suffered from a bad case of the holiday blues. Hilda Johnson lived down the street from Grasso and also spent Christmas alone. Grasso entered Johnson's home in Tulsa, Oklahoma, tightened an extension cord around her neck and strangled to death the 87-year-old woman. He then took her VCR and a small amount of cash.

From Tulsa, Grasso fled to New York, where a year later he committed a similar crime when he strangled an 81-year-old boarding house resident and stole his meager possessions. This time Grasso got caught. He pled guilty to the murder and received a 20-years-to-life sentence. The New York sentencing judge told him, "You're the worst piece of humanity that could stand in this court. I hope that 20 years from now I'm writing letters to the parole board so you can rot away your entire life in prison."

After sentencing, New York sent Grasso to face the Tulsa charge, to which he confessed. He pleaded guilty and received the death penalty. Grasso was apparently satisfied with the sentence. It was a way out of spending the rest of his life in prison. He immediately announced to Oklahoma authorities his desire to be executed as quickly as possible. His

Gary Gilmore, volunteer for execution in Utah in 1977.

mother, who advocates the death penalty for murderers with no exceptions, supported her son's decision. The Oklahoma Supreme Court conducted a rapid mandatory review of the case. Grasso's death sentence was upheld and an execution date set for October 19, 1993. While Grasso and Oklahoma eagerly awaited the death date, New York Governor Mario Cuomo intervened, and a federal judge blocked the execution 12 hours before it went down. Cuomo wanted Grasso back in New York to first serve the 20-years-to-life sentence.

Oklahoma and Grasso's mother objected. "I believe in capital punishment," said an irate Ruth Grasso. "I can't turn around and say I don't believe in it no more because it's my son. Let it get done with!"

As a matter of law, Cuomo got his way. The federal court ruled that the Interstate Act on Detainers agreement gives the sending state (New York) the right to have Grasso returned to have his first sentence served before carrying out the second. Cuomo, an outspoken opponent of capital punishment, told reporters that Grasso is "asking for mercy, choosing what he sees as the easiest penalty." The Oklahoma public defender representing Grasso in his death wish conceded to Cuomo's assessment. "It's not that he wants to die," said attorney Johnny O'Neil. "He just doesn't want life without parole." Grasso admitted, "I don't see any point being locked up for the rest of my life when I can just be executed in another state."

While Oklahoma appeals the federal court decision, Grasso sits in a cell at Attica, New York, a volunteer denied a death chamber. In devising schemes of payback for the New York governor, Grasso hopes to become Cuomo's worst nightmare in the upcoming gubernatorial elections. "I'm going to do everything in my power propaganda-wise, media-wise, to disgrace that man," he told the media. Cuomo realizes the possible consequences. "I got murdered on Grasso," the governor told reporters. "That kind of issue can be very bad for you." Grasso has indeed become a thorn in Cuomo's side.

Most attorneys who oppose the death penalty believe that it is in their clients' best interest to save their lives—irrespective of their clients' wishes. "You have to be extremely wary of uncritically accepting statements as to what [volunteers] want," said California ACLU attorney Michael Laurence. "If they had any judgment, they wouldn't be on death row."

"When an inmate condemned to death decides to consent to his own state-ordered homicide, we end up fighting him *and* the state," said Louisiana's ACLU director and death penalty attorney Denise LeBoeuf. "These are hard fights. Legally, it is difficult to find someone with standing to intervene in a criminal case. These battles take energy and time away from the real enemy—the state. A prisoner who consents to his own murder is, in a sense, saying to the rest of the guys on the row that there is nothing wrong with the death penalty. It's like giving aid and comfort to the enemy in a war. Not that I blame the prisoners themselves. It is the system of capital punishment that creates and dispenses the torment that leads to influencing these guys into giving up their lives."

On the other hand, some defense attorneys see death as in the best interest of their clients. Such was the case of Westley Allen Dodd, who raped and killed three boys, then requested execution by hanging. In his fight to thwart the ACLU and other death penalty opponents, Dodd received legal assistance from Washington defense attorney Darrell E. Lee. After Dodd swung from the gallows on January 5, 1993, Lee told reporters that if "ever there was a case for the death penalty, this would be it. I think society was well served by this execution. I know I was, and Westley was, too."

Dodd did not go to his death as quickly as he had anticipated. It was a slow process as the anti–death penalty network (lawyers, paralegals, writers, religious factions, and activists) worked hard to prevent the execution. Of the 29 volunteers, all have needed, to one degree or another, legal assistance to carry out their death wish. Once a death row prisoner tosses in the towel, a strange thing occurs; everyone connected with the case shuffles into different positions. The buddies become the enemies, the enemies becomes the buddies, and the volunteer becomes the centerpiece of attention by placing himself in a macabre tug-of-war.

Confessed serial killer David Mason robbed and murdered four elderly people in Oakland, California. After his 1981 arrest he strangled to death a fellow prisoner in the county jail. Mason sat on death row watching the years crawl by. Out of despair he finally decided enough was enough. Over objections from his attorneys he announced his death wish. At that, the California organization called Death Penalty Focus flooded Mason with 200 letters in an attempt to change his mind. His attorneys, family members, and the ACLU filed writs to stop the execution.

Mason didn't answer the letters, fired his attorneys, and told the media, "I have desperately tried to keep the ACLU out of my life."

As the legal battle waged, Michael K. Brady, a California defense attorney specializing in capital cases, stepped in. Brady represents murder defendants, yet also condones capital punishment. Taking on Mason's case, Brady joined forces with the state attorney general's office. "It's a very strange experience for me to be on the other side," Brady told the *Los Angeles Times*. "But I'm not advocating that Dave be put to death. I'm just making sure his right to choose is protected."

On August 24, 1993, Mason walked into the gas chamber, told the warden thank you, and triumphantly sucked in the lethal cyanide. According to California officials, Mason is the first volunteer in the state's history.

Lawyers such as Brady and attorneys for the state generally hold in high esteem a prisoner's freedom of choice to be executed. But because of the restrictions placed on what exactly it is the prisoner has to choose from, it is more of a sound-good tactic than a legitimate argument. If that same prisoner chooses to be given a life sentence, his choice, obviously, will be ignored. "They don't have any choice about whether they're going to live," said death row spiritual advisor and Catholic nun Helen Prejean. "The state is going to put them to death, regardless."

"Citizens in 35 states have decided through their legislature to require that all appeals be heard before an execution," said Coleman McCarthy (*Washington Post*). "While the traditional role of the attorney is to follow the instructions of the client, many believe that death is different," wrote abolitionist and author Lisa Radelet (*Consensual Executions, LIFElines*). "Here, the right of the individual must take a back seat to preserving the integrity of the law. If we allow an inmate to drop his appeals and forego review by the federal courts, we allow for the possibility of a miscarriage of justice. We allow the inmate to choose execution when the courts may have found grounds for reversal."

"Condemned prisoners can keep fighting their sentence, if they choose. But if they decide to quit, that's their right," Angola Warden John

Whitley told *The Angolite*. "People have a basic right to end their lives if that's what they want to do. I'm not talking about committing suicide just because you're unhappy or depressed. Hell, if that were the case, everybody would be killing themselves at some point. I'm talking about persons who know they are going to die in the very near future. They should be able to do it calmly, painlessly and with dignity, if that's what they choose."

Although states take aggressive action when trying to put a prisoner to death—horrifying the public with heinous facts of the crime and pushing death row appeals through the system as fast as the law will allow—these same states generally take a hands-off position when it comes to a volunteer. While the prisoner opposes his execution he is on the state's hit list. But when he chooses to be a volunteer he becomes the state's ally.

State time and energy in consensual executions concentrates on anyone opposing the volunteer's death wish. "We remain prepared to oppose any other federal or state action that is brought by anyone in any venue," said California Attorney General, Dan Lungren during the heated battle surrounding the execution of Dave Mason. Deputy Attorney General Catherine Rivlin confirmed to reporters that the state had "agreed all along that [Mason] can have a first petition [in federal court] if *he* wants it. All he needs to do to stop the execution is say, 'I want to stop the execution.'" According to prison officials, the appeal option was left open until the cyanide pellets were dropped.

Stanford University law professor Robert Weisberg criticizes the actions of those who aggressively interfere with a death row inmate's choice to die. Weisberg told reporters that these "zealous opponents" of capital punishment have a "simple goal to reduce executions, any way possible, and don't give a damn about the autonomy of the client, or not a big damn." (*New York Times*).

Agreeing with Weisberg's assessment is the vice dean of Columbia Law School, Vivian Berger, herself an opponent of capital punishment: "One has to be very careful about putting the cause ahead of the client. I myself would be very inclined to listen to a client who says, 'I don't want you working on this when I'm strapped in the chair.'" Berger, also general counsel to the ACLU, presently represents an inmate on Georgia's death row—one fighting to stay alive.

"I recognize that [anti–death penalty attorneys] have a right to file whatever they want, but I don't think it's right that they oppose the inmate's wishes when he has, for whatever reason, decided to quit fighting," commented Warden Whitley. "The decision to end appealing is his, nobody else's. It's his life, his right. These attorneys generally fight it on principle, in which case they forget the man."

James Brown, Episcopal bishop for the southeastern portion of Louisiana, predicts another repercussion resulting from the actions of volunteers: "The more appeals made, the more it reestablishes the free exercise of the appellate right," said Brown. "Say, in this prison, there was a wave of consensual executions. It would, I think, tend to undermine the other prisoners' feelings over the right to appeal. So there is a certain social element of responsibility, when possible, to use the appellate process." Like a muscle, when a right is not exercised, it weakens.

The general attitude of the anti–death penalty network is that no execution, consensual or otherwise, should be carried out. However, there do exist differences within the network over whether consensual executions are acts of homicide or suicide.

In a 1993 policy resolution the National Coalition to Abolish the Death Penalty (NCADP) took the homicide stand: "It is important to remember that what is *not* at stake in such cases is suicide. It is the state that proposes to execute the offender, his or her wishes notwithstanding. A consensual execution is not a state-assisted suicide (Justice Marshall's phrase to the contrary), but at best a prisoner-assisted homicide. We respect the pain of life on death row and the torture of waiting for the possible lethal outcome of protracted litigation. But that pain is imposed by the system of capital punishment."

Sister Helen Prejean, chairperson of the board of directors for the NCADP, sees no middle ground. "Taking the life of another person is homicide. If it were anything else they'd have a choice. This is not a Dr. Kevorkian–type situation," explains Prejean. "Suicide is really a person's own choice. Here it is the state that kills them—no choice. Somebody says, 'We got you here, we're going to kill you.' I think that distinguishes it from suicide. There are no options left open." While Prejean understands the psychological torture of death row and the suffering death row family members face, she affirms that consensual executions should be resisted.

It is peculiar that of all the major discussions concerning consensual executions, death row prisoners have not been included. *The Angolite* conducted a survey in late 1993 to which 19 of the 42 prisoners confined to Angola's death row responded. Though limited, the survey is significant in that it provides an outlet for voices too often misunderstood or forgotten. The poll indicates the condemned have strong opinions concerning consensual execution, and those opinions are, like the rest of the nation, divided. The majority believe a prisoner has the right to choose to be executed, and that consensual executions are another form of suicide, but most agree that anti–death penalty attorneys should fight against a volunteer's quest for death.

Most anti–death penalty attorneys view a client begging for execution as mentally incompetent, or in such a deep state of despair that he or she cannot make a rational decision. "In society, we don't let people like that make decisions about life and death without a lot of hedging," said LeBoeuf.

"Depression," attorney Clive Stafford-Smith told *The Angolite,* "is something that deserves treatment, not death. The death row environment is a deplorable and depressing place. It's quite understandable the degree of despair condemned men and women fall prey to."

Most death row prisoners at some point think about throwing in the towel. They may only contemplate it in the solitude of their cells, never mentioning it to another, but they do think about it. Their despondent situation encourages death as the easier way out. It is no different from the man or woman in the free world who is laid off, goes through a divorce, suddenly finds life nothing but pain and anguish, and uses suicide as a quick-fix solution. Thus, consensual execution is relief from depression and despair. And as with most suicides in the free world, where the easiest way out is generally used—connecting a hose to the muffler and shutting the garage door, taking a overdose of sleeping pills, stepping out of a high-story window— so the death chamber can be used as a suicide vehicle. It is an option over sitting in a cell and painfully slicing the wrists.

Treatment available to the despairing person in the free world is different from that offered the death row prisoner. Serious bouts of depression and despair can be treated through medication (mood elevators), which to some degree is available to prisoners. But the more effective treatment prescribed by psychiatrists is impossible in the prison setting. They recommend patients take a vacation to get away from the environment that is causing the depression. They recommend walking through the mountains, breathing the fresh air and smelling the wildflowers. They encourage closer family bonds of love and understanding. To the condemned, denied contact visits and stuck in a cell 23 hours a day, none of the above apply. Instead, they wallow in despair and, if they are not strong enough, will turn to the death chamber as treatment for their serious "down-home" blues.

Some volunteers refuse to commit suicide in the privacy of their cell for religious reasons. They do not want to commit what they perceive as the unpardonable sin. Yet, they have no problem using the death chamber to accomplish the same result. They feel that if the state does it—simply carries out the sentence—it is different, it is not suicide.

Baton Rouge Catholic Bishop Alfred C. Hughes offered his opinion on the religious concerns of consensual executions. "If they've given up because of no hope, that's not healthy. But if they've given up because they think that the appeal isn't going to go anywhere, and they believe in eternal life and want to know the fullness of salvation, then that's *another* matter."

"That's just what the state wants to hear," said Prejean, author of *Dead Man Walking*. "Obtaining the fullness of God by dying, casting the state in the roll of helper to obtain that fullness. Under those conditions what you're basically saying is, 'Yea, I'm going to God, therefore I will cooperate with the state to achieve my death.' That's not good."

In 1983 Michael Allen Durocher shot his girlfriend and their six-month-old son in the back, then stabbed to death his girlfriend's daughter. The three bodies were not discovered until 1990. Meanwhile, Durocher killed a man in a 1986 robbery and two years later beat a roommate to death. In 1991 Durocher sat on Florida's death row carrying the weight of three death sentences and two life sentences. His expectation of execution was high; any hope he could envision stopped short of spending the rest of his life in prison. Crippled by despair, Durocher tossed in the towel, only to find out that his plans for an easy execution would not develop. "I had assumed I need not do anything, just sit back and wait for it to happen," he said. "I did not expect such opposition."

In his fight against death penalty attorneys and capital punishment opponents, Durocher devised a scheme. He wrote letters to Florida Governor Lawton Chiles, a stern capital punishment proponent, begging the governor to carry out the execution as quickly as possible. The governor and Durocher found common ground. In May 1993 Chiles signed the death warrant, and Durocher sent him a thank-you card. On August 25, 1993, he was executed.

The speed at which Durocher's execution was carried out infuriated death penalty opponents. "The reaction has been, 'If he wants to die, let him go ahead and do it,'" said Susan Cary, a Florida death row attorney who counsels prisoners nearing execution dates. "We wouldn't do that if he were holding a gun in his hand."

Cary is right. Society frowns upon suicide. Even though it remains a crime in only two states, suicide is an affront against humanity. Few will calmly watch a person hook a hose to a car muffler, slide it through the wing window, start the engine, and crawl into the back seat. The natural human impulse will be to stop that person from killing himself.

Charles deGravelles, a volunteer Episcopal chaplain at Angola, does not see consensual executions as acts of suicide. He feels the choice of life or death resides with the prisoner. DeGravelles, who once worked on a suicide crisis center hotline in Baton Rouge, expressed his views, noting they do not necessarily represent his church's position on the matter:

"You're acknowledging that society has the right to create and enforce laws. Philosophically, I subscribe to that. Otherwise, we would have anarchy. Even if you don't agree with capital punishment, which I don't, here's a guy who has been duly sentenced to death by a court of law. He has appeals he can take, but that's entirely in his prerogative to take them or not. I would say absolutely that man has the right to end his life."

Suicide is against prison law. If an inmate attempts to take his life, he is punished for his efforts, usually by being placed in an isolation cell and strapped to a bunk by a four-point restraint. In the meantime he will be issued a disciplinary report for self-mutilation.

Active measures are pursued to prevent suicide by Louisiana's condemned. The one-man cells are searched regularly for contraband, particularly sharp objects and hoards of medication. When an execution date draws near, the condemned man is placed on suicide watch and moved to the front of the tier where he can be more easily observed. As the date with death draws closer still, the prisoner is transferred to the death house, where his every move is under close surveillance. These preventive actions are testimony to the acute awareness prison officials have concerning the despair that encases death row. "It is sure ironic," said anti–death penalty attorney Nick Trenticosta, "that even if the state sees the suicide aspect [of consensual executions] clearly, they will do everything in their power to prevent the inmate from getting materials to kill himself prior to the execution date." It's standard procedure: the state's way and no other.

Twelve of the 36 executing states in the country have carried out consensual executions. Of those 12 states, Nevada sticks out like a sore thumb. The five men it has executed have all been volunteers. This is in striking contrast to Louisiana, which has executed four times as many prisoners (21), but not one has been a volunteer. Louisiana's death row is one of the most severely restricted in the country, according to *Corrections Compendium.* Yet no one has given up.

Death row is a prison within a prison. Angola death row prisoners sit in their cells 23 hours a day, cannot work, have little counseling available, and have no constructive activities to pursue. It is a place of purgatory where the condemned languish between life and death. Hope is the essence of life. Life in prison, for many, is as hopeless as death. There is nothing substantial to strive for. It is the same old misery day in, day out. And depression is the norm rather than the exception. It may not be acceptable to some, but it is certainly understandable why a death row prisoner would volunteer for a quick way out.

Those choosing execution give various reasons: shame, remorse, religious conversion. But none seem as clear as despair. In any environment, clinical depression and despair foster death as a relief. Volunteers view spending years on end squeezed into a small cell as no life at all. They toss in the towel, knowing that surviving for nothing *is* nothing.

Divided Opinions from Those Who Count

Nineteen of the 42 Louisiana death row prisoners in 1993 participated in a poll conducted by *The Angolite*. The other 23 prisoners either were not asked owing to obvious mental health problems or simply declined to answer. Following are the poll questions and responses. Along with yes and no answers were comments illustrating the prinsoners' reasoning.

> Do you believe a death row prisoner has a personal right to choose to be executed if that's what he wants?
>
> 11-Yes: *"Living on death row amounts to torture, mental torture, and if one chooses to no longer endure, then that's his choice!"*
>
> 8-No: *"In my opinion, this would display a severe mental disorder."*

BOX 8.1   DEATH CHAMBER ATTRACTS SUICIDAL

There exists the possibility that consensual executions can lure the suicidal into committing capital murder: "Consensual executions can definitely encourage murder," said abolitionist and longtime prison reformer John Cole Vodicka. "Lloyd Hampton is the perfect example."

Illinois death row inmate Lloyd Wayne Hampton killed a 69-year-old retired janitor during a 1990 robbery. Found guilty and given the death penalty, Hampton abandoned his appeals in hopes of a speedy execution—his plan all along. A career criminal who spent a third of this life behind bars, Hampton was sick of living. "I had given up trying to make it," he told the *Chicago Tribune* (11/7/92). "I decided I either had to put myself in a position of being killed by somebody or committing suicide. At that point I had strong beliefs about not killing myself. So I put myself in a position to have the state kill me."

Less than three hours from his 1992 execution, Hampton changed his mind—apparently due to the pleas of his sister—and reinstated his appeals. However, Hampton's case demonstrates the possible attraction state death chambers have on the suicidal who harbor feelings of anger and despair.

Do you consider a consensual execution as just another form of suicide?

14-Yes: *"You are playing a key role in your decision to die. You are the one giving up your appeals that could result in vacating the death sentence."*

5-No: *"Being a Christian, I believe murder is a sin that can be forgiven by God, but self-murder wouldn't give you any time for repentance, so you couldn't be forgiven."*

If you gave up your appeals and chose to be executed, do you think your attorneys and anti-death-penalty organizations should fight against you?

11-Yes: *"I think a person that would do that could never be thinking right, or be in any condition to make any decision for themselves. If my attorneys believe my execution is wrong, to do otherwise would be hypocritical."*

8-No: *"I don't think they should. But I can understand them fighting against me or anyone else. They do it because they care.*

If you had absolutely no hope of ever getting out of prison, would you rather die or spend the remainder of your life in prison?

9-Live: *"I'd rather live in prison. Life is precious no matter where a person is."*

"I now live only for the hope of getting a life sentence. I don't really see much chance of ever getting out."

10-Die: *"I have told my family, attorneys and court that if it came to a choice of life in prison or death, then I want death. It would not even have to mean no hope. After 20 or 30 years I would not wish to try again."*

"If I get to the point I have no hope of ever getting out, I'll be dead anyway—walking around but dead inside. So yes, I'd just as soon be dead."

Postscript: Thomas Grasso got his wish. He was executed in Oklahoma on March 1, 1995, but only after Mario Cuomo lost his reelection bid to Republican George Pataki, who promised voters he would send Grasso to Oklahoma for execution. Grasso's mother, Ruth, told reporters, "I'm glad Pataki won, because it was our only hope." Grasso, in his final statement, conceded, "Let there be no mistake, Mario Cuomo was wright [sic]. All jurors should remember this. Attica and Oklahoma State Penitentiary are living hells." Cuomo responded by tagging the execution as a "tragic blunder" that relieved the double murderer of a "fate worse than death."

From Gary Gilmore in Utah (January 17, 1977) to Stephen Wood in Oklahoma (August 5, 1998), there have been 59 volunteers. Texas, which leads the country in executions, has had the most, 16. Louisiana, with 25 executions through early 1999, remains volunteer-free.

Table 8.1 presents statistics on consensual executions.

TABLE 8.1

Sixteen Years of Volunteers: Consensual Executions: 1977–93

Name	Date Executed	Race	State
Gary Gilmore	01-17-77	W	UT

Crime: Shot university student to death in robbery

Reason Given: Said he didn't want to rot in prison.

Comment: Career criminal, most of his life incarcerated.

Jessie Bishop	10-22-79	W	NV

Crime:

Reason Given: Career criminal. Said execution was an "occupational hazard" he was willing to accept.

Comment: When asked if death penalty was deterrent, he responded, "Did it stop me?"

Steven Judy	03-09-79	W	IN

Crime: Raped and strangled a 21-year-old woman, then drowned her three children.

Reason Given: Remorse. Did not want to spend life in prison.

Comment: "If society is not ready to help or correct people like me, they might as well do away with us."

Frank Coppola	08-10-82	W	VA

Crime: Robbery/murder of a woman.

Reason Given: To die with dignity. Wanted to lessen the suffering of his children.

Comment: The first four years on death row insisted he was innocent.

Stephen Morin	03-13-85	W	TX

Crime: Killed three women over a five-week crime spree.

Reason Given: Conversion to Christianity. "I am willing to resume my appeals if I could have a competent Christian attorney," he wrote the governor two days before the execution.

Comment: Because of his severe drug abuse it took technicians 40 minutes to fine a vein for the lethal injection.

Continued

TABLE 8.1 — (CONTINUED)

Name	Date Executed	Race	State
Charles Rumbaugh	09-11-85	W	TX

Crime: Murdered a jeweler during a robbery.

Reason Given: Told friends that execution was his way of escaping from Huntsville Prison.

Comment: Attempted suicide while on death row. Last words were, "All I can say is goodbye. I'm ready to begin my journey."

William Vandiver	10-16-85	W	IN

Crime: Stabbed to death, then dismembered his father-in-law.

Reason Given: Said he could no longer take the deplorable conditions of Indiana's death row. Thought the execution would stop the suffering of his family.

Comment: Botched execution, took 17 minutes and required five jolts of electricity.

Carrol Cole	12-06-85	W	NV

Crime: Strangled a woman. Convicted of a total of five murders.

Reason Given: Said he did not want to spend the rest of his life in prison.

Comment: Claimed to have killed 35 people and if set free would kill again.

Jeffery Barney	04-16-86	W	TX

Crime: Raped and strangled a 54-year-old woman.

Reason Given: Said he did not want to spend the rest of his life in prison and that he deserved to die.

Comment: Asked to administer the lethal injection himself.

Ramon Hernandez	01-30-87	H	TX

Crime: Shot a service station attendant to death during a robbery.

Reason Given: Remorse. Did not want his family or the victim's family to despair. Wanted to get execution over with.

Comment: Jumped up on the lethal injection bed and told witnesses he was ready for "the rocket to take off."

Continued

TABLE 8.1 — (CONTINUED)

Name	Date Executed	Race	State
Elisio Moreno	03-04-87	H	TX

Crime: Shot and killed a state trooper during a rampage in which he also killed five other people.

Reason Given: Believed his execution would help change the law to give other convicts the right to represent themselves.

Comment: "He has a misconception of the law," said an attorney. "He doesn't want to die, but his point ain't going to help him."

Arthur Bishop	06-10-88	W	UT

Crime: Kidnaped and murdered five boys in a four-year period.

Reason Given: Admitted he did not want to die, but believed his execution would help the families of the victims get on with their lives.

William Thompson	06-19-89	W	NV

Crime: Convicted and sentenced for killing three people.

Comment: Last words were, "Thank you for letting me die with dignity."

Sean Flannagan	06-23-89	W	NV

Crime: Convicted and sentenced for strangling a homosexual; claimed to have strangled and dismembered another homosexual.

Reason Given: Converted to Christianity on death row; wanted to go to heaven instead of spending his life in prison.

Comment: Smiled and shook the prosecutor's hand when he received the death sentence.

Gerald Smith	01-18-90	W	MO

Crime: Beat his former girlfriend to death; killed another death row inmate.

Comment: Waived and resumed his appeals several times while on death row.

Continued

TABLE 8.1 — (CONTINUED)

Name	Date Executed	Race	State
Jerome Butler	04-21-90	B	TX

Crime: Killed a Houston cabdriver.

Reason Given: Said he did not want to spend his remaining years in prison.

Comment: Spent half his life behind bars.

| Leonard Laws | 05-17-90 | W | MO |

Crime: Took part in the robbery/murder of four elderly people, then burned their house down.

Comment: At one point a court reversed his death sentence, but the state appealed and a higher court reinstated the death penalty.

| Thomas Baal | 06-03-90 | W | NV |

Crime: Stabbed to death a bus driver during a robbery.

Comment: Former mental patient who had brain damage. History of suicide attempts.

| Ronald Simmons | 06-25-90 | W | AR |

Crime: Killed 16 people, 14 of them members of his family.

Reason Given: Shame and remorse.

Comment: After his arrest, he said, "I've gotten everybody who wanted to hurt me."

| James Smith | 06-26-90 | W | TX |

Crime: Robbery/murder of a Texas businessman.

Reason Given: Said he wanted to die because "do-gooders" had already robbed him of his time in the next world.

Comment: Claimed innocence and said in his final statement: "I will not humiliate myself. I will let no man break me." Once requested a lump of dirt for his last meal, but officials refused, say it was not part of the regular prison menu.

| Charles Walker | 09-12-90 | W | FL |

Crime: Killed a couple for beer money.

Continued

TABLE 8.1 — (CONTINUED)

Name	Date Executed	Race	State

Reason Given: Could see no hope, no future. "Why should I appeal; I'm going to lay in a cell for 10, 15 years and then die."

Comment: Warned a clemency board that he would kill again in prison if given a life sentence.

| Steven Pennell | 03-14-92 | W | DE |

Crime: Tortured and slayed two women in 1988; murdered two other women in 1989.

Reason Given: Wanted death to put his case to rest and ease the suffering for his wife and two kids.

Comment: Maintained his innocence to the end but requested a speedy execution.

| Westley Dodd | 01-05-93 | W | WA |

Crime: Raped and killed three young boys.

Reason Given: Wanted death rather than to spend his life in prison. Expressed some remorse.

Comment: Long criminal record for sexually abusing children. At his request he was hanged, just as he had hanged one of his victims.

| John Brewer | 03-03-93 | W | AR |

Crime: Murdered his pregnant fiancee and had sex with the corpse.

Reason Given: "I committed this crime and I feel it is an appropriate penalty for the crime."

Comment: His mother said he had been suicidal since age six.

| James Allen Red Dog | 03-03-93 | NA | DE |

Crime: Killed a man and kidnaped and raped a woman.

Reason Given: This was a Sioux Indian who refused to appeal because it would violate his warrior code. Last words: "You can all kiss my ass."

Comment: Had been under the federal witness protection program for his testimony against prison gangs and the American Indian Movement.

| Andrew Chabrol | 06-17-93 | W | VA |

Crime: Kidnaped, raped, and strangled a woman who had earlier resisted his advances.

Continued

TABLE 8.1 (CONTINUED)

Reason Given: "He's made up his mind, and it's been up for a long time," said his attorney. "He's a bright individual. It's an informed choice."

Comment: Pleaded guilty and after automatic review refused to pursue further appeals.

| David Mason | 08-24-93 | W | CA |

Crime: Strangled and robbed four elderly people; choked to death a fellow prisoner.

Reason Given: "I accept responsibility for my actions. I believe in the most serious penalty for the most serious crime."

Comment: Had a history of suicide attempts. Thanked the warden just before the cyanide pellets were dropped.

| Michael Durocher | 08-25-93 | W | FL |

Crime: Killed his girlfriend, her five-year-old daughter, and his six-month-old son.

Reason Given: In a letter to the governor of Florida, Durocher stated that he was a "believer in capital punishment and that I respectfully request that justice now be served."

Comment: Sent Florida Governor Lawton Chiles a thank-you card once the death warrant was signed.

| Anthony Cook | 11-10-93 | W | TX |

Crime: Kidnaped, robbed, and murdered a man leaving a motel.

Reason Given: Said spiritual conversion caused remorse and a willingness to be executed.

Comment: Was on parole at the time of the crime. Wrote the DA a letter stating his desire to be executed. "I'm the one who did it. I can no longer lie about it," he wrote.

Continued

9

Death Row Donors

LANE NELSON

From *The Angolite,* January/February 1995, Angola, La: Louisiana State Penitentiary.

Jack "Dr. Death" Kevorkian, best known for assisting terminally ill people to commit suicide, is supporting a Texas death row inmate's request to donate body organs upon execution. So far that request has been denied. The Texas Department of Corrections, the American Medical Association, and various human rights organizations, adamantly opposes the surgical procedure on legal and/or moral grounds. According to the Human Rights Watch, condemned prisoners in the United States are prohibited from donating organs for transplant purposes because of pressures such as coercion, intimidation, and inducement—vulnerabilities that can infringe upon a prisoner's genuine free consent. But, as with assisted suicides, Kevorkian disagrees with the law. He believes death row prisoners not only have the right to donate body parts, but that the medical profession has a duty to accept the organs to save the lives of people in dire need.

Certainly, potential recipients far outnumber organ donors nationally and internationally. On a January 1995 edition of NBC's news program, *Dateline,* a physician said that eight to ten people die daily in this country waiting for organ transplants. According to an Associated Press release in October 1994, 500 people in Italy, including 80 children, are on the waiting list for heart transplants, and most will die waiting. On the surface, Kevorkian's contention appears a noble, humanitarian proposition. But underneath this death row donor push stews a pot of potential atrocities—atrocities that bubbled quickly to the surface in China's death row donor program.

The Human Rights Watch/Asia has published a report, *Organ procurement and Judicial Execution in China,* that reveals a wide range of human rights and medical ethical violations regarding organ transplants among China's death row prisoners. The 1994 report asserts that China's high annual execution rate, which often reaches into the thousands, is due in large part to that country's organ transplant program.

It was not until 1991 that mounting evidence and persistent pressure from outside human rights organizations forced China to admit a death row donor program even existed. Chinese officials have downplayed that admission by asserting body organs are taken "only in rare instances and with the consent of the [condemned] person." The Human Rights watch report says otherwise: In August 1992, a recently released Chinese prisoner informed a Hong Kong newspaper that "a team of doctors was always on hand at execution grounds in major cities such as Beijing, Shanghai, and Guangzhou, and, once the prisoners had been shot, the doctors immediately dissected the bodies and removed the organs required."

A former People's Republic of China (PRC) surgeon, who for reasons of personal safety could not be identified, in August 1994 recounted to a

Western journalist how he had removed, for transplant purposes, the kidneys of several condemned prisoners in a major Chinese city in 1988 on the evening prior to their execution.

According to a BBC television documentary screened in late 1992, Hong Kong physician Dr. Man Kam Chan "referred more than a hundred patients to China for kidney transplants and he knows where the corpses are coming from. . . . Chan, a prominent renal specialist who is among the few doctors in Hong Kong that refers patients to the mainland for the operation, said, 'Almost all kidneys transplanted in China come from executed prisoners. That's the main source, along with a few donated by living relatives. . . . No consent for organ removal is given by either the prisoner or the family.'"

While Chinese law provides guidelines for the removal of organs from condemned prisoners, those provisions are often sidestepped. The 1984 publication, *Temporary Rules Concerning the Utilization of Corpses or Organs from the Corpses of Executed Criminals,* stipulates that organ removal take place only under three circumstances: (1) the body is not claimed; (2) the condemned prisoner volunteers for dissection; and (3) the family consents to the dissection after execution. These stipulations, which are usually encroached through coercive tactics, were established more for a good humanitarian appearance than adherence. In the rare cases where consent is given, it is under duress and intimidation owing to the conditions of China's death rows. As described in the *Organ Procurement and Judicial Execution in China* report by a retired Chinese prison guard, there is a special place inside the jail for holding condemned prisoners that consists of a long chamber comprising several solitary quarters, one cell for each felon. The door to the chamber is lined with black rubber, very heavy, like an entrance to hell designed by some devil. The corridor is dark and deathly quiet. No sounds at all can be heard apart from the footsteps of guards and the clinking of ankle-fetters. Each criminal is kept all alone in a tiny, narrow cell. The four walls are lined with thick, springy sheets of leather, and the cell is as dark as a coffin. If they wish to talk to the guards, prisoners must stand and speak through a surveillance hole in the door. All of the prisoners are in handcuffs and leg irons, which will not be removed before the time of their execution. In order to eat, drink, or go to the toilet, they have to be helped by general duties staff ("zayi," prisoners serving light sentences). Condemned prisoners are denied access to the latrine and are barred from reading newspapers or listening to the prison's education broadcasts. The only recreation left to them is to doze lethargically or just sit there in blank contemplation. In effect, criminals sent to the solitary quarters have lost their souls, for what awaits them is death.

Under such intolerable conditions, it's not hard to perceive what a prisoner will agree to for an hour's walk in the sunshine, or polite conversation and a cup of coffee with a guard. Moreover, condemned prisoners are not notified that their one guaranteed appeal has been denied until just a few hours before their execution, allowing no time to inform authorities they do not want their bodies dissected. Executed people in China are cremated, making it impossible for families to know whether the bodies were used for medical purposes.

Even when a condemned prisoner does give voluntary consent for removal of body organs upon execution, the likelihood of negligent atrocity exists. "An incident that occurred recently in Taiwan, a country which has stricter laws on prisoner consent and considerably more effective judicial safeguards than China, illustrates the type of horrifying misuse of medical resources that can occur as a result of this practice," the *Organ Procurement* report explains. "When the sentence of a consenting prisoner scheduled to be an organ donor was carried out, he was not killed by the first bullet shot to the head. He was rushed to a hospital, where doctors were able to improve upon his condition. Later, after consultation with the Ministry of Justice, the medical staff agreed upon a convenient time to reschedule the execution. Saving life and taking life became hopelessly intermingled."

The report also emphasizes the prevalence of torturous tactics used by Chinese "law enforcement officials bent on extracting confessions to meet government pressure for *speedy arrests and speedy punishment.*" From the moment of their arrest, Chinese prisoners are isolated from family members, and from a defense lawyer until just days before the trial begins. The wait of several months to a year before going to trial gives authorities plenty of time to coerce confessions and obtain wrongful convictions. "An official newspaper stated in October 1993 that a total of 1,687 cases of police and justice officials extracting confessions by torture had occurred nationwide since 1988." The report claims that pressure applied for speedy arrests, convictions and punishments is linked to organ transplants of executed prisoners.

Wrongful convictions in China have been rampant. "[D]uring the Cultural Revolution (1966–76) no less than 725,000 persons were wrongly convicted by the courts." Most of these were for counterrevolutionary convictions that often warrant the death sentence—easily obtained in a pro-Communist court setting that provides weak judicial safeguards for the accused. Judicial abuses and executions continued to climb after Mao's death in 1976. "[T]his was the very period described in the *Journal of Chinese Organ Transplantation* as having 'a high tide of kidney, liver, heart and lung transplants across the country.'" With Deng Xiaoping's rise to power in 1978, and with the establishment of an "elaborate system of laws and judicial rudiments," the prison population and executions somewhat declined.

Increasing protests and activism against the government caused the military to clamp down in China. The 1989 Tiananmen Square Massacre is the most graphic example. "China's prisons are now more heavily stocked with political and religious prisoners than they were in the mid-1980s," the *Organ Procurement* report declares. "Nowhere are judicial failings of the regime more evident than in China's current extreme reliance on the use of capital punishment. Not only are there far more prisoners in Chinese jails today than there were prior to 1983 (according to one official source, the prison population has doubled), but far more people are now being condemned to death and judicially executed each year in China than at any time since the early 1950s." According to some Chinese scholars and international humanitarians, a conservative estimate of executions in China is well over 1,000 a year. An article in the *Law Review* of Wuhan University by a Chinese legal scholar calling for an end to mass executions notes that "around 35% of the [200 or so] criminal offenses specified in the Criminal Law are now punishable by death."

Perhaps most chilling of all is China's method of execution: a pistol shot to the back of the head. The method itself is not so shocking. It is the purpose behind the method. Executing prisoners in this manner *allows the undamaged harvesting of such organs as kidneys and livers*. Moreover, the report cites evidence provided by various Chinese officials to explain that "executions are sometimes botched so that the victims' bodies can be kept alive longer, thereby making organ transplantation procedures more viable. . . . In other words, vivisection sometimes occurs." Additionally, prisoners are sometimes shot in other parts of the body when a head injury would damage coveted organs. As one former Shanghai police official put it, "In order to preserve the eyes, the prisoner was shot in the heart. This is what happens. If they need the heart, the prisoner would be shot in the head instead."

There is an overwhelming need in Asian countries for body organs. "In Hong Kong, for example, only 55 kidney transplants were performed in 1990, but there was a waiting list of some 600 patients." This grave shortage in Hong Kong, China, and other Asian countries is "due in large part to a traditional belief that bodies should be buried intact and that desecration of the body is to be avoided," states the *Organ Procurement* report. Evidently, in China this religious belief takes a back seat where condemned prisoners are concerned, and thus patients in Hong Kong and elsewhere travel to China for organ transplants. Because of crucial medical timing involved with organ transplants, high-paying foreign patients are told the exact day and time the transplant surgery will take place. Such a scheduling procedure "suggests that execution dates are scheduled to conform with patient transplantation needs, rather than with the strict requirements of legal due process," explains the report, which also claims that younger, healthy men are more likely candidates for execution.

Organs retrieved from executed prisoners generally go to high-ranking government officials and well-to-do citizens, or they are placed on the international trade market for high-paying foreign customers. The death row organ donor program's influence over China's judicial system is exemplified through a documented example detailed in the report: "Doctors at the Shenzhen People's Armed Police Hospital told a former Intermediate Court judge that they would be particularly happy to accommodate his request to obtain a donated kidney for his brother, since they wanted the court to help in arranging a steady supply of executed prisoners' organs."

Still, advocates for a death row donor program in the United States argue that China's abuses could never be repeated under the American criminal justice system. Heads in the sand, they ignore the fact that habeas corpus is being stripped to a meaningless shell; that blacks are four times more likely to receive the death penalty than whites; and that actual innocence is no longer an appealable issue. In a land where prosecutors routinely withhold exculpatory evidence, and 15-year-olds are given life sentences for drugs, the potential for abuse of a death row donor program is enormous. The people cry for vengeance and tax cuts in equal measure. A death row donor program could bring them both.

> The use of corpses or organs of executed criminals must be kept strictly secret. . . . A surgical vehicle from the health department may be permitted to drive onto the execution grounds to remove the organs, but it is not permisible to use a vehicle bearing health department insignia or to wear white clothing. Guards must remain posted around the execution grounds while the operation for organ removal is going on.
>
> *Chinese directive*

◆ DEATH PENALTY GAINS POPULARITY

During the 1970s and up until the early 1980s, the total number of those sentenced to death and executed in a particular province of China had never reached triple figures. But from 1983 onward, the number has consistently been in the three-figure range annually—in fact, some years it has almost reached quadruple figures. And during the annual crackdown campaign in a single city administered by that province, the number of those sentenced to the death penalty in a six-month period alone not only went into triple figures, it even exceeded the total number of death penalty sentences passed each year throughout the entire province during the 1970s.

◆ VISIBLE MAN

On August 5, 1993, Paul Jernigan was put to death in Texas for beating, stabbing, and killing an elderly man during a burglary. When the lethal injection pumped to his heart, Jernigan's soul may have taken flight but his body stayed around. According to the *Houston Chronicle,* immediately after execution the body was transported to the University of Colorado at Denver, where it was kept in cold storage at temperatures of 50–60 degrees below zero. Once thoroughly frozen, the corpse was removed, braced upright, and sliced from head to toe into 1,871 pieces. Each piece, thinner than a slice of bread, was photographed and stored digitally. The layered images were then stacked on top of each other electronically in a computer database. Paul Jernigan was reborn as the "Visible Man" online on the Internet computer network.

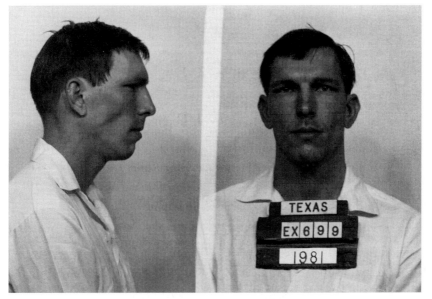

Paul Jernigan, Texas inmate who donated his body to science.
(Copyright: Texas Department of Criminal Justice.)

"It's a virtual reality thing," said Michael Ackerman, who came up with the high-tech idea and headed the Visible Man project. According to Ackerman, the program will take up 15 gigabytes in storage space, equivalent to about 5 million typewritten pages of text. The multidimensional map of Jernigan's body can be used to help teach and enhance surgery skills to medical students, and help doctors explain more clearly to their patients just where and why surgery will be performed. Jernigan's body was not the first choice. Other cadavers were rejected because of abnormalities or injuries. But after examining Jernigan's corpse before it was frozen, Ackerman knew he had a winner: "It's the perfect cadaver. There's no injuries, right? There's no debilitating illness. Which is exactly what we wanted—someone who looked like he was alive."

Although Jernigan's body was whisked out of Huntsville's death chamber nearly a year and a half ago, the Visible Man project was kept secret until November 1994. There are now questions being raised as to whether this type of death row donor procedure violated any state or federal laws. Jernigan himself kept his death wish quiet. Annabelle McHenry, Jernigan's mother, didn't know until her son told her the day before the execution. "He told me he wanted to do something good," McHenry told a Houston reporter. "It was a gift," said Jernigan's appeal attorney, Mark A. Ticer. "He wasn't going to laud himself, pat himself on the back. We didn't send embossed announcements that 'Paul Jernigan has donated his body to science and this is his ticket to redemption. . . .' Uh-uh. He didn't think that way."

While many applaud Jernigan's donation as a gesture of goodwill—even the murder victim's nephew responded favorably to the news—his accomplice, now out on parole, sees it differently. Roy Lamb said Jernigan hoped a true-crime book would be written about the murder, allowing the proceeds of the book to go to his family. According to Lamb, the final gesture of donating the body to science was thought by Jernigan the key to sealing the deal.

Postscript: Before Georgia executed Larry Lonchar, a volunteer, in November 1996, Lonchar made a last request: to donate his kidney to the ailing detective who arrested him for a triple murder. Upon hearing the request, detective Melvin Ferguson contacted Lonchar's lawyers, telling them he knew from the murder investigation their blood types matched and that he would gladly accept the donation. But state and prison officials refused to cooperate and denied the last request. Lonchar was put to death—healthy kidneys and all.

10

Killing the Lawyers

Lane Nelson

The first thing we do, let's kill all the lawyers.

William Shakespeare, *Henry VI,* Part 2

From *The Angolite*, January/February 1996, Angola, La: Louisiana State Penitentiary.

Before the state executes someone, the condemned should have a fair trial. Politicians, lawmakers, and the general public agree on this point. The U.S. Supreme Court requires it. Justice demands it. But only dedicated, skilled post-trial representation for the condemned can ensure it.

In 1988 Congress mandated a federally funded program aimed at recruiting skilled lawyers to break the logjam of unrepresented prisoners piling up on the nation's death rows. Less than 10 years later, in 1995, Congress pulled the plug. The solution, congressional leaders said, had become the problem.

The 20 death penalty "resource centers" set up across the country, small offices of lawyers, paralegals, and investigators specializing in death sentence appeals, have used the last of the $19.8 million total annual allotment. Some have shut down; others are trying to survive on limited state funding. Although no one is certain what effect the defunding will have, death penalty advocates hope it will speed up the appeals process and hasten executions.

South Carolina Attorney General Charles Condon initiated the push to defund the centers. To paraphrase Shakespeare, Condon did not want to kill all the lawyers, only the death penalty defense lawyers. Frustrated that his state was not carrying out executions fast enough, he turned to Representative Bob Inglis (R-SC) and other hard-line congressmen for help. Early last year, speaking at a House judiciary subcommittee, Condon painted a picture of how the $19.8 million was misspent: "The [centers] have been known to insinuate themselves to spread confusion at every stage of the process, operating as a kind of anti–death penalty group subsidized at public expense."

Condon's rebuke came on the heels of an exhaustive report recommending expansion of the Post-Conviction Defender Organization program. That report, submitted to the committee by a panel of federal judges, was ignored, and the committee recommended eliminating all funding.

Later the defunding bill was added to a broader appropriations package and passed through the House without debate. It then went to a Senate committee for approval. Senator Phil Gramm (R-Texas) chaired that committee. Gramm, a presidential candidate, strongly supports the death penalty. "Representing clients and lobbying to do away with the death penalty seem to be on an even scale for death penalty resource centers," said Gramm's spokesperson Larry Neal. "[Federal efforts] should be on increasing funding to law enforcement, putting people in prison and keeping them there, not the other way around." The bill cleared the Senate subcommittee with no problem, passed the full Senate, and became law at the end of summer.

Death penalty advocates, like Michael Rushford of the Criminal Justice Legal Foundation and Kevin Washburn of California's Citizens for Law and Order, are pleased. "The money that's being used is used to delay the carrying out of a death sentence for sometimes as long as 15 years," Washburn stated on National Public Radio. "The centers have functioned like brakes," Rushford told *USA Today.* "Congress is taking the brakes off."

Ironically, support for center funding has sprouted from unusual sources. Former Texas Attorney General Jim Mattox, a vocal death penalty advocate who helped send 36 men to the execution chamber, views the elimination of federal funding as a step backward. "This should be a no-brainer for Congress: Conservatives should love these defender offices because they make the death penalty faster and cheaper," he wrote in *USA Today.* "Liberals should love them because decent lawyers, through habeas corpus, help guard against the execution of innocent people and the violation of constitutional liberties."

Maryland Attorney General Joseph Curran voiced similar concern over the defunding and quality of representation that will now be afforded death row prisoners. "The scales of justice demand that there be a level playing field, with highly qualified counsel for both the state and the accused," Curran told the *New York Times.* "We're not talking about a shoplifting case where there might be a $100 fine."

In the years following reinstatement of the death penalty, attorneys unfamiliar with the complexity of death penalty law caused frustrating problems and delays for both federal and state judges. The federal judiciary committee, along with reports from federal judges, district attorneys, attorney generals, and criminal defense lawyer associations, convinced Congress to establish death penalty resource centers as a way to provide death-sentenced prisoners competent legal representation on appeal. Centers sprang up across the country, attracting skilled, dedicated attorneys willing to work for peanuts. They assisted with or took over appeals, saving states and the federal government the greater expense of paying hourly fees to attorneys to represent indigent death row prisoners.

The idea worked. Almost immediately death penalty cases started moving through the system faster, and representation for people sentenced to the ultimate punishment climbed back to constitutional standards. But that was then, when a tough-on-crime Bush administration created and sustained the resource centers for economic and judicial efficiency.

"The last thing the courts need right now is to have the lawyers who are best trained put out of business," George Kendall told *The Recorder,* a Washington-based legal publication. Kendall, a lawyer with the NAACP Legal Defense and Education Fund, specializes in death penalty cases. He foresees massive chaos in the wake of eliminating center funding. "[It will have] apocalyptic consequences on the administration of justice."

Gerald H. Goldstein, president of the National Association of Criminal Defense Lawyers, said large law firms will now hesitate to offer pro bono services in death penalty cases. "The silk-stocking firms do not want to take on these cases unless they know they can rely on the centers for training and a lot of practical help along the way," Goldstein explained to the *New York Times*. "It takes a special person to walk between a citizen and his execution. It's not an inviting place to be, and even fewer people will want to be there without the centers to back them up."

Experts suggest defunding will result in hundreds of cases being abandoned by the estimated 140 center lawyers nationwide. "We'll be back to the pre-1988 horror story where we had lots of people on death row whose cases were stalled because they couldn't get a lawyer to represent them on appeal," said Bryan Stevenson, director of the Alabama Capital Punishment Resource Center. "What the government will now do is spend thousands, millions of dollars even, paying lawyers to get up to speed just to get where we would otherwise already be."

Florida Supreme Court Justice Ben F. Overton told the *Tampa Tribune* that all prisoners under a sentence of death in Florida are entitled to an attorney—not just legal representation, but competent representation such as provided by center lawyers. Because judges will now be forced to search for competent lawyers to take death penalty cases, Overton believes the legal process will slow down and cost more. "I don't think there is any question about that."

Fifty-nine prisoners are on Louisiana's death row. The Loyola Death Penalty Resource Center (LDPRC) in New Orleans monitors and helps in one form or another with all appeals for Louisiana's condemned. That assistance ranges from investigating claims of innocence to full legal representation, including making a last-ditch plea to the clemency board and sitting with a client in those last hours before the execution. Most beneficial, however, is the center's ability to recruit private attorneys to take death penalty appeals on a pro bono basis. These are attorneys from large law firms that have the financial resources to handle the high cost of litigating capital cases. Because death penalty litigation is a complex, arcane area of law, recruited attorneys rely on help from center lawyers. The result is death row prisoners are provided constitutionally sound legal representation. This is what Congress had in mind when it created the resource centers in 1988. What Congress did not foresee was how effective the centers would be in both finding flawed convictions and keeping their clients alive.

"In the early to mid eighties, law firms were being recruited to take death penalty cases for free. But these firms wouldn't take cases if they couldn't get some backup from people who knew death penalty law. That's why the resource centers were established initially," said LDPRC director Nick Trenticosta. "Congress and federal judges knew what was happening wasn't working. The fact of the matter now is, we work too well. And because we work well, they take the money away."

Louisiana death row prisoner Tracy Lee, represented by Trenticosta, shares the same opinion: "Because these centers were eventually filled with dedicated and selfless attorneys who are willing to work hard for little pay, and because these skilled attorneys have been successful in what they do, Congress now wants to, and for the most part has, stopped them."

Supporters of defunding have a different view. "The idea it will get worse without these centers is laughable," Condon told *USA Today* shortly after the bill passed. "It can't get any worse. Most death row inmates die of old age." Condon has his facts wrong. From Gary Gilmore's execution in January 1977 to October 31, 1995, 302 prisoners were executed in this country. During that same period, 95 death-sentenced prisoners either died of natural causes or were killed on death row while appealing their cases. An additional 43 committed suicide.

"Only four death row inmates have been put to death in our state since the late 1970s," Condon told the *Charleston Post* in 1995. "And I can assure

Nick Trenticosta and the staff attorneys of the Loyola Death Penalty Resource Center. (Copyright: Wilbert Rideau, The Angolite.)

you that the people of South Carolina are fed up with a system that is clearly not working in the public interest. . . . [The centers] have effectively blocked the State of South Carolina from having a death penalty." A Charleston prosecutor from 1980 to 1994, Condon sent 11 men to death row. He once suggested the state use "electric sofas" to hold multiple executions.

John Blume heads South Carolina's resource center. "They're like a schoolyard bully beating up on little kids," he told the *Charleston Post* concerning Condon and his supporters. "Before the organizations were created, they were facing lawyers who really didn't know what they were doing. And now that some kid almost their own size shows up, they turn home screaming to their mama, 'It's not fair, it's not fair.'"

"It's a classic shoot-yourself-in-the-foot argument," said David A. Sellers, spokesman for the federal court system in Washington. "These defendants have to receive counsel, there's no question about that. The question is who should be doing it."

Not center lawyers, according to Bob Inglis (R-South Carolina). Inglis told the *ABA Journal* that he favors a defendant's constitutional right to counsel but feels the centers "serve as think tanks for legal theories" with the sole purpose of preventing executions. "I think it's really humorous," Inglis said. "It's really ironic that people who wake up in the morning thinking of ways to stop the implementation of the death penalty argue that [the existence of resource centers] speeds up the implementation of death sentences."

Illinois defense attorney Michael Metnick isn't laughing. "I take offense to suggestions we are obstructionists or thwarting the process," he told the *Springfield State Journal-Register*. "We just want to make damn certain, before the state executes an inmate, that that inmate is guilty of the crime."

The most troubling aspect of capital punishment is that a certain number of innocent people will be convicted and executed, with no means to correct the error. Alabama resource center director Bryan Stevenson took over Walter McMillian's death penalty case in the late stages of the appeal process. McMillian had always claimed his innocence in the murder and robbery of a dry-cleaning clerk. Stevenson spent thousands of hours combing records and revisiting witnesses. His investigation revealed the state had withheld evidence that proved the key witness against McMillian had lied. In 1993 the conviction was overturned and McMillian was set free. According to Stevenson, he made $28,000 a year working with the center. "If this were about money," he told *USA Today,* "it would never make any sense."

In 1983, 10-year-old Jeanine Nicario was abducted from her home in Naperville, Illinois, raped, and murdered. Rolando Cruz, Alejandro Hernandez, and Stephen Buckley were arrested. Cruz and Hernandez were convicted and sentenced to death. Buckley was acquitted. Cruz's court-appointed attorney, John Hanlon, continued to defend Cruz, believing in his innocence. He went to the Capital Resource Center and sought help. In a combined effort, thousands of hours and dollars were spent discovering and compiling evidence that proved Cruz was innocent, and proved that prosecutors and police detectives had manufactured evidence of guilt. The state supreme court reversed the conviction. At his third trial in November 1995, Cruz was set free after a conscience-stricken police lieutenant testified that two of his detectives had concocted Cruz's "confession."

Hanlon publicly acknowledged his gratitude for the assistance of center lawyers and admonished the move by Congress to eliminate resource centers. "People like Rolando Cruz, who are innocent, are going to be executed if things like this happen," he told the *Naperville Metropolitan* a few days after Cruz's release.

"Crazy Joe" Spaziano spent 20 years on Florida's death row for the rape and murder of a teen-aged girl. At his trial, the prosecution had no physical evidence, only the testimony of a teenager who said Spaziano had killed the woman. That testimony, unbeknownst to the jury, had been enhanced through hypnosis. "If we can't get in the testimony of Tony DiLisio," the prosecutor told the judge during the trial, "we'd have absolutely no case whatsoever."

In 1995 DiLisio recanted his testimony and admitted he lied about having any knowledge of the crime. Spaziano, a member of the Outlaws motorcycle gang, faced the terror of numerous execution dates. He now faces a new trial, but it is doubtful he will again be found guilty. Still, Spaziano's imminent release from death row did not come easy. It took a group of skilled death penalty attorneys years of work to finally convince a court of Spaziano's likely innocence and the miscarriage of justice in the case.

Due in large part to center attorneys, five Louisiana death row prisoners since 1991 have argued their innocence and won new trials. Clarence "Smitty" Smith, originally sentenced to die for the 1981 car bomb killing of an FBI informant, was acquitted at his second trial in 1994. Like Spaziano, Smith was also a member of the Outlaws and was originally convicted and sent to death row on the testimony of one witness. That witness, an ex-Outlaw, received total immunity for several murders and other felonies in exchange for his testimony. No physical evidence linked Smith to the state of Louisiana, let alone the crime. Some have suggested Spaziano and Smith were the victims of a concerted law enforcement effort to break up the Outlaws. Had these men not received help appealing their cases from skilled death penalty attorneys, they would still be on death row, or executed.

The vast majority of defendants on trial for capital murder are indigents represented by public defenders. This is where the problem of unequal justice starts. "Far too often," reports the Death Penalty Information Center, "people are given the death penalty not for committing the worst crimes, but for having the worst lawyers."

Much of Trenticosta's time and funding on post-conviction death penalty work has been spent trying to correct crucial mistakes made by inexperienced trial counsel. "In most cases it's not because the lawyers were bad lawyers," he said. "It's that the lawyers could not perform effectively, either because of inexperience or lack of funding to prepare the case." A study of death penalty representation in the South conducted by the *National Law Journal* concluded that capital trials are "more like a random flip of the coin than a delicate balancing of the scales [because defense attorneys are] too often . . . ill-trained, unprepared, grossly underpaid." In the death penalty appeal case of *Martinez-Macias v. Collins,* the appellate ruling stated, "The state [of Texas] paid defense counsel $11.84 per hour. Unfortunately, the justice system got only what it paid for."

Condemned prisoner Keith Messiah was found guilty of murder after a one-day trial. In the rush to justice, he was represented by an underpaid, overworked, under-skilled New Orleans public defender. The penalty phase of the trial lasted only 20 minutes. Trenticosta and his team appealed Messiah's case for five years. Last year Messiah received a life sentence without parole.

To present a proper defense, some investigation is required. But court-appointed lawyers seldom have the time or resources to conduct proper investigations. The situation described in *Hafdahl v. Texas* is typical: "[D]efense counsel Mallory Holloway was told that he had better not ask for investigation funds, since he had already drained the county's budget by insisting on co-counsel."

Andrew Golden, a former teacher and law-abiding citizen who had never received a traffic ticket, was sentenced to die in 1991 for the drowning death of his wife. Ardelle Golden's body was found inside the family car in a lake at the end of a boat ramp, and Andrew was arrested for capital murder. The prosecution speculated insurance money as the motive. Golden's inexperienced attorney did not prepare for the trial and presented no defense. As a result, the jury heard only the state's side of the story, found Golden guilty, and sentenced him to death. Had the attorney performed an adequate investigation, the jury would have learned of the likelihood that Ardelle committed suicide. She was depressed about the recent death of her father. Four notices about her father's death were near the body inside the car, and a coffee mug was wedged between the brake and accelerator of the submerged automobile.

Golden's family hired an experienced death penalty lawyer to handle the appeal. In 1994 the Florida Supreme Court, presented with the exculpatory evidence, threw out the conviction and sentence of death. Golden was freed and charges against him dropped.

Problems exist with court-appointed trial lawyers handling capital cases: low pay, overwhelming caseloads, limited availability of investigative and paralegal assistance. But most alarming are public defenders who *just don't care.* Joe Frank Cannon, a Houston court-appointed attorney, has 10 clients on Texas death row and, according to the *Wall Street Journal,* boasts of speeding through trials "like greased lightning." Candelario Elizondo, former president of the Harris County Criminal Lawyers Association, said Cannon is a favorite among Houston judges, "because he delivers on his promise to move the court's docket."

California attorney Ron Slick has at least eight clients on death row. He spends only a few days defending a capital murder case. Slick gives "new meaning to the words speedy trial," said the *Los Angeles Times.*

The late U.S. Supreme Court Justice, Thurgood Marshall, once said that "the *Federal Reports* are filled with stories of counsel who presented no evidence in mitigation of their clients' sentences because they did not know what to offer or how to offer it, or had not read the state's sentencing statute."

According to Alabama center attorney Ruth Friedman, the elimination of center funding by politicians like Condon, Inglis, and Gramm is wasteful political pandering. "It's grandstanding," she said. "Lawyers who don't know the law are not going to do these cases faster. And it's going to cost more money to pay them on an appointed, hourly basis. Talk about wasting people's money."

Chief Judge Richard Arnold, U.S. Eighth Circuit Court of Appeals, calculates that center lawyers receive about $55 an hour, while court-appointed lawyers receive anywhere from $75 to $125 an hour. Arnold heads the policy-making body of the federal judiciary. "The [centers] are clearly a cheaper way of providing the service, and they tend to be a better quality way," he said. "They don't do anything but death penalty work, which is highly specialized and complicated." In a letter to the Senate this past summer, Arnold urged against eliminating such a beneficial program: "If they are eliminated, we will experience significant delays in trying cases because it will be difficult to find qualified counsel. . . . I know you are committed to the goal of reducing the federal deficit, but I believe that elimination of the [centers] will . . . cost more."

According to a study by the U.S. General Accounting Office, the average cost of center lawyers representing death row inmates in 1993 was $17,200 per case. It was $37,000 in cases handled by private, court-appointed attorneys.

Trenticosta, who started working with the center in November 1988, a month after it opened, estimates he and the other four lawyers at LDPRC receive $33 an hour. He believes the centers are cost-effective, even more so when they advise private attorneys who are working death penalty appeals pro bono. "If you put me in the tax code," he explained, "I would malpractice the case. I'm not trained in that area of the law. Our specialty is death penalty law—habeas corpus law and Eighth Amendment law—which is deep and complex. I've never worked with a law firm that hasn't benefited from us getting into the case."

Of the $19.8 million allotted to the 20 centers, the New Orleans center received $600,000 the last year of its life, less than most other centers. But the need is not as large as it is in states that hold hundreds of prisoners on death row, states like California (425), Texas (401), Florida (340), Pennsylvania (200), and Illinois (154). Trenticosta refuses to give up his fight to afford death-sentenced prisoners constitutionally mandated legal representation on appeal. He remains cautiously optimistic. "Fortunately, we are in a lot better shape than other centers," he said. "Other places have been forced to shut down completely. . . . Because of the changes in the state public defender system in Louisiana, we can now get funding for direct appeal work, if we get appointed to the cases. That has helped us maintain our office expenses. Some of us are doing trials now so we can receive the $57 an hour for that, which again keeps the operation going." When funding for LDPRC expired, Trenticosta and his small crew moved to a smaller, less expensive office. Everyone in the crew took a reduction in salary.

Trenticosta has assured Louisiana's condemned that no cases presently being handled by his office will be abandoned. "We made a commitment," he said. "We are not going to abandon those we now represent, not by any means. If we have to hold bake sales and dances to raise money, that's just what we'll do. We are not going to let Congress tell us we can't represent our clients."

Nevertheless, good intentions only go so far. "What we've learned, and this is no secret to anyone in this country, is that resources make things happen," admitted Trenticosta. "If we can't jump into a car and drive 400 miles to talk to a witness who may have information on a case, then we can't do our job."

With federal funding eliminated for resource centers, some courts will appoint lawyers of their choice to handle death sentence appeals. The Cannons and Slicks of the lawyer world will be handed their share, and the possibility of executing innocent people will increase.

Close to 3,000 people now live on death row, about 1,000 more than the year the centers opened and the most ever in the history of this country. Last year 56 men were executed, more than twice as many as in 1987, the year before the centers opened. It is not clear how withdrawing federal funding for resource centers will grease the execution process wheels. Many death penalty cases on appeal will likely stall in midstream because of the search for and appointment of new attorneys, inexperienced ones at that. Courts will be hard-pressed to find pro bono attorneys willing to take on capital cases without knowledgeable center attorneys to guide them.

Texas, the capital of capital punishment, may be hit harder than other states. It accounts for more than a third of all executions carried out over the past 20 years. Mandy Welch, director of the now defunct Texas Resource Center, told a reporter in August 1995 that they were in a state of shock and denial over the defunding. "People [on staff] are trying to determine how long they can go without income, so they can continue representation. I had someone tell me, 'I could live on credit cards for one month, maybe two.'" Five months later, only 2 of the 18 center lawyers in Texas are still hanging on.

Moreover, according to the Texas Justice Information and Management System, 155 capital prosecutions were underway in the state in May 1995. And in Louisiana last year more people were sentenced to death than in any other year since reinstatement of capital punishment in 1976. The state's death row now holds more condemned prisoners than at any other time in its history. Prosecutors are seeking the death penalty more often, at least in Louisiana and Texas, and that will continue to swell death row populations. The arithmetic is not hard to add up.

What was an experiment in capital-case justice has proved an exercise in frustration. Retired U.S. Supreme Court Justice Harry A. Blackmun stated in 1994, "When we execute a capital defendant in this country, we rely on the belief that the individual was guilty, and was convicted and sentenced after a fair trial, to justify the imposition of state-sponsored killings. . . . My 24 years of overseeing the imposition of the death penalty from this Court have left me in grave doubt whether this reliance is justified and whether the constitutional requirement of competent counsel for capital defendants is being fulfilled." What would he say now, when the only knowledgeable defense lawyers in the field are being scattered to the winds?

◆ THE BUDDY SYSTEM

Court-appointed attorneys reside near the bottom of the legal food chain. Many are young, inexperienced, and scramble for the small fees criminal defense work provides. Consequently, they are more inclined to stay on the good side of the judge who appoints them than to vigorously defend their clients. And judges with overloaded court dockets tend to appoint lawyers, especially in capital cases, who don't clog the system with long, drawn-out trials.

"[L]awyers basically are much more loyal to the judge than to their clients," Yale University law professor Stephen Bright told the *Houston Chronicle,* "because the clients don't have anything to do with it. The clients didn't get them their jobs, they're not paying them." Bright is a noted lecturer, lawyer, and head of the Southern Center for Human Rights in Atlanta, Georgia, a nonprofit organization that helps prisoners, the homeless, and the mentally impaired. He and his tiny staff are currently assisting with 50 death penalty cases. Bright's statement coincided with a study issued by the Death Penalty Information Center documenting instances of judge-attorney relationships that outweighed attorney-client representations.

Both Bright and the study point out that elected judges sensitive to the public's overwhelming endorsement of the death penalty are reluctant to appoint aggressive attorneys in capital cases. These judges, said Bright, do not want to damage their popularity in the polls. As a result, a defendant on trial for his life fights against the prosecution, the judge, and his own lawyer. Thirty-four of the 38 capital punishment states elect judges.

Said Bright, "Judges face a dilemma: whether to do the right thing—that is, what is required by the Constitution and the law of the United States. Judges have a duty to follow the law, whether it's popular or unpopular. And yet in [capital cases], if the judge does enforce the law, he or she is signing his or her political death warrant."

States do not pay court-appointed attorneys enough to do a proper job, whether they want to or not. According to Bright, Alabama's maximum fee for handling a capital case is $1,000. He estimates it takes 500 to 1,000 or more hours to properly prepare for trial. "With all that time required," he said, "that comes out to about [one dollar] an hour. It's awfully hard work to get any lawyer to work for [a buck] an hour."

Postscript: In 1997, 74 executions were carried out. In 1998, 66 men and two women were executed. As of October 1, 1998, the nation's death row population exceeded 3,500.

Eighty men and one woman were confined to Louisiana's death row at the end of 1998. From sheer determination to offer the condemned in Louisiana a constitutional level of legal representation, the LDPRC is still functioning—though its name has changed to the Post-Conviction Relief Center and lawyers have dropped in numbers. Helping to pick up the slack from Trenticosta and his crew is a new organization in New Orleans, the Louisiana Crisis Assistance Center. Attorney Clive Stafford-Smith is its director. LCAC handles first-degree murder trials—trying to prevent the death penalty from ever being imposed—as well as appeals for death-sentenced prisoners. Still, the odds continue to be overwhelming. The arithmetic has not changed: more people are being sentenced to death in the state while fewer skilled lawyers are available to to work the appeals.

Clive Stafford-Smith of the Loyola Death Penalty Resource Center. (Copyright: Burk Foster.)

11

The Great Writ—
Re: The Condemned

LANE NELSON

From *The Angolite,* May/June 1996, Angola, La: Louisiana State Penitentiary.

On April 24, 1996, President Bill Clinton signed into law the Anti-Terrorism and Effective Death Penalty Act. With a military band playing, American flags waving, Clinton was cheered by family members of those who lost their lives in terrorist attacks over recent years in Oklahoma City and at the New York World Trade Center. But terrorists have less to fear from the new law than do run-of-the-mill death-sentenced criminal offenders whose use of habeas corpus has been severely restricted and their impending executions fast-forwarded.

Habeas corpus is the remedy a person in custody has against illegal confinement. The *Great Writ,* as it is called, has been in existence since the framing of the Constitution, and according to James Liebman, professor at Columbia University of Law, the Supreme Court granted the first habeas petition in 1806. He explained in a March *New York Times* Op-Ed article that as the use of incarceration as punishment increased, so did the use of habeas corpus applications. Liebman, a noted legal scholar, warned just before the bill was enacted that "if Congress passes its anti-terrorism legislation, prisoners would have no remedy for the first time since 1789."

It was the use of habeas corpus by lawyers and courts to delay and even thwart the execution of the condemned on the nation's death rows that generated political and judicial flak and cries for change. For many years forces in Congress had sought to enact restrictions on the writ's use by death-sentenced prisoners, to no avail. But the outrage produced by last year's Oklahoma City bombing was the nail in the coffin of habeas corpus use against the death penalty.

The primary provisions in the Effective Death Penalty Act (EDPA) will lead to severe restrictions on federal court review of a prisoner's challenges to state court decisions. The new law mandates that the "State court shall be presumed to be correct," and the prisoner "shall have the burden of re-butting the presumption of correctness by *clear and convincing evidence.*" Second or successive habeas attempts are barred. The condemned, with a new constitutional claim, can no longer enter federal district court at will. Any habeas petition filed after the first one must now go directly to a panel of three federal judges, who will decide whether the petition should be considered. That decision must be based upon one of three things: (1) "the claim relies on a new rule of constitutional law, made retroactive to cases on collateral review by the Supreme Court; (2) the factual predicate of the claim could not have been discovered previously through the exercise of due diligence"; (3) the facts in the claim, if proved, would establish "by clear and convincing evidence that, but for constitutional error, no reasonable fact finder would have found the applicant guilty of the underlying

President Bill Clinton at the signing of the Effective Death Penalty Act of 1996.

offense." The panel's decision to deny a second or successive application is final, not appealable to any court.

A condemned prisoner now must also file his or her application for habeas corpus relief "not later than 180 days after final State court affirmance of the conviction and sentence on direct review or the expiration of the time for seeking such review." In order for the 180-day requirement to apply, a state must have some provision by which the condemned is furnished legal counsel during state post-conviction proceedings. While many states do, Louisiana does not. Mandatory appointment of counsel in the state ends when the direct appeal is final. Death-sentenced prisoners in Louisiana and other states that do not provide post-conviction appellate counsel are allowed, under EDPA, an additional six months to file. Still, the new law is a severe restriction. Prior to it, Louisiana's condemned prisoners were under no time constraints to get through state court and into federal court.

The one-year period starts the day the prisoner's direct appeal becomes final in state courts. Time stops on the day the prisoner files his post-conviction petition, then starts again after the highest state court has denied it. How that time will be computed while in state court is yet to be determined by judicial interpretation. What is clear, however, is that the death-sentenced prisoner must file a post-conviction petition with unprecedented speed. This can be disastrous for condemned prisoners who do not have an attorney to immediately pick up the case once direct appeal is final.

Former Senator Bob Dole and Representative Bill McCullom (R-Florida) led the successful effort in 1995 to eliminate federal funding for the 20 death penalty resource centers throughout the country. Since 1988 those centers have provided post-conviction assistance to condemned prisoners, guaranteeing them constitutionally required legal representation in the complex area of habeas law. With elimination of the centers went the majority of skilled lawyers who swiftly picked up death penalty cases after direct appeal was exhausted. Now, without the assistance of qualified state-appointed lawyers, and with pro bono representation in capital cases harder to obtain, the condemned will be hard-pressed to come up with a meaningful solution within the one-year time limitation.

The worst scenario under EDPA is that condemned prisoners will not be able to find attorneys to handle their cases before the one-year filing period expires. They will then be barred from presenting their claims in federal court regardless of their merit, denying them the right to habeas corpus review. Alternatively, at the last minute, the desperate prisoner, crippled by ignorance, may cobble together a poorly researched, poorly argued petition that is doomed to fail. In either case, he or she dies.

But even if the condemned prisoner quickly finds a lawyer, the attorney may have to rush to file a post-conviction petition in state court, with little time to do research, preparation, and investigative work. Yet, the attorney had better not overlook anything. Issues not presented at the state level cannot be brought into federal court. Larry W. Yackle, professor of law at Boston University, warns, "It is now more important than ever that lawyers identify and litigate federal claims in state court as fully as possible. In many instances, state court dispositions of federal claims will be effectively final. When subsequent federal habeas litigation is available at all, its value will depend in large part on the quality of the record made previously in state court."

Federal courts are now under time limitations to rule on capital cases. The new law requires that capital cases "shall be given priority by the district court and by the court of appeals over all noncapital matters." A district court judge has 180 days to review and rule on a capital habeas application. In turn, the court of appeals has 120 days to make its ruling. These time constraints include "the preparation of all pleadings and briefs, and if necessary, an [evidentiary] hearing." The Administrative Office of the United States

Courts is charged as the watchdog for Congress in ensuring compliance to these new time restrictions.

The stage is set to speed up executions. The only thing standing in the way is the U.S. Supreme Court.

Ellis Wayne Felker, under sentence of death in Georgia for the 1981 rape and murder of a college student, filed his second petition for habeas corpus in the federal court just as EDPA took effect. A three-judge panel denied him permission to file. They also refused him a rehearing or permission to appeal their decision. Within days of Felker's scheduled execution the U.S. Supreme Court issued a temporary stay and agreed to hear his arguments challenging the constitutionality of the new law.

At issue was whether Congress has the power to restrict the judicial branch in hearing habeas corpus petitions. The gist of the argument is separation of powers: Has Congress unduly infringed on the constitutional authority of the federal judiciary?

The Supreme Court also wanted the state to answer "whether application of the Act in this case is a suspension of the writ of habeas corpus?" If so, it could violate Article I, Section 9, of the Constitution: "The privilege of the writ of habeas corpus shall not be suspended, unless when in cases of rebellion or invasion that public safety may require it."

Death penalty attorneys, prosecutors, legal scholars, and especially death row prisoners immediately turned a sharp eye to the Felker case. The Court put it on the fast track—granting review on May 3, hearing oral arguments on June 3, and pushing to render a decision before their 1996 summer break.

Four justices, considered the "liberal" minority, dissented over the accelerated scheduling, saying it was "both unnecessary and profoundly unwise. . . ." During oral arguments, Justice Stephen Breyer asked Georgia prosecutor Susan Boleyn whether the new procedural laws would allow the Supreme Court to intervene in cases such as Felker's *if* there was a possibility of innocence. Boleyn, according to the *Associated Press,* said it would not. "We want extraordinary relief to be even more extraordinary," she told the Court, adding it is Congress's intention that claims of innocence be handled only by state courts and governors.

Henry Monaghan, Felker's attorney, pointed out that the historical basis for habeas relief in capital cases has to do with preventing an innocent person from being executed.

Both sides were challenged by questions from the Court, and the toughest were aimed at Boleyn, who did not come unprepared. Supporting her position were several friend-of-the-court briefs, including one submitted by Senator Orrin Hatch (R-Utah) and signed by 54 members of Congress who, not unexpectedly, claim that the new act they created does not restrict the Supreme Court's authority.

U.S. Solicitor General Drew Days told the Court the bill does not strip the Court of all its power, and that it simply solves a problem the Court and country have been plagued with for years—long, drawn-out delays in executions.

Less than a month later the justices unanimously upheld Congress, ruling that the three-judge "gatekeeping" requirement did not suspend the writ of habeas corpus, nor interfere with the high Court's authority to entertain habeas petitions filed directly to the Court under "exceptional circumstances," though they acknowledged "[t]hese writs are rarely granted." Georgia's attorney general estimated Felker would be executed within six weeks of that decision.

What is intended to speed the death penalty review process may slow it to a crawl. The Felker decision will not end the legal battle. Each provision in the habeas reform section of EDPA is ripe for constitutional challenge. A sea of litigation is expected, which could delay executions for a few years.

New Orleans death penalty lawyer Denise LeBoeuf sees the three-judge panel requirement as the most detrimental provision of EDPA. She explained that in most cases of innocence, facts and evidence turn up years later and only after painstaking investigation. "If a prisoner facing death can't come back around with a second habeas petition claiming meritorious constitutional error and have it fairly reviewed by the federal court, what is the sense of having due process of law in this country?" said LeBoeuf. "This three-judge panel can block substantial claims of innocence and leave the petitioner nowhere to turn. It is not the fault of the man or woman sitting in a cell on death row that a claim wasn't discovered until later."

Professor Liebman, an expert on habeas corpus proceedings in capital cases, discovered that "between 1978 and October 1995, the Great Writ was granted in 40 out of every 100 cases in which a death sentence had been imposed." Many of those rulings came not on the first writ filed, but on a second or successive writ, after skilled attorneys took over the case, and adequate preparation and investigation revealed reversible errors having to do either with the conviction or death sentence.

According to a *New York Times* Op-Ed article coauthored by Benjamin Civiletti (attorney general under President Jimmy Carter) and Elliot Richardson (attorney general under Richard Nixon), EDPA is unconstitutional for several reasons, most notably because it violates due process of law and effectively suspends the Great Writ. "One bite of the apple cannot become no bite," they wrote. They also mentioned a similar bill introduced into Congress nearly three decades ago. At the time Hugh Scott (R-Pennsylvania) told legislators it "would have about as much chance of being held constitutional as the celebrated celluloid dog chasing the asbestos cat through hell." Congress in that era rejected that bill, but the Supreme Court today has so far endorsed EDPA.

In 1994 a congressional judiciary committee researched the possibility of innocent people being executed in this country. Their findings were published in a report titled *Innocence and the Death Penalty: Assessing the Danger of Mistaken Executions.* It lists 52 death-sentenced prisoners from 1975 to 1994 who were released from death row after authorities determined they were innocent. Those were the lucky ones, fortunate enough to have had competent legal counsel and to have been allowed back into court with newly discovered evidence of their innocence. One must wonder how many of the nearly 350 executed since 1975 were innocent and unlucky.

"It is now irrefutable that innocent persons are still being sentenced to death," the report stated, "and the chances are high that innocent persons have been or will be executed. . . . Most releases from death row over the past 20 years came only after many years and many failed appeals. The average length of time between conviction and release was almost seven years for the 52 death row inmates released." Had the EDPA been passed prior to those 52 people prevailing on their claims of innocence, the majority would have been executed.

In recent years the U.S. Supreme Court has incrementally limited the use of habeas corpus for all prisoners. Warren McCleskey was sentenced to death in Georgia in 1978 for the killing of an off-duty police officer during the robbery of a furniture store. He wanted a second chance in federal court for review of a claim his lawyers failed to properly raise in his first petition. On his second try the Supreme Court picked up the case to clarify and stiffen the procedural rule of abuse of the writ. The Court ruled that habeas petitioners only get one bite of the apple, not two, and that McCleskey's claim would not be reviewed. He was executed in September 1991, shortly after the decision.

The Supreme Court in 1993 told Leonel Herrera, a Texas death row prisoner, that he was not entitled to a federal hearing on his claim of innocence based on newly discovered evidence. The Court told him to go to the Texas clemency board. He did, and was executed in May 1993.

Habeas review has already been restricted by the nation's highest court to the point of emasculating constitutional due process of law. Now comes the "Effective" Death Penalty Act, which allows the "Great Writ" to keep its name but not its purpose. The new law prioritizes executing prisoners as quickly as possible, with little regard for constitutional due process or innocence.

Assembly-line executions have yet to begin, although the last two years have seen a significant increase. Litigation continues to challenge the due process restrictions of the new law. It's anybody's guess how the Supreme Court will eventually settle the entire issue. But one thing is certain, "get-tough" advocates will not stop until execution follows conviction as night follows day—swiftly and inevitably.

The 3,000 prisoners on death row have reason to worry. Congress, with this new act, tells death-sentenced prisoners, isolated in their cells, that if they do not have a court-appointed lawyer to rush them to federal court in six months, they had better find one on their own or compose their own habeas corpus application within a year. If they cannot find a skilled lawyer who wants to handle such stressful work, if they cannot read or write or interpret law well enough to file their own habeas properly, then that is tough luck. They might as well sign up on the list of "volunteers"— condemned prisoners who give up their appeals in exchange for a quick execution.

Justice Thurgood Marshall once wrote: "A state has no legitimate interest in killing a man sooner than later. If there is any chance that a defendant has a valid objection to his conviction or sentence, elementary principles of justice require that his attorneys be afforded a full opportunity to present that claim before the issue is rendered moot by his death." These are simple words that signify what Constitutional due process in capital cases should be—simple words that signify the American concept of justice. Congress responds with the Anti-Terrorism and Effective Death Penalty Act, a hate-inspired piece of legislation comparable to Hitler's infamous Nuremberg laws, which also singled out groups of "undesirables" for special treatment by the courts: gypsies, criminals, the mentally ill or retarded and, of course, the Jews.

Postscript: So far, the EDPA has withstood all legal challenges, and death penalty cases are speeding through the courts in comparision to what once was. Nevertheless, death penalty attorneys have not thrown in the towel and are still hurling litigation at what they consider unconstitutional legislation.

As for the Georgia attorney general's prediction that he would have Ellis Wayne Felker killed within six weeks of the court decision, he was off, but not by enough for Felker, who was executed November 15, 1996, about three months behind schedule.

12

A Practice in Search of an Ethic: The Death Penalty in the Contemporary South

BURK FOSTER

In 1920, after the rape and murder of a little girl, Kentucky amended its death penalty statute, which called for electrocution of capital offenders, to provide that when a rape was involved, the execution was to be carried out by hanging in the county jail yard in the presence of at least 50 witnesses. One of the men to whom this law would be applied was a 22-year-old black man, Rainey Bethea, who was executed at sunrise on August 14, 1936, in Owensboro, Kentucky. Bethea has been convicted of raping, robbing, and killing Mrs. Elza Edwards, a 70-year-old white widow, on June 10, barely two months earlier.

No one had been hanged in public in Daviess County for more than a generation. Folks from all over came to town for the spectacle. They began arriving in Owensboro the day before. By dawn on execution Friday, the crowd had grown to between 10,000 and 20,000 white people. Extra lawmen had been called in to keep the crowd from getting out of hand.

The sheriff of Daviess County, Mrs. Florence Thompson, who had succeeded her late husband in office, presided over the hanging. She had retained the services of Arthur L. Hash, a former Louisville policeman, as executioner, and G. Phil Hanna of Illinois, as technical advisor, to perform the hanging.

Amid the boisterous crowd yelling taunts and encouragements to the execution party, Bethea knelt on the gallows in prayer and stood up to face the east, trying to watch one last sunrise before the hood was placed over his head. The trap was sprung at 5:28 A.M. Sixteen and a half minutes later, he was pronounced dead by two doctors. Members of the crowd charged the gallows at this point and tore off pieces of his death hood as souvenirs of the execution.

On the same day in Tennessee, in exactly the same amount of time that it took Rainey Bethea to die, three black men were electrocuted for unrelated murders, one right after the other, in the same electric chair—three executions in 16 minutes. But it is Bethea's hanging that became the memorable historical event—the last public execution in America.

In some respects, the hanging of Rainey Bethea may have marked the high point of capital punishment in America. The number of legal executions peaked in the latter half of the 1930s, increasing to 199 in 1935, 195 in 1936, and 190 in 1938. After the 1930s legal executions began to decline, from an average of almost 170 per year in the 1930s to 130 per year in the 1940s and 70 per year in the 1950s.

Popular support for capital punishment waned to the point that by the May 1966 Gallup Poll, more people were opposed to capital punishment than in favor of it. That year only one man was executed in the United States, the next year only two. Then executions stopped altogether as we

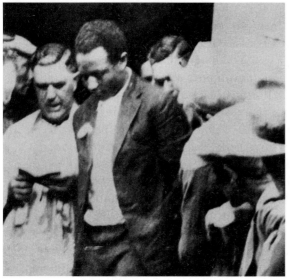

Sam Woodward was hung in public in Lafayette Parish, Louisiana, in 1927. (Copyright: Lafayette Clerk of Court Collection.)

awaited a definitive U.S. Supreme Court ruling on the constitutionality of the death penalty. This ruling finally came with *Furman v. Georgia* (1972), declaring the death penalty as it was then being practiced "cruel and unusual punishment."

It was over; the death penalty had been abolished. Well, not exactly. In 1997 the 25th anniversary of *Furman v. Georgia,* the United States executed 74 men, a total not reached in this country since 1955. How did this practice, once thought to be so near dead, find a vital new place in end-of-the-millennium America? The people who attended Rainey Bethea's hanging could probably explain it to us.

Thirty-eight states, the federal government, and the military have capital punishment laws on the books today, but the death penalty is pronounced and carried out most often in the South. Every Confederate state and every borderland Southern state except West Virginia has the death penalty, all have people on death row, and all except Tennessee have carried out executions in the past 20 years. Sixty percent of the men and women on death row are confined in the 16 southern states; without California's huge death row, the South would have over two thirds of death row inmates. Last year, 85% of America's 68 executions were in the South, half of them in the two states of Texas and Virginia.

The death penalty remains hugely popular in the South today, both among the public and among the legal officials who make it work. It has an important place in an enduring Southern tradition—the cultural tradition of violence. This violence can be channeled in two ways. As interpersonal violence, it is responsible for high rates of criminal assault and homicide. As legal violence, it is directed against those criminals who have themselves committed the worst of those crimes of interpersonal violence.

Many scholars have addressed the problem of Southern violence. One of the best known is Sheldon Hackney. In his 1969 article, "Southern Violence," he drew from many sources to first quantify the problem, then discuss possible reasons for its existence. He cited H.C. Brearley's study of Southern homicide rates in the 1920s. Brearley, who found that Southern homicide rates in this era were two and a half times greater than the rest of the country, defined the South as "that part of the United States lying below the Smith and Wesson line."

Another researcher, writing at the same time as Brearley but from a different perspective, came to much the same conclusion. Frederick L. Hoffman, consulting statistician with the Prudential Insurance Company, studied American homicide rates in the 1920s. Hoffman wrote in the June 1928 *Current History:*

> The homicide problem in America is not diminishing, but increasing in seriousness. . . . The homicide death rate is highest in the city of Memphis, which for many years has maintained an unenviable distinction. In 1927 the Memphis homicide rate was 69.3, against an average of 10.4 for all cities considered. In other words, the Memphis homicide death rate was seven times the normal for the country at large. . . .
>
> In the case of the Southern cities, the situation is seriously complicated by the negro element, which is much more prone to murder than the whites. This explains in part the excessive homicide rate in Detroit, which has a substantial increase in the colored population in recent years. In 1927 the Detroit rate was 18.7, while that of New York was only 6.1 and that of Boston 3.9. The Chicago rate for the same year was 13.3. . . . the outstanding fact of the homicide problem . . . can be traced to the ease with which firearms are obtainable and the common habit of "gun-toting" in many sections of the country. That the situation is much worse in the South than elsewhere is shown by the fact that during the same seven years only 48.4% of the deaths from homicide were caused by firearms in the City of Boston. In Birmingham, where conditions again are typically Southern and where gun-toting is a common practice, the proportion of homicide deaths by firearms was 73%. As is well known to every student of the homicide problem, the countries in which the murder death rate is lowest are the countries in which the carrying or possession of firearms is permissible only under strict Government regulations. All efforts to curtail the traffic in firearms have met with determined opposition on the part of the interests concerned.

In his article a generation later, Hackney showed that Southerners remained much less likely to commit suicide but far more likely to commit homicide than non-Southerners. In his discussion of possible explanations, he reviewed such possibilities as

> The impact of the frontier experience in shaping individualism.
>
> In the aftermath of slavery, heightened black aggression, most often directed intraracially, resulting from alienation against the dominant social order.
>
> The white Southerner's worldview of himself as a victim.
>
> A siege mentality that denies responsibility and places fault with external forces.

Hackney does not solve the problem of Southern violence. No one really has yet. In a 1996 article titled "Law, Social Policy, and Violence: The Impact of Regional Cultures," appearing in the *Journal of Personality and Social Psychology*, Dov Cohen of the University of Illinois has pointed out that

> Acceptance of violence is present in almost all parts of American society. . . . [but] violence will be most condoned in the South and West because the frontier tradition is strongest in these regions. An important element in this tradition is the acceptance of violence used for self-protection and defense. In addition, the legacy of the dehumanizing and violent institution of slavery should make the South even more approving of violence, specifically when it is used to coerce, punish, and maintain social control.

Cohen suggests that whereas Southerners and Westerners both "talk" violence to a greater degree than Northerners, Southerners actually practice violence more, including state-sanctioned execution.

In a study of changes in state and regional homicide rates from the 1970s through the 1990s, Michael Neustrom and Burk Foster found that although homicide rates in two thirds of the states declined during these two decades, in some Southern states and in other more urbanized states homicide rates increased. Southern homicide rates remain more than twice as high as those of other states. If you lived in Louisiana in 1992, for instance, you would have been more than 10 times as likely to be murdered than if you lived in North or South Dakota, New Hampshire, Maine, or Iowa. And most of Louisiana's nation-leading homicide rate in the 1990s is directly attributable to a sharp increase in the murder rate in New Orleans, which has 10% of the population but 40% of the murders. This once led to the facetious proposition that the easiest way to reduce Louisiana's murder rate, to below the Southern average, was to simply expel Orleans Parish from the rest of the state—leaving everyone else feeling much safer.

It is in the South, with its climate of high rates of personal violence of many forms—domestic, neighborhood, drug- and alcohol-related, and predatory criminal—that support for the legal system's use of the death penalty flourishes. It has been so for 300 years in the South, from the colonial period to the present. In regard to the death penalty in the South, let's make three historical observations:

1. Capital punishment historian Watt Espy, who operates the Capital Punishment Research Project in Headland, Alabama, has established that from colonial times to the present, about 55% of all legal executions in America have taken place in the South. Many of these occurred under local government authority before states assumed control over executions.

Espy's data does not include the several thousand lynchings or extralegal executions that took place in local communities, particularly in the period between the Civil War and World War II. Various sources estimate that there may have been over 5,000 lynchings, mostly in the South, alongside the legal executions being carried by state and local governments.

2. In the modern era of capital punishment, which is said to have begun in 1930, 455 men were executed for rape, that is, nonhomicidal rape in which the victim survived. All 455 were in the South; 405, or 89%, were black men, the great majority of whom were convicted of raping white women. Of the 14 men who were electrocuted for rape in Louisiana in the 1940s and 1950s, all were black, and 13 of the 14 were convicted of raping white girls or women.

3. The death penalty, both as a pronouncement and as an act carried out, remains highly popular in the contemporary South. The 16 southern states have death row populations ranging from 17, in Delaware and Maryland, to about 450 in Texas. Of the 12 states with death row populations of more than 100, seven are in the South—Texas, Florida, North Carolina, Alabama, Oklahoma, Georgia, and Tennessee.

Since capital punishment resumed in 1977, there have been just over 500 executions in America. Eighty-three percent of these have been in the South, led by Texas with 167, exactly one third of the total, by itself. In terms of persons actually executed, all of the top 10 states are in the South.

Delaware, although small in numbers, actually qualifies as the leading death penalty state in America. It has a much lower homicide rate but gives death sentences at a much higher rate than states like California or Texas, and it carries out executions at the highest rate of any state. If Delaware had the same population as Texas, it would have given more than a thousand death sentences and executed more than 200 people in the past 20 years. Don't kill anyone in Delaware.

Why does the South not only believe in the death penalty but practice it with religion-like zeal? The traditional rationales for the use of the death penalty focus on how the penalty will affect society. These include three principal purposes: deterrence, incapacitation, and retribution, all of which, it can be argued, are of declining significance, to the point of irrelevance today. Even prosecutors who argue for death rarely cite these purposes as justifications.

Deterrence suffers from declining support, except in conjunction with speeding up the appeals process. We simply do not kill enough murderers fast enough for capital punishment to have any demonstrable deterrent effect. Even when we did kill more of them faster, no short- or long-term deterrent effect could be proved.

Incapacitation, as protection from society's mad dogs, finds an occasional supporter, with the line that no executed criminal has ever come back from the dead to kill again. But with the availability of true life sentences and secure prisons today, the need to execute to protect has diminished. As the pope once said (in St. Louis), the death penalty is "unnecessary in modern society," because we have the means to securely restrain our worst murderers for life.

Retribution, based on equivalence, may be slightly more relevant than the other justifications today, but its form has been altered from retribution for the victim or society and to retribution for the victim's family.

Philosophical justifications matter little to contemporary decision makers. The death penalty is justified as a political expedient, a tough but direct action people can take in the war on violent crime. The emergent ethic of the death penalty in the South is made up of three parts:

1. *Respect for victims of crime, not just the dead but the family as well.* This could be called the "victim deference factor." What are the victims' wishes? Do they want the death penalty or not? The victims who complain the loudest get what they want from the prosecutor, even to dictating death penalty trials. "Victim impact," the concept that allows survivors to express their sense of loss, has become an important part of the penalty phase of the first-degree murder trial. To whatever extent the death penalty is based on objective criteria—that is, the gravity of the offense and the blameworthiness of the offender—the loudness of the family's cries ought to be a minimal force. Politically it is becoming just the opposite today.

Douglas Dennis, in an article in *The Angolite* prison magazine, had these observations on "victimhood:"

Victimhood is a ragingly popular philosophy nowadays, but some warn it is morally bankrupt. It endorses self-pity and gives license to divisiveness and hatred. . . .

Lost in all the raw, physical pain and emotional anguish suffered by crime victims is the perfectly sound reason why this nation's founding fathers barred them from the judicial process: Justice cannot be fair and equitable unless it is unbiased. Prosecutors and judges were invented so cool heads could dispense justice. "For the first time since the Normans and Danes went around hacking each other to pieces," said syndicated columnist Joe Bob Briggs, "you have all these angry revenge-seeking people in the courtroom, demanding blood for blood.

"In other words, we forgot the whole reason for having state prosecutions in the first place. It was to keep these people out of it, to make sure it was fair by not having any emotional revenge speeches in the courtroom." "Victims' rights" is not progress, it is a regression to justice by vendetta.

2. *Moral repudiation.* To be on a death penalty jury, you must be willing to vote for death. These jurors, then, agree in principle that death is the appropriate punishment for certain criminals committing specific criminal homicides. They agree on the death penalty because they think killing is wrong. Their position is moral and absolute; they are taking a stand that brooks no argument. They have in effect taken the moral high ground, leaving the moral "low ground" to those who would argue that mitigating circumstances would merit a penalty other than death.

3. *The "good citizen" obligation.* Your civic duty requires you to make a difficult decision in the war on crime. Responsible citizens have to take a stand. "We sentence you to death because it is our public duty to do so." A juror in a Louisiana capital trial said as much last year: "We felt it was our obligation to the community to sentence this man to death."

The effect of the death penalty on society or on other criminals does not matter. The focus is on the courtroom—the situation immediately at hand. We owe it to the victim and the local community to impose the death penalty. The emphasis is not on some possibly beneficial philosophical purpose, but on the act of achieving consensus, which occurs in three steps:

1. The prosecutor recommends it.
2. The jury decides it.
3. The judge approves it.

In this scenario, there is no effect on society, no underlying purpose. The death penalty in the South today is means-driven, not ends-driven. What is important is achieving the consensus of moral condemnation.

There are no objective standards of when an offense merits the death penalty. Heinousness, like beauty, is in the eye of the beholder; it is purely situational. It allows certain prosecutors and judges and certain populations, acting as jurors, to think and do their worst, while others around them do very nicely with minimal use or no use at all of the death penalty.

What it takes for a particular legal jurisdiction to get a lot of death sentences today is a prosecutor willing to take the trouble to seek the death penalty, a public-spirited citizenry looking for some people to give death sentences to, and judicial officials willing to let nature take its course—they unite in a symbolic act expressing sympathy with the victims and solidarity with their fellow human beings.

Sears and Kinder in 1971 described symbolic attitudes as "almost wholly abstract, ideological, and symbolic in nature." Such attitudes are not concrete, instrumental, or goal oriented, but expressive. They "have almost no conceivable personal relevance to the individual, but have to do with his moral code or his sense of how society should be organized."

Phoebe Ellsworth and Samuel R. Gross of the University of Michigan have written about the importance of emotion and symbolism to the death penalty. In a 1994 article titled "Hardening of the Attitudes: Americans' Views on the Death Penalty," they suggest that symbolic collective representations, such as public attitudes toward the death penalty, are "value expressive, emotional, and closely tied to the deep, fundamental beliefs of a culture." They go on to say,

> Research over the last 20 years has tended to confirm the hypothesis that most people's death penalty attitudes (pro or con) are based on emotion rather than information or rational argument. People feel strongly about the death penalty, know little about it, and feel no need to know more. . . . [M]ost people's attitudes toward capital punishment are basically emotional. The "reasons" (to be for or against) are determined by the attitudes, not the reverse. . . .
>
> Whatever the relationship between crime and support for the death penalty, it is not driven by personal experience. Many studies have shown that people who have been victimized themselves, or who fear for their personal safety, are no more likely to support the death penalty than those who have been more fortunate, or are less fearful. . . . If there is any one emotion that mediates between crime and support for the death penalty, it is probably frustration rather than fear. Year after year we live with high crime rates, we see graphic coverage of violence, we hear politicians promise to win the war against violence, against gangs, against drugs, against crime—but nothing changes. It is not hard to understand why many people support capital punishment even though they believe it

does not deter crime and is not fair. The death penalty is concrete, it is forceful, and it is final (which nothing else seems to be); it is something, and being for it means that you insist that something be done.

How does this symbolic act fit into the legal system of the South today? As a practice, the death penalty is not pervasive, like a stain spreading evenly across each state of the South. Rather, the pattern resembles blood spatters, drops of blood falling here and there, across the geography and ecology of the South. We talk about the "death belt," reaching from Texas and Oklahoma across to the Atlantic Coast, but what we really have are "death pockets" within the larger boundaries.

Using Louisiana as an example, Orleans Parish has about five times as many homicides as each of the three next largest parishes—Jefferson, East Baton Rouge, and Caddo. But in the decade of the 1990s, Orleans has given 12 death sentences, while East Baton Rouge has given 17, Jefferson 12, and Caddo 6. Fewer than half the parishes in the state have given anyone a death sentence in the past two decades; only 14 parishes (of 64) have given more than two.

James Liebman, a law professor at Columbia University, said in a 1995 *New York Times* article, "Lots of states have death belts. In southern Georgia, there are lots of death sentences; in northern Georgia, there aren't. In Tennessee, there are tons of death sentences in Memphis and East Knoxville, but not in Nashville."

The same article points out that of 254 counties in Texas, only 42 had sent any inmates to Texas's death row, and half of those only one. Almost a third of Texas's death row came from one jurisdiction, Harris County, where district attorney Johnny B. Holmes is famous as the "deadliest prosecutor" in America.

Most states have similar "death pockets," judicial districts with disproportionately high rates of death sentences. What you expect to find in such a locale is

1. A hard-core, conservative, politically popular prosecutor.
2. Judges who generally go along with the prosecutor's office.
3. A jury pool in which white conservatives predominate.
4. A small lower class, including significant numbers of blacks and Hispanics, that commits enough death-qualified crimes (usually felony murders such as robbery and rape against middle-class white victims) to generate a significant number of prosecutable capital cases.

The real death pocket of America is not Houston, Texas, but the "City of Brotherly Love," Philadelphia, whose district attorney, Lynne Abraham, seeks the death penalty in over half of all homicides and finds it very often: more than half the inmates on Pennsylvania's death row come from Philadelphia. William Penn and the correctional reformers who founded the American penitentiary would be shocked at this strange turn of events.

The appellate courts, which according to *Gregg* are supposed to be assuring proportionality in the application of death sentences across the state, ignore any notion of national or statewide standards in favor of local autonomy. The result is a system far more arbitrary and capricious than the one described in *Furman v. Georgia* a quarter-century ago, but with a far less critical Supreme Court looking at it.

How would one rationally counter this political spirit that promotes high rates of capital punishment in the South today?

1. *By citing numbers,* like those indicating recent decline in the homicide rate. The murder rate has fallen off sharply in recent years. It now stands at about 7.0 per 100,000 population nationwide; in many cities, murder rates are back to the levels of the 1960s, rates that were, incidentally, much lower than they had been at other times in the American past, including one homicide peak in the 1930s. Of course, proponents of the death penalty suggest that the decline in murders is due to the increase in executions. We should keep the execution rate high to keep murders in decline.

2. *By arguing costs*—namely, that it is more expensive to execute than imprison. The most rigorous studies suggest that putting someone to death costs two to three times as much as a real life sentence. The increased costs are mostly legal expenses associated with appeals. Proponents of capital punishment would argue that the way to reduce these costs is to speed up and reduce appeals, which many states and the federal courts are apparently trying to do.

3. *By selling fortuity,* the 1-in-60 chance of getting a death sentence. There were 20,000 murders last year and barely 300 death sentences. The death penalty is applied so capriciously, no one even tries to argue that it is done fairly. But proponents argue that we need *more,* not fewer death sentences. Increasing the number of death sentences would distribute them more fairly by state, by district, by race, by class, by gender, by age, and by any of the other discriminatory criteria.

4. *By proposing alternatives,* such as the true natural life sentence. More states are turning to real life sentences that carry no chance of parole. Louisiana has almost 1,000 first-degree murderers serving real life sentences, most of them at our well-known Angola penitentiary. Proponents argue that real life sentences lack the impact of death. Abolitionists argue that what Professor Eric Trump calls "death in prison"—irrevocable,

endless confinement at hard labor for a full lifetime—is a more severe punishment than early death.

Will any of these (or all of these in combination) make a difference? Not likely. Two other possibilities, however, might:

1. *Changes in the makeup of the U.S. Supreme Court.* Some death penalty abolitionists, giving up on popular opinion and state legislatures, see a more liberal Supreme Court as the only short-term hope for abolition of capital punishment.

2. *Pressures in the world court of public opinion.* Consider the protests in Mexico and Canada when their citizens were about to be executed, or the international outcry at the execution of Sean Sellers in Oklahoma, condemned for three murders committed at age 16 and finally executed in February 1999. But what does international opinion matter to a popularly elected district attorney in the South? In a word, nothing.

Built upon a tradition of personal violence in which state violence is a perfectly legitimate, even necessary response, the death penalty has found an ethic for survival for at least one more generation in the South, and likely in most of the rest of the country as well, though not to the same extent in practice. Other nations, and even some of our own United States, have done well without the death penalty for a long time.

Michigan was the first state to abolish the death penalty, in 1847, followed by Rhode Island in 1852 and Wisconsin in 1853. The last execution in Michigan was carried out in 1830. But the death penalty, as we have already determined, will not stay dead. The restoration of capital punishment was debated in the Michigan legislature no fewer than 25 times between 1885 and 1952. Restoration was defeated in the legislature 23 times, vetoed by the governor once, and rejected once by popular vote. One commentator wrote,

> Michigan is one of eight states sufficiently civilized to have abolished capital punishment, but on April 16 its Senate voted 21 to 10 to restore the death penalty. If concurred in by the House and signed by the Governor, the measure will have to go before the people for a popular vote. The Senate's action is a backward step, and final approval of its measure would be a disgrace to the State and a set-back for the cause of law-enforcement in this country. . . .

A recent testimonial to that effect is from Frederick L. Hoffman, consulting statistician of the Prudential Insurance Company, as a conclusion to his analysis of the homicide figures for 1928. Writing in *The Spectator,* an insurance journal published in New York City, Mr. Hoffman says,

If we are not willing to enforce the death penalty, it would certainly be much better to do away with it. That we are not willing to enforce it is made clear in nearly every trial for murder of the first degree, in which the resources of the law are exhausted to save a convicted person from the electric chair, the hangman's rope, the lethal gas chamber, or the firing squad. . . . Certainly the states in which the death penalty is enforced show a higher murder death-rate than the States in which it is not enforced. A good illustration is the State of Rhode Island where the death penalty has not been enforced since 1852. During the year under review, Providence, R.I., had a homicide death rate of only 3.8 per 100,000, while Pawtucket, R.I., had no deaths from homicide at all during 1928, nor for that matter during 1927. . . . Or Providence, R.I., with 286,000 population and 11 deaths from homicide in 1928 may be compared with Houston, Texas, with 275,000 population and 72 deaths from homicide. This argument could be extended to practically every section of the country and no evidence can be produced to show that capital punishment acts as a deterrent or hindrance to even the worst of murder records conceivable. The death penalty, rather to the contrary, acts a deterrent to swift and adequate justice, imposes heavy burdens upon the taxpayers as the result of long trials, fosters sensationalism of the worst possible type, and stains the civilization of those who enforce it.

The numerous violent deaths in the United States do little credit to our supposed high civilization. One way of reducing this toll is through swift and sure justice, and one way to swift and sure justice is to do away with that relic of barbarism, capital punishment. Michigan should stand by the law it has.

This prophetic article was from the May 1, 1929, *The Nation.* In this instance, capital punishment was once more resigned to the ranks of the restless undead, at least in Michigan, though sponsors have promised to bring it back again (as a referendum to amend the state constitution) in the 1999 legislative session.

Away from the northern borders of the contiguous 48 states, and particularly in the South, the death penalty has made a spirited comeback. The year of 1997, with 74 executions, took us almost back to the "happy days" of 1955. Soon, perhaps this year, we will return to the Korean War of 1951, the last year with more than 100 executions. If we persevere, within the next decade we can return all the way back to Rainey Bethea and the 195 executions of 1936 Depression-era America. Who can say how far back into the past the future of the death penalty may take us?

13

An Unholy Tradition

WATT ESPY

From *The Angolite,* January/February 1988, Angola, La: Louisiana State Penitentiary.

In 1754 the soldiers garrisoned at Cat Island in the Gulf of Mexico mutinied, murdered their cruel commander, a sadistic officer named Duroux, and threw his body into the Gulf. They escaped, made their way to the mainland, and had started for the English Colony of Georgia when they were captured by a band of Choctaw Indians and returned to New Orleans for trial.

The French Governor, Kerlerec, a stern disciplinarian, was determined to make a suitable example of those he deemed the ringleaders. Three of them were strapped naked to a wheel, their bodies stretched taut, and each bone broken with a sledge hammer. They were then left to languish without sustenance until death.

A more unique punishment, possibly the most bizarre in the annals of American capital punishment, was reserved for the fourth condemned man, a Swiss mercenary. In order to impress the enormity of the offense on his fellow countrymen who were also serving the French, Kerlerec decreed for this man a death then used in Switzerland, a country that has long since abolished the death penalty.

The culprit was sentenced to be securely nailed into a wooden box, which was then sawed in half. Lest the deterrent factor be diminished, the other Swiss mercenaries were ordered to serve as the executioners.

The 1754 executions, considered by any standard barbaric, were not Louisiana's first experience with executions, nor would they be the last. The first confirmed execution in Louisiana was that of a black man who in 1722 was publicly burned alive for the murder of a Frenchman. In September of

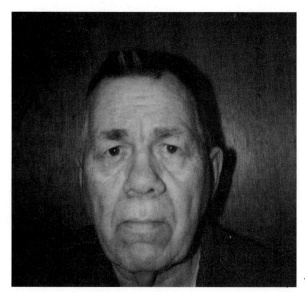

Watt Espy (Copyright Watt Espy.)

the same year two white men were hanged for theft after having undergone five days of continuous torture.

In 1730 the slave Samba and six of his followers made an unsuccessful insurrection. Their attempt at freedom cost them dearly. They were broken on the wheel. The only conspirator to escape this form of punishment was the lone female in the group, who was hanged.

In October 1777 Clement and Jacob, slaves of Don Pedro Cabaret, were charged with the murder of a fellow slave, Pierre. Clement avoided torture by confessing and was hanged in what is now Jackson Square in New Orleans. The interesting portion of the sentence, which was carried out in February 1778, was the judge's additional stipulation that after death "his body will be put into a leather sack with a dog, a viper, a monkey, and a cock, the mouth of the sack sewed up, will be pitched into the river. . . ."

Jacob refused to confess and was tortured. He was chained to the barrel of a cannon for three days, as a fire built underneath the cannon slowly roasted him. When he still refused to make a confession, he was absolved of the murder but declared guilty of theft and condemned to receive 200 lashes at the foot of the gallows.

Louisiana holds the dubious distinction of being the only state that actually used decapitation as a means of execution. (Utah's original constitution gave a condemned person the choice of hanging, the firing squad, or decapitation. After none had selected the latter, it was subsequently dropped.) In January 1811 slaves in St. John the Baptist Parish revolted and marched on New Orleans, 400 strong. The militia from New Orleans and Baton Rouge engaged the rebels 25 miles north of the city. The slaves broke and ran, leaving 65 of their number dead and 16 others captive. After a speedy trial the 16 captives were beheaded in the Place d'Armes, and afterward their severed heads were placed on poles set at intervals on the banks of the river to serve as a terrifying warning to others held in bondage.

As in other states, the overwhelming majority of executions in Louisiana were by hanging. Among the 884 legal executions that have been confirmed in the Pelican State, 756 were by hanging. The gallows, used exclusively in Louisiana from 1811 (after the decapitation of the 16 slaves) to 1941, was in many respects as cruel as earlier forms of execution. Things could go wrong, and many times they did. When the drop was too short, the neck was not broken and the victim slowly strangled. If the drop was too long, the head could be torn from the body or the feet could touch the ground, making it necessary for several stout men to pull the victim up by the rope and hold him until death occurred. Occasionally, the rope would break, making it necessary for the officers to drag the condemned man back up to the top of the gallows, procure a new rope, and do it again.

In 1941 Louisiana substituted the electric chair for hanging. Taking a cue from neighboring Mississippi, Louisiana used a portable electric chair that was hauled from parish to parish—carrying out the execution in the jurisdiction of conviction. Generally, those earlier electrocutions were conducted inside the parish jail or in some other location within the parish courthouse.

In 1957 the law was again changed so that all executions were to take place within the walls of the state prison at Angola. Once before, for a brief period (1910–1918) all hangings had taken place in the old Baton Rouge Penitentiary.

Many states had preceded Louisiana in substituting the chair for the gallows, and it was done, invariably, because legislators considered it "more humane." The several states that opted for the gas chamber did so for the same reason most states have opted for lethal injection today. We continue to seek a more sanitized way of killing.

All methods have their drawbacks. A malfunctioning electric chair can burn the body almost beyond recognition, and there have been cases where after the attending physician pronounced the prisoner dead, he began breathing again. The law, of course, had to be followed, so these prisoners were taken back to the chair for another shot of juice. The entire

The Angola electric chair, in which 86 men and one woman were electrocuted between 1941 and 1991. (Copyright: Chris DeLay.)

civilized world was shocked when, on May 29, 1947, Louisiana electrocuted Willie Francis at St. Martinville a second time, the original execution a year earlier having failed due to a malfunction of the chair.

Cyanide gas, another method proposed for carrying out the death penalty, was made odious by Adolph Hitler's Nazis, who used it to such monstrous ends in an effort to rid themselves of those they thought unworthy of life in their new world order. Death by inhalation of cyanide is not pleasant. The searing fumes burn through to the lungs, and death does not occur instantaneously.

Even the most recent innovation in dealing death to ones whom society would eliminate, lethal injection, is hardly something that should be condoned by a civilized people. Stephen Morin, executed in Texas on March 13, 1985, had to suffer intensely as technicians prodded his veins for over 40 minutes with needles before they were able to find a vein capable of receiving the tubes which carry the solutions of death into the body. Several others who have died by this same means have suffered the same torment. There will be many, many more as condemned persons are executed who have small, rolling veins, or whose veins have dried up over the years because of intravenous drug use.

It appears that instead of debating which manner of killing is the "most humane," we should be considering the more fundamental question—whether there is any "humane" way to kill another human being.

Postscript: Watt Epsy, whose 30-year research has made him the foremost authority on legal executions in the United States, is head of the Capital Punishment Research Project in Headland, Alabama. The preceding information was originally contained in an article in the *Shreveport Journal* in November 1987 and reappeared in a reprint in *The Angolite.*

Execution statistics generally utilized date back only to 1930, when the federal government officially began keeping records. Epsy's inventory of 15,669 confirmed executions goes further, dating back to colonial days and including executions in the Philippines during the period it was an official commonwealth of the United States, prior to full independence.

Virginia tops Espy's list for executing more citizens than any other state, followed by New York, Georgia, and Pennsylvania. Louisiana, with 894 executions, ranks fifth—a point worth noting in light of Louisiana's status as the nation's execution capital at the time this information first appeared in print. "It is really depressing to see the large numbers, particularly in Louisiana, that are being executed following the McClesky decision in the Supreme Court," Epsy told *The Angolite* at the time. "It horrifies me to think that very shortly we may be killing people at the same rate as in the mid-1930s (almost 200 per year), and our people will not even be aware of it. Percentage-wise, your state seems to be determined to lead them all, and this is something which no civilized person should be proud of."

Several states, including Texas, Virginia, Florida, and Missouri, have moved ahead of Louisiana in post-1977 executions.

14

The Executed Warden

LANE NELSON

From *The Angolite,* January/February 1997, Angola, La: Louisiana State Penitentiary.

Wardens of American prisons have always held absolute power over those in their charge, more so in the South than elsewhere, and more so in the past than today. The only accountability wardens of the past had was for the size of their budgets and the number of escapes and disturbances. Excess in any of those three categories could and did ruin careers. But until the 1970s, when federal courts began looking at prison conditions, few wardens were held accountable for mistreating, brutalizing, or killing their prisoners.

Many Southern prisons—Angola, Huntsville, Parchman, to name a few—have been hellholes of disease, deprivation, and death, but no prison in this country, it can be argued, was ever worse than Andersonville. Set up in Georgia during the Civil War by the Confederacy to hold Union prisoners of war, it was officially named Camp Sumpter. During its brief 14 months of existence, 12,912 inmates died within its walls. The warden was a Swiss expatriate who had settled in Louisiana, Henry Hartmann Wirz. He is the only warden ever executed in this country because of the way he ran his prison.

Wirz was born in Zurich, Switzerland, on November 25, 1823. He received an elementary education and dreamed of becoming a doctor, but his father, a tailor, insisted his son follow in his footsteps. From 1843 to 1846, Wirz worked with his father, married, fathered two children, and got into money trouble. It is unclear what that trouble was—perhaps embezzlement—but he served a short prison sentence and his wife divorced him. When Wirz was released from prison, the Swiss government banished him. He sailed to America.

Wirz arrived in Massachusetts in 1849 and found work in a clothing factory. Five years later he traveled to Kentucky, became a physician's assistant and, on May 28, 1854, married a widow, Elizabeth Wolf. He tried to establish his own medical practice in Kentucky, but the effort failed when local doctors protested his scheme to pose as a certified physician. Angry and shamed, Wirz and his family drifted south, to Milken's Bend, Louisiana. There he found work on the Marshall Plantation, doctoring slaves and livestock. Perhaps for the first time in his life, in the serene environment of the South and able to practice his "medicine," Henry Wirz found contentment and joy. Then came the Civil War.

On June 16, 1861, he joined the Fourth Battalion Louisiana Infantry and fought for the Confederate cause. He quickly earned the rank of sergeant, and at the battle of Fair Oaks/Seven Pines, near Richmond, Virginia, he was promoted to captain. During that battle he was shot in the right arm. The wound, which pained him constantly after that, became a reminder of his enemy, the North.

Out of the infirmary and back in uniform, Wirz was detailed to General John Winder, the man in charge of war prisons in Virginia (comparable to the head of the state's department of corrections). His loyalty to Winder enabled him to hold brief wardenships over several prisons confining Union soldiers. Andersonville, his last military responsibility, gave Wirz a place in American history.

Located in Sumpter County, Georgia, Andersonville was built to ease overcrowding in other Southern military prisons. Designed to hold 10,000 captives, the open stockade consisted of 23½ acres. Construction began in late December 1863, with 500–600 slaves brought in from areas of Georgia and Florida to clear pine trees and build a 20-foot-high, thick wooden wall around the stockade. Five feet of the wooden wall were below the ground to discourage prisoners from tunneling their way to freedom. A clear running stream cut through the middle of the prison, and just outside the gate sat a small infirmary.

Inside the stockade a "deadline" was set up 16 feet from the wood wall—an invisible line marked by intervals of sticks. Inside the deadline was dead space, literally. Prisoners who crossed into it, by mistake or intentionally, were shot by guards in sentry boxes. It was not uncommon for prisoners no longer able to endure the atrocious conditions to suicidally step into the dead area. Others prisoners were baited over the line by bored and trigger-happy Confederate guards. One Southern soldier from the First Georgia Regiment wrote in a letter to his wife, "Some of [the guards] would like nothing better than to shoot one of the scoundrels just for the fun of it. Indeed, I heard one chap say that he just wanted one to put his foot over the line when he was on post, and he would never give him time to pull it back. Many would murder them in cold blood."

On February 25, 1864, the first 500 prisoners marched into Andersonville. Let loose in the stockade to fend for themselves, they scrounged enough leftover lumber to build crude shanties. The thousands of prisoners who came afterwards, like Union private John Ransom, found no lumber. "My blanket keeps us all warm," wrote Ransom, who later published a diary of his imprisonment. "There are two or more in our [group]. Daytime the large spread is stretched three or four feet high, on four sticks, and keeps off the sun, and at night taken down for a cover."

Ransom arrived at Andersonville in the middle of March 1864, about the time Captain Wirz took over as warden. He was greeted by the news that he and all prisoners would soon be released. Andersonville authorities informed its prisoners on nearly a daily basis to remain comfortable, that their stay would only be a few weeks, until an exchange for Confederate soldiers held in Union prisons could be worked out. "Such talk would not go down any longer," Ransom eventually scratched in his diary. "We had been fooled enough, and paid no attention to what they told us."

Wirz, not unlike other wardens, purposely encouraged false hope to pacify the prison population. Desperate acts by hopeless men would thus be less likely to occur. For the most part the strategy worked. There was never any mass stampede on the walls and gates of Andersonville. Instead, thousands of men wasted away and died dreaming of freedom. "The slightest news about exchange is told from one to the other," wrote Ransom, "and gains every time repeated, until finally it's grand, good news, and sure exchange is immediate. The weak ones feed upon these reports, and struggle along from day to day. One hour they are all hopeful and expectant and the next hour as bad as the other way." Andersonville prisoners, as people in wretched circumstances often do, manufactured hope out of thin air.

Conditions of utter horror prevailed at Andersonville. On April 1, 1864, the prison held 7,160 Union soldiers. By May 1, the population had grown to 12, 213, and already 728 men had died. Exposure to freezing winter nights and, later, sweltering summer days, plus the foul water and dire shortages of food and medicine caused rampant disease, added to the universal malnutrition.

As the population increased, rations decreased. In his book, *History of Andersonville Prison,* Ovid L. Futch describes the food situation:

> Ohio cavalryman David Kennedy, whose chief complaint at first was the monotony of a diet of fat bacon and cornbread, soon began to deplore the increasing scantiness and inferior quality of his food. On May 23 he wrote [in a diary]: "Rations getting short and very poor. Cornbread, corn ground cob, and all." The next day he was given rice, which he described as half rice and half dirt, "not half-cooked, brought in an old soap barrel, very strong of soap, enough to make a body puke to look at." On the Fourth of July, when the population exceeded 25,000, Kennedy wrote, "It is a sorrowful Fourth. Hunger gnaws our vitals as we have not drawn any rations for two days. We draw this evening spoilt beef and maggoty mush alive with worms."

The blankets that shielded some of the imprisoned soldiers from the sun's heat were of no use in pouring Southern rains, especially on winter nights when temperatures dipped to freezing. Clothes were not issued to prisoners. The South could not afford to properly clothe its own soldiers on the battlefields, let alone its prisoners. So Andersonville prisoners had to make do with the uniforms they came in with, until the material wasted away and fell off their bodies. Afterward they lived naked.

The once sparkling stream that cut through the prison turned foul. The cookhouse that sat above the stockade emptied its grease and food wastes into the water. About a quarter mile above the cookhouse, two companies of Confederate soldiers bathed and emptied their latrines into the stream. All that muck flowed into the stockade, and prisoners were forced to dig wells to find drinking water. What they found was water so high in sulphur content that it made many sick. The prison hospital quickly became overwhelmed with starved, wounded, and diseased prisoners. Much of the sparse medicine dispensed was contaminated, adding to the death toll.

By August, 33,000 prisoners were squeezed into the stockade. Those who arrived that month were not only aghast at the staggering conditions, but also appalled by the reaction of the prison population. The dead lay everywhere, and men fought over possession of the corpses, wanting to carry the bodies outside the gate for the chance to pick up wood on the way back in.

Early on, Wirz sent groups of prisoners under armed guard into the woods to collect firewood, but those special details ended after too many Union soldiers escaped. The warden did keep one detail intact, consisting of slaves and trusted "convict guards," to build him and his family a comfortable, wood-frame house about a mile from the prison. These so-called convict guards were prisoners who, holding to Southern penal tradition, Warden Wirz allowed to work outside the stockade and perform some guard duties. In return for their loyalty to Wirz, they were provided with extra rations, better housing, and sometimes freedom.

For more than a century after the Civil War, convict guards were used regularly in Southern prisons, and their abuse of authority wreaked havoc on prison populations. In Mississippi and other states, convict guards were granted full pardons for killing escaping prisoners. It was not until federal courts intervened in the operations of state prisons that convict guards were eliminated. Louisiana's shotgun-toting convict guards were retired in the early 1970s.

Escape attempts were a daily occurrence at Andersonville. What may have been the best means of escape was devised when the death toll rose. Collecting dead bodies and carrying them outside the stockade became routine. Bodies were hauled to a large shack and piled until mass burials took place. Prisoners would fake death to be brought outside and tossed onto the pile. Once the sun went down they would crawl off into the woods. That escape route ended the day too many tried at the same time and a Confederate guard noticed the "resurrection." After that, Wirz gave explicit orders that the dead be checked before being carried outside. "Checking" came by way of kicking the body hard a couple times, or putting a rifle to a prisoner's head, sometimes pulling the trigger.

The most frequent method of attempted escape, however, was tunneling. Groups of prisoners dug tunnels all over the stockade hoping to get far enough under and away from the outer fence to make a fair break into the woods. Many tried; few made it. Even the ones who did make it to the woods had to contend with bloodhounds that tracked them and often tore them to pieces. These Union soldiers were in the South, after all, where Southerners had been chasing runaway slaves for many years before the war began.

But chase dogs were not the main concern for escaping prisoners. "Tunnel traitors" were. Confidential informants scurried through the stockade searching for tunnels in progress, then sneaking to Wirz to inform him of the location of the tunnel. As a reward these tunnel traitors received a chunk of meat or a plug of tobacco. There were 604 deaths not attributed to disease or other natural causes that occurred at Andersonville during its operation. Some of these deaths were no doubt tunnel traitors, killed by their fellow prisoners.

Adversity can change people, sometimes for the good, sometimes for the bad. In a cruel environment where oppression continually grows worse and the only thing to look forward to is something else to lose—such as at Andersonville, where adequate food, wood, and water became practically unobtainable—some will do anything to survive. Even though Andersonville held prisoners of war and not criminals, groups of soldiers banded together and attacked the weaker among them, stealing whatever meager items they could. During the summer of 1864, these roving gangs of thugs were responsible for a marked increase in beatings and even killings in the prison population.

Rumors of intolerable conditions at Andersonville caught the attention of the Southern War Department, which issued orders to have the prison inspected. Confederate Colonel Daniel T. Chandler, a one-time Union sympathizer, was sent on the assignment in early August 1864. Among his findings were that Andersonville's Confederate "troops are entirely without discipline, and their officers are incapable of instructing them, being ignorant of their own duties." He also reported horrid conditions inside the stockade and recommended the immediate transfer of thousands of prisoners to relieve overcrowding. Chandler noted how the dead were treated, "their hands in many instances being mutilated with an ax in the removal of rings," and being piled in trenches without coffins for burial.

Wirz, who guided Chandler around the prison, admitted to deficiencies in cooking and baking but took exception to the rest of Chandler's report and recommendations. He filed a rebuttal, saying, "I saw very soon that [Colonel Chandler] would be made the plaything of cute Yankees, who would give him most horrible descriptions of their sufferings . . . owing doubtlessly to the sympathy which his looks indicated he had for them."

Another inspection of Andersonville was authorized. Confederate Surgeon General Samuel P. Moore sent Joseph Jones, a renowned Southern physician and medical professor, to Andersonville to investigate the high mortality there. When Jones reached Andersonville in mid-August 1864, Wirz refused him entrance to the stockade until ordered to do so by a higher authority. Yet another who later inspected Andersonville wrote that Wirz "was exceedingly profane." A detective serving under General Winder agreed, saying that Wirz was "an extremely profane man and very strict in the discharge of his duties, oftentimes severe toward prisoners."

At the end of September 1864, with Union forces driving deeper into the South, and taking into consideration the reports of Chandler and Jones, most of the inmates at Andersonville were transferred to other prisons. Because the Andersonville atrocities were well-known to the North, citizens of Sumpter County and the outlying areas feared an onslaught by General Sherman or other Union generals. A Confederate soldier at the time said that it would be better to face the Yankees anywhere else "than here in South-West Georgia, for the horrors of the stockade have so enraged them that they will have no mercy on this county." The soldier had reason for alarm. Cutting his way into the South, General Sherman told his officers that he would "make Georgia howl."

But Andersonville was spared a bloody onslaught; instead, Union forces pushed toward Atlanta. The invasion of the Union Army called every available Confederate soldier to the battlefield. By November 1864 only 1,359 Union soldiers were held at the prison under a skeleton force of guards who were mostly youths and old men.

With the South falling, Union prisoners at Andersonville—not told how close the North was to winning the war—were given the chance to swear allegiance to the Confederacy and enlist in its service. In March 1865, just one month before the war ended, 138 Union inmates switched sides. Apparently, this opportunity had been available for some time. Historical records reveal that during Andersonville's 14-month existence a total of 338 Union prisoners joined the Confederate army. Generally, when prisoners chucked their allegiance and switched sides they were put in uniform and placed on the front lines of battlefields, having no choice but to fight to stay alive.

On April 9, 1865, Confederate General Robert E. Lee surrendered to General Ulysses S. Grant at Appomattox, Virginia. The bloody Civil War had ended, but not before it had claimed the lives of almost half a million Union and Confederate soldiers.

The end of the war brought an end to Andersonville, but not to its reputation. Northerners considered Henry Wirz a devilish monster, and General John Winder, Wirz's superior, worse. In the book, *The Tragedy of Andersonville,* Union general and military judge advocate N. P. Chipman credits Winder with being "the moving spirit of evil" at Andersonville. "It was [Winder] who suggested to Colonel Chandler that it was better to let the prison relieve its congestion by death than by enlargement—a sentiment in harmony with the policy pursued by his faithful subordinate Wirz. The removal of Winder was urged by Colonel Chandler, but he was not only not removed but was promoted." Winder escaped the North's wrath by dying, apparently of a heart attack, in February 1865.

With news that the war was over, wardens and officials from other Southern prisons—the Turners at Richmond, Major Gee of Salisbury, and Lieutenant Boisseux of Belle Island—quickly packed up and took off. Knowing their lives were at stake, they slipped into obscurity. But not Wirz, who remained, defiantly or foolishly, with his family in the house he had built at Andersonville. This is where Union Captain Henry Noyes found him in May 1865, sitting at home with his wife and two step-daughters.

Noyes had orders to arrest Wirz and transport him back to Washington, DC, to stand trial for war crimes. To make his job easier, he lied to the Wirz family, saying the former warden would return after a debriefing by government officials. Wirz, suspecting otherwise, quickly penned a letter to Union Major General James Harrison Wilson, who was in charge of restoring and keeping order in Macon, Georgia:

> I am a native of Switzerland, and was before the war a citizen of Louisiana, and by profession a physician. Like hundreds and thousands of others, I was carried away by the maelstrom of excitement and joined the Southern army. . . . [In my charge at Andersonville] I was only a medium, or, I may better say, the tool in the hands of my superiors. This is my condition. I am a man with a family. I lost all my property when the Federal army besieged Vicksburg. I have no money at present to go any place, and, even if I had, I know of no place to go. My life is in danger, and I most respectfully ask of you help and relief. If you will be so generous as to give me some sort of a safe conduct, or what I should greatly prefer, a guard to protect myself and family against violence, I should be thankful to you; and you may rest assured that your protection will not be given to

one who is unworthy of it. My intention is to return with my family to Europe, as soon as I can make the arrangements. . . . Very respectfully, your obedient servant.

Wirz's plea was ignored. Although he went calmly, it was no easy task getting him to Washington. Several times Noyes and his small guard ran across Union soldiers who recognized the warden and wanted to hang him on the spot. "Whenever I got him where there were any of our soldiers I had to hurry him off and get him under a strong guard in order to save him," Noyes recounted as a witness at the Wirz trial. "I think that but for the guard I had, and my personal presence, they would have taken hold of him, and if they had got hold of him I do not suppose he would have ever reached Washington."

Once in Washington, Wirz was arraigned on charges of murder and conspiracy to commit murder, with several specified acts of inhumane treatment at Andersonville detailing each count. He pleaded not guilty. The most publicized charge was an alleged conspiracy: Confederate President Jefferson Davis and high-ranking Confederate officers supposedly systematically designed the deaths of Union soldiers in Southern prison camps, with Wirz and others like him their willing tools. But neither Davis nor any other Confederate leaders were tried for war crimes.

At trial, Wirz and his attorneys flatly denied some charges and defended against others by saying he was just following orders. Wirz continually insisted he was not even at Andersonville in August, when the death toll reached its peak, but had taken a vacation. Yet, reports of the several inspections that occurred that month noted his presence.

Trial records show the proceeding was a spectacle, fueled by heated Northern opinion, sensationalist journalism, and political grandstanding. Although no evidence showed that Wirz had killed anyone by his own hand, witness after witness testified of Wirz's brutality and disregard for his prisoners. Wardens, like sea captains, are responsible for their "ships." The dead of Andersonville doomed Wirz from the start.

Southern revisionists have taken exception to the prosecution and execution of Wirz. They argue that he was a hero, a martyr. In 1909 a 45-foot granite memorial honoring him was unveiled at Andersonville. Wirz's memory is still honored with special annual events and ceremonies. Today the town of Andersonville is quiet, sparsely populated, and caters to tourists who stop to see the Civil War museum, a national cemetery that holds the bodies of thousands of Civil War soldiers and the Wirz memorial.

In a book edited by J. H. Segars and published in Atlanta, Georgia, by Southern Heritage Press, *Andersonville: The Southern Perspective—Journal of Confederate History Series, Volume 13,* Segars says the North's failure to continue with the prisoner exchange system caused immense overcrowding in Southern prisons and thus was responsible for the tragic events at Andersonville. He provides official documents and excerpts from letters written by Confederate guards and physicians stationed at Andersonville, a few Union soldiers imprisoned there, and Wirz's relatives, some of whom still reside in Louisiana, that describe Wirz as a kind-hearted man who did the best he could under dire circumstances.

Andersonville held a total of 45,613 inmates according to official records. On August 8, 1864, it held its greatest number of Union prisoners: 33,114. The most deaths that occurred on a single day were 127 on August 23, 1864. Two hundred and fifty Confederate guards also died at Andersonville. Not counting the guards, 12,912 men died at Andersonville. "I found the stockade extremely crowded," said William John Hamilton, a Southern priest who visited it in May, "with a great deal of sickness and suffering among the men. I was kept so busy administering the sacraments to the dying that I had to curtail a great deal of the service that Catholic priests administer to the dying, they died so fast." The average death rate during the 14 months of the prison's existence was nearly one man every 45 minutes.

Even Southerners concede Andersonville was a horror. Eliza Frances Andrews, a cultured Southern belle and zealous rebel, who later became the first woman accepted in the International Academy of Literature, wrote about the prison in 1865: "It is dreadful. My heart aches for the poor wretches, Yankees though they are, and I am afraid God will suffer some terrible retribution to fall upon us for letting such things happen."

Warden Wirz was held accountable for the abuses at Andersonville only because the South lost. Union wardens guilty of somewhat less atrocious but similar mistreatment of Confederate soldiers in Northern prisons never appeared in the dock. Nevertheless, Wirz was no martyr. Reflecting traditional Southern indifference to the well-being of minorities and prisoners, he at best turned his back and allowed nearly 13,000 inmates in his care to waste away and die. That number is one and a half times more than the total deaths of Confederate POWs held in the 25 Union prisons during all of 1864.

Wirz could have tried to improve the conditions and alleviate the misery of those in his charge. At the very least he could have looked the other way as Union prisoners, those who still had the will and energy, tried to escape. Instead, he insisted they wallow in the misery of Andersonville until death claimed them.

Warden Henry Hartmann Wirz was found guilty as charged and sentenced to death. On November 10, 1865, to the cheers of Northern sympathizers, he was led to the scaffold and hanged, paying the price for his part in the creation of the hellhole Southern prisons.

◆ POW EXCHANGE SYSTEM

A prisoner exchange system, motivated by dwindling resources and humanitarian reasons, was worked out through written contract signed by representatives of the Union and Confederacy in 1862. The manner, rate, and time periods for exchange were specified in the agreement. One general or admiral would be exchanged for a person of equal rank or 60 privates, an army captain his equal or 6 privates, and so forth. It was also agreed that "all prisoners of whatever arm of service are to be exchanged or paroled in 10 days from the time of their capture, if it be practicable to transfer them to their own lines in that time; if not, as soon thereafter as practicable."

The exchange system worked for a while, but then problems surfaced. The South accused the North of violating the agreement by not releasing the appropriate number of Confederate soldiers once Union soldiers were let go. The South was correct, but the reason the North reneged was because of the South's refusal to agree that black Union soldiers and white officers in command of black regiments qualified for exchange. Rather, the South punished black soldiers, often to the point of death. This infuriated the North, and by the middle of 1863 the exchange system was only words on paper. Although some exchanges did take place afterwards, it was only under special circumstances. Instead, both sides concentrated on building more stockades to hold prisoners of war for the duration of the conflict.

Following is a diary entry from Private Ransom for March 27, 1864, which offers further chilling details of the horror that was Andersonville:

> We have issued to us once each day, about a pint of beans, or more properly peas (full of bugs), and three-quarters of a pint of meal, and nearly every day a piece of bacon the size of your two fingers, probably about three or four ounces. This is very good rations, taken in comparison to what I received before. Prison gradually filling from day to day, and situation rather more unhealthy. Occasionally a squad comes in who have been lately captured, and they tell of our battles, sometimes victorious and sometimes otherwise. Sometimes we are hopeful and sometimes the reverse. . . . Take all the exercise we can, drink no water, and trying to

get along. It is a sad sight to see the men die so fast. New prisoners die the quickest, and are buried in the near vicinity, we are told in trenches without coffins. Sometimes we have visitors of citizens and women, who come to look at us. There is sympathy in some of their faces, and in some a lack of it.

◆ NORTHERN PRISONS FOR CONFEDERATE POWS

Stories of cruelty that filtered out of Andersonville prison sparked Union congressional retaliation. In 1864 Senator Henry Smith Lane introduced House Resolution No. 96. The preamble read: "Rebel prisoners in our hands are to be subjected to a treatment finding its parallels only in the conduct of savage tribes and resulting in the death of multitudes by the slow but designed process of starvation and by mortal diseases occasioned by insufficient and unhealthy food and wanton exposure to their persons to the inclemency of the weather."

Supporters of the bill promised it would force the South to provide clothing, medicine and better treatment for Union prisoners. Other Northern politicians and military officials disagreed, saying that the South was bankrupt and could not afford the better treatment demanded. After rounds of legislative debate, the bill was tabled in the 1864 session and never again introduced. But news of the resolution spread, and Union wardens acted on it as if it were law.

At Camp Douglas, Illinois, Confederate soldiers were forced to ride the "Morgan Horse" in freezing weather. With no blankets, many died during minus-40 degree winter nights. At Point Lookout, Maryland, lack of firewood led to pneumonia that spread through the prison population like fire in a cotton field. In the stockade at Elmira, New York, the stream used by prisoners quickly became contaminated from human waste and other toxins, causing many deaths.

No investigations were ever conducted into the conditions of Northern prisons, and no Union warden, officer, or prison guard ever had to answer for the mistreatment of Confederate prisoners of war. In his book, *Civil War Prisons and Escapes,* Robert Denney explains why: "The victor writes the history." Table 14.1 presents some statistics on deaths at Northern POW prisons.

TABLE 14.1

Population and Deaths of Confederate POWs at 25 Northern Prisons: 1864

	Prisoners	Died
January	36,290	801
February	35,762	779
March	34,535	675
April	34,211	413
May	33,949	357
June	44,746	436
July	50,279	715
August	51,631	793
September	57,810	879
October	57,870	772
November	56,061	818
December	51,909	1,084
Total:	545,053	8,522

Source: N. P. Chipman, *The Tragedy of Andersonville.*

15

"Goodbye, Toni Jo": The Electrocution of Annie Beatrice Henry

BURK FOSTER

_____

From *The Angolite,* May/June 1995, Angola, La: Louisiana State Penitentiary.

She believed in her fate: she said she always knew there was a God running the show. When she was six, her mother, who had named her Annie Beatrice, died of tuberculosis. At 13 she ran away from home and became a prostitute. By 17 she was a drug addict and full-time whore in Shreveport's red-light district, working under a new name: "Toni Jo Hood." She escaped the street life to marry her one true love, a tough guy named "Cowboy" Henry, only to have him torn away to serve 50 years in a Texas prison.

On Valentine's Day, not long after her 24th birthday, she murdered a salesman in a rice field south of Lake Charles. She had to do it, she explained in one of her confessions: it was all part of her scheme to get Cowboy out of prison. Less than two months later, a Calcasieu Parish jury gave Toni Jo her first death sentence. In the next two years she would get two more. In jail she converted to Catholicism, and the young priest who baptized her became her closest friend as she waited in jail to be put to death.

On the Saturday after Thanksgiving 1942, in the Lake Charles courthouse, Toni Jo Henry was executed in Louisiana's portable electric chair.

Toni Jo Henry in court. (Copyright Lake Charles American Press. Computer enhancement by Leslie D. Schilling.)

She was 26 years old, described in the local newspaper as "the prettiest murder defendant in these parts in our time," and she was one of a kind: the only woman ever electrocuted in Louisiana.

The murder of Houston salesman Joseph P. Calloway on St. Valentine's Day 1940, and the subsequent trials of Toni Jo Henry and her male companion Finnon Burks, eventually resulting in the execution of both defendants in late 1942 and early 1943, made up one of those local, media-driven cultural events that we label a "crime of the century." These crimes are almost invariably not the "worst" crimes or the most heinous; they merely attract the most publicity, for reasons that often have little to do with the gravity of the offenses.

People around Lake Charles still recall Toni Jo's quirky violence because it seems to bridge the gap between the pre–World War II gangster era—the days of the "gun moll"—and today's "criminal as society's victim" school of thought.

For the 1940s the murder of Calloway by Henry and Burks had all the elements necessary for media melodrama: a beautiful defendant with a very troubled past; a passionate love story between a Texas convict and the prostitute-drug addict he had diverted—if only temporarily—from a life of crime; a chance meeting between an Army deserter and the anguished wife that led to a horrific criminal act; a victim's family and a legal system bent on exacting life-for-life retribution; and a terrific legal battle that continued up to the last few days before each defendant was executed.

No wonder the public was fascinated with the case for the three years it was in the limelight; its combination of glamour, violence, sadness, weirdness, and inexplicable mystery are the stuff antiheroes are made of. No wonder that the *Lake Charles American Press,* in its 50-year retrospective on the case in November 1992, used the headline, "Toni Jo's execution was national sensation."

Had she not shot to death Joseph Calloway in a Calcasieu Parish rice field, it is unlikely that Toni Jo Henry's life would ever have attracted national attention. But it is also evident that once the attention was focused on her, she made the most of it, enjoying favored attention and celebrity status up to the day she died.

Toni Jo Henry was as well-known for her crime in her day as Patty Hearst or Jean Harris in our era, or Bonnie Parker and Ma Barker, in her own. Parker and Barker had been dead only about five years when Toni Jo committed her murder, and there is more than a hint of the influence of the 1930s-style female desperado on Toni Jo's public image, as portrayed in her own public statements, her life history, and in media accounts of her relationship with her convict husband, Claude "Cowboy" Henry.

Toni Jo's early life suggests that she might have had a lot of problems as she grew up, particularly in her relationships with men, but there was no clear predictor that she would one day take a pistol and shoot a kneeling, praying, naked man in the head because she needed his car. Her crime must have shocked her own family as much as it did that of the victim, Joseph P. Calloway, who was by all accounts simply a good Samaritan who happened to be in the wrong place at the wrong time, driving a new Ford coupe that was just the car Toni Jo had been looking for. It was the car that got him killed, Toni Jo said later, the car that made her a murderer and sealed her fate as well as his.

Toni Jo Henry was born Annie Beatrice McQuiston in Shreveport on January 3, 1916. Today we would call her family life dysfunctional; then they just called it unhappy. Her parents, John and Ella McQuiston, did not get along. Annie, as she was called until she took to the streets, was the third of five children.

The family broke up early. Annie's aunt, Emma Holt, who was a key witness for both prosecution and defense in the three trials of Toni Jo Henry, testified that Annie was about four years old when Ella McQuiston contracted tuberculosis. "Her mother had T.B.," Mrs. Holt said, "and this woman came to live with him; he left his wife and children and lived with this woman."

Annie was six when her mother died. John McQuiston married the woman he was living with, who became Annie's stepmother, and retrieved Annie and her two younger siblings from their grandmother's house. The stepmother "run the two older children off," Mrs. Holt testified, but kept Annie and the two babies at home until Annie finally ran away for good.

Mrs. Holt's testimony, which was offered as what we would today call mitigation evidence, was virtually the same in all three trials. She was very emotional as she told how she had tried to help the little girl, to take her out of the home, but "I couldn't get her because she had a father." Mrs. Holt testified that Annie begged her to take her into her home, on many occasions, from the age of 6 until the age of 13, when she finally left home. Mrs. Holt described Annie's accounts of how the stepmother had taken Annie with her on dates with other men while she was married to Annie's father.

When Annie was 13, she and her two older sisters had part-time jobs in a Shreveport macaroni factory. The manager fired them when he learned of the family history of tuberculosis. Not long after, John McQuiston gave Annie a severe beating, and she left home for good.

Mrs. Holt testified that she saw Annie only once in the next three years. Annie was not living in Shreveport. Annie Beatrice McQuiston had in fact ceased to exist, except on legal documents. In her place was a small time prostitute and hustler whose street name was Toni Jo Hood.

Mrs. Holt testified that she saw her niece, who now insisted that she be called "Toni Jo," smoking marijuana and drinking alcohol at the age of 16. Mrs. Holt arranged for her niece to marry a young man the next year, thinking he might be able to take care of the young girl and save her from her sordid life. But the young man did not support his wife, and he and Toni Jo both ended up living with Mrs. Holt.

They lived with her only a few weeks, and Toni Jo left to take up residence in a house of prostitution on Common Street, in Shreveport's red-light district, or what the locals referred to as "the District." She no longer sought any other lawful means of employment. She was a working prostitute.

Mrs. Holt said Toni Jo lived in the District for two or three years, until she was about 20, when she left Shreveport. She did not see Toni Jo again until the early morning hours of February 16, 1940, about 1:00 or 1:30 AM, when Toni Jo appeared at the Holts' home on the Mooringsport road north of Shreveport and announced, "Aunt Emma, I shot a man."

In four years on the road, Toni Jo had apparently drifted into southwestern Louisiana and across the Sabine River into South Texas. She was known to have worked as a prostitute in Lake Charles, Beaumont, Houston, and San Antonio. She had also become addicted to cocaine.

In Texas she met Claude Henry, whose nickname was "Cowboy." Cowboy was from Los Angeles, not Texas, but he had a reputation for toughness (and a criminal record) that was appropriate to a Texas outlaw. It was said that Cowboy and Toni Jo were made for each other—like opposite sides of the same rough coin. In a 1942 jailhouse interview, Toni Jo said this about Cowboy:

> No one ever cared about me before him. That guy is the king of my heart. He gave me a home and he got that drug monkey off my back—and that drug monkey is a big, strong thing.
>
> I remember the day I told him I was a cokie and the look on his face. He thought I just smoked marijuana. But when I told him my train went a lot further than marijuana, he took me to a hotel room and I lay there in bed for a week and he would come in now and then and ask me how I was doing. He'd slap my face with iced towels and we'd both laugh.

Cowboy is always referred to as "an ex-boxer." There is no clear record of any lawful employment of either Cowboy or Toni Jo during this time, but it is clear that both were well-known in the underworld of South Texas.

Toni Jo and Cowboy bought a marriage license in the Calcasieu Parish Courthouse on November 25, 1939. Their wedding ceremony was performed that day by a Sulphur justice of the peace, James A. Johnson. Mr. and Mrs. Cowboy Henry returned to Texas, a cloud hanging over the newlyweds' future from the start.

Cowboy had shot to death a former San Antonio police officer in 1938. Those homicide charges were still pending when he and Toni Jo married. He may not have taken them seriously, but he should have: the blissful honeymoon of Cowboy and Toni Jo, which probably would not have lasted very long for the two of them under the best of circumstances, would be over within a few weeks, and with it their married life together.

When Cowboy's case came to trial, he was found guilty of murder. On February 8, 1940, the Bexar County judge sentenced him to 50 years in the Texas penitentiary. When Toni Jo heard the sentence pronounced, she exploded in anger. "Those bastards have got my man," she is supposed to have shouted in the courtroom. She swore that she would get Cowboy out of prison as quickly as she could. Cowboy was taken into custody and sent to the Texas prison at Sugarland; he and Toni Jo would be together only one more time in this life.

Toni Jo was not one to mince words, nor to procrastinate once she had made up her mind. Within four or five days of Cowboy's sentencing, she was in Beaumont, drinking a Coke with two girlfriends, when they ran into an old friend of one of the girls. He was an ex-convict who had just deserted from the Army in San Antonio. "Arkie," the girl called him. Toni asked Arkie if he had any guts. He told her, "Yeah, I got guts," and asked what she meant.

She told him the kind that would make quick, easy money, and he suggested they go up to a little town near his home in Arkansas and rob a bank. Toni Jo said, "I was going to help him because I wanted the money to help get my husband's sentence cut and he would have been eligible for parole."

That same night, which was the evening of Tuesday, February 13, 1940, Toni Jo recruited two teenage boys to break into a secondhand store and steal some guns. The boys were very successful, but they should have been given more complete instructions: they brought back a suitcase full of 16 pistols, but ammunition that would fit only one of the handguns.

On Wednesday Toni Jo and Arkie left Beaumont, headed to Arkansas to rob the bank. They caught one ride and then another, with a fellow in a Lincoln Zephyr, to the bus station in Orange. Toni Jo told Arkie she did not want that car, so they walked across the Sabine River Bridge into Louisiana and waited for another ride.

Just after dark, outside a Highway 90 honky-tonk called the Night Owl, a light-green deluxe Ford Coupe with Texas plates stopped. The driver invited them to get in. He told them his name was Joseph P. Calloway. He was 43, a tire salesman in Houston. Toni Jo said later he was a very cordial and nice fellow. The car was new. Calloway was delivering it to Jennings, Louisiana, as a favor to friends who ran the Younger Brothers Trucking Company there. Toni Jo whispered to Arkie that this car would do. Arkie would have to drive. Toni Jo lacked one basic skill of the gun moll: she could not drive a car.

Toni Jo had in her purse the only gun they had with bullets in it. Arkie had an old automatic with no bullets. Past Lake Charles, they pulled out their guns. "What's this?" Calloway asked.

Toni Jo told him, "Don't be so dumb."

Calloway told them if it was money they wanted, they could have all he had. Toni Jo told him it was the car they needed. They turned north off Highway 90 and made him stop the car. Arkie went through Calloway's pockets, took his money and his watch, and made him get in the trunk (which in those days everyone called the turtle or turtle back). Arkie drove back south, crossing Highway 90 again, looking for a deserted spot.

Flares from oil field fires cast too much light, so they continued on south for several miles, coming to an area called Plateau Petit Bois southeast of Lake Charles. They pulled off the side of the gravel road into a small trail that led into Earl Daughenbaugh's rice field. Arkie unlocked the turtle, and Calloway got out. Arkie and Toni Jo escorted Calloway over a barbed wire fence and into the field, stopping next to a stack of rice straw.

Toni Jo told Calloway to take off his clothes. He did, and she wrapped them in his overcoat. When he was taking his clothes off, Calloway asked Arkie and Toni Jo, "Don't you people know you're going to the penitentiary for this?"

Toni Jo told him to shut up and think about where he was going. He asked if it was all right for him to pray for them. Calloway was sitting, or kneeling, naked on the icy ground of the rice field when he was shot once above the right eye with a .32 caliber bullet. He slumped over, dead on the spot.

Toni Jo and Arkie got back into the Ford and drove away. They stopped in Lake Charles and bought gas, then drove to Shreveport by about midnight and on to El Dorado, Arkansas. They continued on up Highway 167 to look over the bank in Harrell that Arkie had promised would be easy to rob, only to discover there was no bank in Harrell. Arkie said later Toni Jo was not in good humor at this point. She had to find some bank to rob. They turned west to Camden to have breakfast and get a room at a hotel. They stopped to burn Calloway's clothes on the road and threw his shoes off a bridge before they got to Camden.

Toni Jo and Arkie argued in the hotel room. In Arkie's account, he was afraid Toni Jo would kill him also. She had locked him in the hotel room with her, and he got out by making up an excuse that he needed to get more bullets for the guns. In Toni Jo's version, she hit him across the face with a gun, and he left the room and never came back.

Later in the afternoon of Thursday, February 15, when it became obvious that Arkie was not coming back, Toni Jo went to the Camden bus station and bought a ticket to Shreveport. She appeared at Emma Holt's house after midnight, early Friday morning.

Aunt Emma knew that something was wrong. Toni Jo was nervous and shaking. At first she would not say what was wrong. She asked about all the family members. Aunt Emma asked her again what was the matter, and Toni Jo said she had shot a man, shot him in the heart. She said the killing had taken place somewhere between Orange, Texas, and Lake Charles.

Aunt Emma and Toni Jo talked until later in the morning, and then Toni Jo fell asleep on the couch. While Toni Jo was sleeping, Aunt Emma looked in her handbag and found a loaded revolver. Aunt Emma must have been in a dilemma about what to do. She resolved it in the evening by calling her brother, George McQuiston, who was Toni Jo's uncle, her father's brother. He was also Captain McQuiston, inspector of the Louisiana State Police.

Captain McQuiston sent two state troopers out to pick up Toni Jo. They brought her in for questioning. Captain McQuiston spoke with Toni Jo privately. He told her he wanted to help her all he could, and if she was in any trouble to tell him what it was. At first she would not say much, then abruptly she repeated what she had told her aunt: that she had killed a man, somewhere around Lake Charles.

Captain McQuiston loaded Toni Jo into a state police vehicle along with Sergeant D. B. Walker and Captain J. L. Atkins of the state police and headed for Lake Charles. From this moment until her death almost three years later, Toni Jo was never free of custody.

They spent the cold, rainy morning of Saturday, February 17, driving around rural areas south of Lake Charles, looking for the body of Joseph Calloway. No one had discovered it yet, and Toni Jo couldn't find it either. The Shreveport troopers went home at noon. Maybe the whole story was a hoax.

Captain John Jones and Trooper Fremont LeBleu took Toni Jo out to continue the search, and this time they were successful. They were driving along a dirt road off Highway 42, when Toni Jo saw the two rice stacks, east and west of the road, that she had been looking for as landmarks. Trooper LeBleu got out of the car to look behind the stack to the west, and there he found Calloway's body, lying face down as it had been left three days before. "She was right . . . here it is," LeBleu said.

With the dead body confirming that a genuine homicide had occurred, the wheels of justice began to turn more rapidly. Sheriff Henry Reid and District Attorney C. V. Pattison were notified, Coroner E. L. Clement assembled a coroner's jury to view the body at the scene, and—most important from the viewpoint of the local citizenry—the news media were notified.

The first news account of the crime, in the *Lake Charles American Press* of Monday, February 19, 1940, had a front-page photo of the body of Joseph Calloway, opaqued below his neck, guarded by the two state troopers, Jones and LeBleu, with a close-up of Toni Jo Henry superimposed over the body. The caption described her as "unemotional, sullen and darkly scowling," and reported that "a full confession had been obtained. Although she claims to have had as a companion, a man who she terms a 'little, yellow rat' but continues to shield, the woman took full blame for firing the fatal shot."

The accompanying news article said that Mrs. Henry—"Toni," as she preferred to be known—walked into the coroner's inquest sullen and defiant but nonetheless jaunty, dressed in red slacks and a short jacket, gave one deliberate glance at the jury members and spectators, then said, "I refuse to make a statement." She also stuck to the underworld code of not "stooling" on her male accomplice for whom police of five southern states were searching.

What amazed the law enforcement officials who were present at the inquest, the newspaper reported, was the emotionless manner in which Toni admitted her part in the Plateau Petit Bois murder without implicating her companion further than that he was with her. Nor could they fathom the motive beyond that they wanted the car, which they could have taken by simply forcing Calloway out.

If Toni Jo was not talking any more, everyone else who knew anything about the case was. Details of several confessions she had made—to Aunt Emma, Uncle George, and various state police and local law enforcement officers—were being reported, and Dr. Clement, the coroner, added fuel to the fire when he revealed during the inquest that Calloway had been "brutally tortured before he was slain." Calloway's hand had been cut to the bone when the turtle back was slammed on it, but an even worse injury had been done.

> Performing an autopsy on the victim, admittedly shot between the eyes by Mrs. Henry of Beaumont, the Calcasieu coroner said he discovered where pliers had been clamped twice to a lower-body extremity—probably when the victim was being led into the rice field.

The distinctive jaw-pattern of the pliers was still visible in the torn flesh, although the body had lain since early Wednesday night until Saturday afternoon where it had fallen after a .32 calibre revolver bullet cut short Calloway's prayer that he be spared.

The idea that Toni Jo had clamped pliers around Calloway's penis to lead him to the spot where he would be killed gripped the popular imagination. Although no evidence of torture was ever introduced in her three trials, and no officials involved in the investigation ever discussed the mysterious plier-mark injuries again, Toni Jo was a torture-murderer from this day on, for readers of papers in Lake Charles and Beaumont, and for readers of other newspapers elsewhere repeating the crime story as they took it off the wire.

The next day, the *American Press* reported that Toni Jo had been taken on a midnight ride to Beaumont to meet with her husband on Monday night. After the "tearful and distraught meeting with her convict husband," at which Cowboy "beseeched her to tell all she knew," Toni Jo identified her accomplice as "Arkansas," the only name she knew for him. She then obligingly looked at mug shots of criminals in the Beaumont Police Department's rogues' gallery until she found the picture of her "little, yellow rat" companion: William Lloyd Adams, alias Kermit Haygood and Finnon Horace Burke. He was reported to be from Oklahoma but had done time in Texas. Why he was nicknamed "Arkansas" no one could say.

The first newspaper photograph of Arkansas showed a mild-looking young man, about five feet eight inches tall, weighing about 140 pounds, with blue eyes, dark chestnut hair, and medium complexion and build. He looked more like an insurance clerk than a desperado. The next night, February 21, exactly a week after the killing, when the local sheriff, his deputy and an FBI agent showed up at his sister's house in Warren, Arkansas, to arrest him, Arkansas acted more like an insurance clerk than a desperado. He walked out and shook hands with the sheriff. "I was not surprised as I was expecting it most any time," he said.

Arkansas's real name, as it turned out, was Horace Finnon Burks. He had served eight months in a Texas prison for an attempted burglary in Athens, Texas, and he had left the Army —he refused to say "deserted"— "because it was muddy and raining and snowing and we was living in tents, and I left to go and turn in at another post somewhere where I would get out of those tents." When he first met Toni Jo in Beaumont, all he was thinking about was going home to Arkansas, or maybe going up to Shreveport to turn himself in. The one point he wanted made clear was that he had nothing to do with killing the man. He had abandoned Calloway's car in Arkadelphia, and he had pawned the dead man's watch in Prescott, those acts he did not deny: but killing Calloway, the idea and the act, that all belonged to Toni Jo.

Calcasieu Parish authorities went up to Arkansas on Thursday, February 22, to return Burks to Louisiana. He waived extradition, and by Thursday night he was back in the parish jail, almost reunited with Toni Jo, whom he had abandoned in Camden the week before.

The Friday *American Press,* in its by now standard daily front page coverage of the crime, came up with a real classic. Its reporter, William Daniels, apparently got the jailer to put Toni Jo and Arkie together in a jail corridor for a posed photo; he then interviewed both of them at length, in their separate cells, for their contrasting accounts of their meeting in Beaumont, the crime, and their actions afterward.

The photo showed Finnon Burks, dressed in jailhouse khakis, staring directly at the camera. Toni Jo, standing at his left side in a colorful print blouse, was perhaps an inch shorter; she was looking crossways past him, as if at another person off-camera. The two showed no sign of recognition, according to the photo caption, which depicted their meeting as undramatic and casual. Toni Jo much resembled Rita Hayworth, as she might

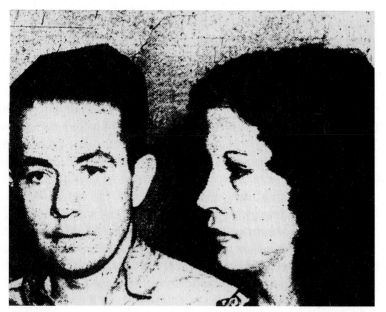

Toni Jo Henry and Finnon Burks reunited in jail, February 1940. (Copyright: Lake Charles American Press. Computer enhancement by Leslie D. Schilling.)

have starred in a 1940s film noir, playing a woman whose fate had become tied to a man so beneath her she imagines he isn't there.

Daniels described the photo session: "As flashlight bulbs popped, Burks smoothed his hair. After a minute or two, Mrs. Henry said smilingly she was 'bored' being surrounded by so many 'ugly men.' Later, indicating her red slacks and flowered waist, she showed concern for her appearance—remarking she'd 'blow her top' if a fresh change did not reach her."

Daniels, in his subsequent long interview with each defendant, found their stories remarkably similar, except for two key differences: how the murder was committed, and how they came to split up in Arkansas. Toni Jo now blamed Arkie for the shooting, which she said took place as she was walking away with Calloway's clothes. Why did she confess? "I just didn't care. I wanted to protect Arkansas. I had nothing to live for." She said that when they quarreled in the hotel room in Camden, he was leaving with all the guns. She grabbed one from his waistband and slapped him, and he left.

Daniels observed that Toni Jo did not mind talking about herself. She was polite and offered the reporter cigarettes. "Woman-like, she pointed out the results of her 'housekeeping' this morning—how she had cleaned the floors and her bathroom and made up her bunk." One thing had aroused her ire, however. That was, "I am not as hard, sullen and that sort of thing like you all have made me out in the newspapers."

When Daniels was leaving, she smiled and said, "Don't worry about finding me, I'll be here any time you want to see me." And getting serious once more, she asked, "What's all this they're saying about me torturing Calloway. Neither of us touched him or did any of the things they're saying we did, and I don't care what the coroner says."

Finnon Burks, in his interview an hour later, said he was walking away from the rice stack with Calloway's clothes when he heard the shot. Then Toni Jo came up to the fence, and he asked her, "What have you done?" The next morning, in Camden, when he had left her on the pretext of getting more shells for the guns, she had threatened to "look him up" if he turned "yellow."

Which of them had done the shooting? The coroner's inquest had already named Toni Jo. Law enforcement officials said it did not matter. Under the felony murder doctrine, both were equally guilty. And Sheriff Reid quoted Toni Jo as saying, "One is as guilty as the other." On February 27, 1940, Toni Jo Henry and Finnon Burks were jointly indicted for the murder. Two days later, on February 29, her attorneys were appointed. These two men, Clement M. Moss and Norman Anderson, would stick with Toni Jo through all three trials, gaining in the process what they did not have when they began: experience in criminal law.

Moss and Anderson maintained from the start that they were civil lawyers and practiced civil law almost exclusively. Anderson was a tax lawyer, and federal tax returns were due on March 15. Nevertheless, Judge John T. Hood (no relation to Toni Jo's made-up identity) confirmed their appointment on March 2, 1940, and, despite their request for a continuance, ordered them to prepare for trial on March 27, exactly 25 days from the official date of their appointment.

On March 14 Moss and Anderson filed a motion for severance to separate Toni Jo's trial from that of Finnon Burks. It had become clear that Finnon, in an effort to save himself from the death penalty, was going to testify that Toni Jo shot Calloway, and Toni Jo was going to do the same. Their separate interests were best served by severance, which Judge Hood ordered on March 15. Toni Jo would be tried first, and the trial of Finnon Burks would follow in May. So much for the reunion of the partners in crime; until the very end, neither would have much good to say about the other.

If Toni Jo's attorneys were rank amateurs at criminal law, the family of Joseph Calloway had gone to extraordinary lengths to ensure that a tough old pro would be on the prosecutor's side. Mrs. Calloway had hired J. P. Copeland, a former assistant district attorney in Hunt County, Texas, and a personal friend of the victim, to be a special prosecutor in the case.

Copeland made no bones about his intentions. He said in a March 6 interview with the Lake Charles paper, "Nothing will satisfy me and the better class of people in Houston but the death penalty for this man and woman." "Nor," he continued, "can the manner of death be too severe." Feelings about the brutal and needless Plateau Petit Bois murder had run "extremely high" in Houston, he said. He went on to say he felt sure that had the crime been committed in Houston, "Burks and Mrs. Henry would have been mobbed." Of "100 persons in Houston to whom I talked about this murder, without exception each said they both should have the death penalty," the attorney said.

Interviewed in Houston on March 25, two days before the trial was to begin, Copeland did not seem to have mellowed much. "I believe this is one of the most cold-blooded murders that has been committed anywhere. I do not think that the annals of criminal law nor the cesspools of hell have ever engulfed a more heinous or atrocious crime than the act that took the life of J. P. Calloway."

Copeland brought with him Calloway's widow and 17-year-old daughter, Lita. One of Calloway's last requests, when he was praying in the field before he was shot, was to be allowed to live so he might see his nine-year-old daughter graduate from college. At some point in the six weeks before trial, the little daughter had aged eight years. In the photograph they posed for on the courthouse steps the day the trial began, March 27, 1940, Lita Calloway looked as fiercely determined as her mother and Mr. Copeland to see Toni Jo and Finnon Burks dead.

Toni Jo would have three trials, in March 1940, February 1941, and January 1942. All three would take place in Lake Charles, after the defense motion for a change of venue was denied; all three would follow Louisiana law in allowing only men to serve as jurors; and all three would result in verdicts of "guilty as charged to murder," which, lacking the jury's "without capital punishment" recommendation, meant a death sentence: hanging, at the first trial, or electrocution, at the second and third.

Court records give no indication about the race or other characteristics of the background of the jurors selected or not selected. Jury selection went much faster than it would in a similar trial today. Prospective jurors were questioned in large panels, and the questioning about their background and beliefs was much more superficial than it would be today. Still, finding un-biased jurors willing to listen objectively to the evidence was a problem. Both sides dismissed many jurors for cause, mainly having formed strong opinions against Toni Jo based on the extensive pretrial publicity, and the defense used dozens of challenges for cause and most of its peremptory challenges in the first two trials.

In the first trial, particularly, conducted within six weeks of the crime, public sentiment against Toni Jo Henry, the torture-murderer, ran very strong. The mood in court was volatile. Spectators filled the seating area, stood around the wall, and finally were admitted to stand inside the railing, ringing the prosecution and defense tables and the jury box. Different esti-mates put the size of the crowd inside the railing at 100 to as large as 400 at different times.

Mrs. Calloway and Lita were given seats inside the railing, facing the jurymen 10 feet away. When defense counsel objected, Special Assistant District Attorney Copeland replied, "If the jury might be inclined to feel sorry for the woman on trial, I want them to see the widow and daughter of the man killed."

Disorder in the court extended to gestures and comments directed at the jury. Spectators were observed making slit-throat motions to jurors in the courtroom. When the jury was coming back from supper for a night session, women members of the crowd outside the courthouse were heard to yell, "Hang her," and "Hang that bitch." As Supreme Court Justice Odom observed in Toni Jo's appeal of her first conviction, "The people generally were intensely interested in the outcome of the trial."

Defense counsel asked Judge Hood to declare a mistrial in view of the fact that "people think this is a holiday." Clement Moss said, "This public clamor seeking to hang the defendant has been done very openly . . . and I don't believe the defendant can secure a fair trial here." The trial went on regardless. Five police witnesses testified to Toni Jo Henry's statements to them. George McQuiston could not be found for the trial, but Toni Jo's Aunt Emma testified, sobbing repeatedly as she told how Toni Jo had come to her house and made her bizarre confession.

Toni Jo was the only defense witness. She was on the stand for an hour and a half. Her attorneys got her version of the killing into the record, with Burks firing the fatal shot "to the heart," as she testified. They attempted to bring out her personal history at length, but the prosecutors objected. Judge Hood sustained the objections on the rules of evidence.

In closing arguments, handled by J. P. Copeland, the special prosecutor held up a glass of clear water, which he said "was as clean as the lives of Mrs. Calloway and her 17-year-old daughter." Then he dropped a few drops of ink into the glass and said the darkened liquid represented "the gloom and heartbreak a slayer's bullet brought to the souls of the widow and daughter."

The jury deliberated six and a half hours, which must have encouraged the defense to hope that a deadlock had occurred. Then the verdict came in: guilty as charged to murder. Toni Jo Henry was sentenced to death on April 24, 1940. Moss and Anderson filed notice of appeal.

The next month Finnon Burks was tried in the same court for his part in the murder. His only real defense was that he did not pull the trigger. He was found guilty of murder on May 23 and sentenced to death on June 8, 1940. The Louisiana Supreme Court rejected his appeal later that year, and for the rest of his life Finnon Burks was mostly waiting to see what would happen with Toni Jo—hoping she would get a break that he could manipulate to save his own life.

Toni Jo did get one big legal break later in 1940. On November 19, the Louisiana Supreme Court overturned her first conviction. Several grounds for reversal existed, the justices agreed: the hostile influence of the spectators on the jury (one observation was that "the jury knew what they were there for"); the prejudicial influence of seating the victim's family inside by the jurymen; questions about the voluntariness of the several confessions Toni Jo had made to the police; and the inflammatory remarks of a prosecutor.

No, it wasn't Copeland who had erred, it was Coleman D. Reed, the Calcasieu assistant district attorney, who spoke to the jury of a case he had prosecuted in Oakdale in which the defendant was released from prison after serving only four years of a life sentence for murder. His point was obvious, and well-made at the time: a life sentence in Louisiana ordinarily meant much less than a lifetime to be served. But the state supreme court said he knew the jury could not be told this. This same prosecutor, in making an enthusiastic argument during the trial, had said of Toni Jo: "She is as dangerous as a poisonous snake." The supreme court clearly found the first trial excessive, in many aspects, and ordered the case returned to Calcasieu Parish.

In the summer of 1940, while her legal appeal was underway, Toni Jo got word to a young parish priest, Fr. Wayne Richard, who had just been assigned to the Church of the Immaculate Conception in Lake Charles, that she would like to talk with him. Fr. Richard, who had been ordained earlier in 1940, was only a couple of years older than Toni Jo. Today Fr. Richard is a retired priest living in Lafayette—the last surviving member of the group closest to Toni Jo while she was in jail, as far as he knows. He has not spoken with any other member of the execution party in half a century.

Fr. Richard recalls that about two years after the execution the Lake Charles newspaper did a long article on the Toni Jo Henry case, focusing on the sudden demise of many participants in the three trials. District Attorney Pattison and Sheriff Henry Reid, Sr., had died (immediately before Finnon Burks's execution) as well as several others whom Fr. Richard no longer recalls.

Fr. Richard was himself reassigned to a different parish, in New Iberia, some time later; it could have been that as the new priest it was his turn to go, or it could have been, as he has always suspected, that the reassignment was meant to remove from the diocese someone so closely associated with the execution. Fifty-two years after she met her fate in the electric chair, Fr. Richard still vividly remembers Toni Jo Henry.

He describes her as tall, about five feet seven or eight, with dark hair that was her crowning glory. Her complexion was dark; she was said to be part-Indian. She was well-spoken, had no accent, and was fastidious about her appearance. But he also describes "a certain rigidity or hardness about her. She was not a very emotional person."

Why did she call for him to visit? He still has no idea. Toni Jo was not Catholic, but she said she had been attracted to the Church: "She said she would walk into a church and light a candle to St. Joseph." St. Joseph was the patron saint of carpenters, and workingmen, and the Universal Church. He was also the patron saint of the dying.

"Toni Jo always felt that she was going to be electrocuted." Did she get religion out of fear of death? Fr. Richard doesn't think so. She wasn't afraid. She was pessimistic. "She thought she didn't have a chance." She did seem genuinely interested in learning about the Catholic faith, though. He would go to visit her in jail two or three times a week. She would ask him questions about religion and the Church, and he would answer those questions, or other times they would just talk. He says they never discussed the crime itself, and they talked very little about her early life, which she generally did not want to discuss.

A newspaper account says that Fr. Richard baptized Toni Jo on August 30, 1940, after three weeks of instruction. Fr. Richard recalls giving her instruction for a much longer period of time, perhaps eight to twelve months, before she was baptized, but he cannot firmly dispute the date.

Toni Jo Henry was a very controversial figure around Lake Charles, but she got along fine with her keepers in the jail. "She had a certain persona that affected the people she came in contact with," Fr. Richard recalls. She was provided with a two-room "suite" in the jail. She furnished it—courtesy of "a friend from Texas"—as one might a small apartment: armchair, dresser, desk, curtains, fan, radio, coffeepot—confining, perhaps, but with all the necessities. The last few months before she was executed, she was even allowed to adopt a jailhouse puppy, a rat terrier that stayed in her cell.

Fr. Richard was aware of local gossip suggesting that Toni Jo was getting special treatment. Rumors circulated that she had become the lover of various local officials—jailers, law enforcement officers, even the courthouse group of lawyers and politicians. He did not believe these stories, and he never saw any evidence that Toni Jo was unfaithful to Cowboy Henry.

Fr. Richard found that Toni Jo "was passionately in love with her husband." She spoke of him often, doing his time in Texas. She wrote him letters every day, and he wrote her back. Correspondence took up most of her time in jail. She received many thousands of letters from all over the country. After her most widely circulated interview in August 1942, 129 pieces of mail came on one day. On another day, closer to her execution, 209 pieces came. Some people sent money. Others sent Bibles. A few letter writers became regular correspondents; some came to see her in jail, travelling across town or across the country to visit.

At home in her spruced-up jail cell, which she called a "death cell right along," Toni Jo was a gracious hostess who enjoyed receiving visitors. She said in her August 4, 1942, interview with Elliott Chaze of World Wide Syndicate:

> I think condemned persons fret more about losing contact with human beings than anything else. You feel so out of it. It's more than these bars; it's more like a hellish battle with long distance when she won't give you a number—anybody's number—not one friendly human being's number. You get so cold and pretty soon you're a freak even to yourself.

Toni Jo Henry in her jail cell. (Copyright: Lake Charles American Press. Computer enhancement by Leslie D. Schilling.)

She passed her time, when she was not visiting or writing letters, in listening to the radio or reading the papers. She liked to keep up with the war news and liked to work the crossword puzzles. As her spiritual adviser, did Fr. Richard ever see Toni Jo reading the Bible? No, he recalls, but she had a lot of time at night by herself when people weren't around. She always seemed thoughtful and well-informed, although she had never finished grade school. She asked intelligent questions and appeared to take what he told her seriously. He never sensed that her interest in the Church was fakery. Jailer Gibbs Duhon, who saw more of Toni Jo than anyone else for three years, commented right before her execution that in his observation she had lived up to the principles of the Church.

Did Fr. Richard ever ask her why she had committed such a terrible crime? No, he says, he did not. But others did. The best answer she gave may have been in the interview with Elliott Chaze on August 4, 1942:

> I'm still not sure why we took his clothes. . . . I said once and I say now, it seemed that would delay pursuit. I'm telling you I shot him, because it's no good lying now. Burks didn't do it. Sometimes I wonder why I didn't knock the man unconscious instead, but it was like being drunk, real drunk.
>
> "Ever pull something when you were drunk and that something seemed the cutest, smartest thing in the world, but it was the awfulest?

Well, me, I was drunk with pressure. I told you about my husband. . . . I always knew there was a God running the show. But I thought maybe I could steal just one little act.

As the parish priest, Fr. Richard often encountered people who expressed hatred of Toni Jo Henry. He met a man on the street one day who said he wanted to "pull the switch." Fr. Richard invited this man to go along on a jail visit. The two men went upstairs and had a long talk with Toni Jo in her cell. When they were walking down the steps of the courthouse to leave, the man told Fr. Richard, "You know, that woman should never be put to death."

Fr. Richard said Toni Jo had that kind of effect on people. From her point of view, the unfortunate thing was that you had to get to know her first; her sympathetic qualities never came across to jurymen in the courtroom.

Her second murder trial lasted from February 3 to February 7, 1941. It was much more low-key than the first. Enough time had passed that public interest was not as strong. Only local attorneys were involved, C. V. Pattison and Coleman Reed as prosecutors and Moss and Anderson returning as defense counsel.

Claude Henry, in a letter written on September 22, 1940, from his prison in Sugarland, Texas, had attempted to hire attorney "J. T. Hawkins," who in reality was Griffin Hawkins, to get a life sentence for Toni Jo. He just needed to know how much it would cost. Griffin Hawkins replied, on September 24, that the fee he had discussed with Cowboy's emissary was for arguing her case before the Louisiana Supreme Court; he could not guarantee a life sentence. After Moss and Anderson were successful in getting the first conviction overturned two months later, Toni Jo and Cowboy must have determined to go ahead with them as counsel—or perhaps they lacked the resources to hire other more high-powered counsel.

A different judge presided, Mark C. Pickrel. Toni Jo did not testify this time. The information about her personal history and family life that the attorneys wanted the jury to hear was related to the jury by Emma Holt when she was recalled by the defense. George McQuiston testified this time about statements Toni Jo had made to him. And Finnon Burks, waiting to be executed in the same parish jail with Toni Jo, testified for the state that she had done the shooting. Absent the histrionics of the first trial, the result was the same: a verdict of guilty as charged to murder, signed by Lane Young, foreman, February 7, 1941. Judge Pickrel sentenced Toni Jo to death again on February 26, 1941.

Moss and Anderson appealed again, and again the Louisiana Supreme Court overturned the conviction. The basis for reversible error this time was in the jury selection process. The court ruled that District Attorney Pattison's questioning of prospective jurors was slanted. It resulted in the selection of several jurors who clearly favored the death penalty. One juror, the Court said, should have been excused because of preconceived opinions about the case. This opinion was issued on June 10, 1941, and *State of Louisiana v. Annie Beatrice Henry* went back to square one.

Toni Jo's third murder trial began on January 20, 1942. By now everyone must have been familiar with the drill. A new team of prosecutors, District Attorney Griffin T. Hawkins and First Assistant District Attorney Joe Tritico presented the state's case, Moss and Anderson defended, and Judge Pickrel presided. This was the speediest and least controversial trial. The death verdict was returned on January 23, signed by foreman D. A. Collette. Toni Jo was formally sentenced to death, for the third time, by Judge Pickrel on January 31, 1942.

The third time was the charm for the prosecutors; finding no major errors, the Louisiana Supreme Court upheld Toni Jo's conviction on June 29, 1942. Getting past this important legal hurdle, the state began to make serious plans to put Toni Jo Henry and Finnon Burks to death. Both would be electrocuted, rather than hanged, as the state had changed its method of execution in 1940. Two men had been electrocuted in 1941, and three more would die in the electric chair in 1942 before Toni Jo's turn came.

Governor Sam Jones, who coincidentally was elected to office the week Toni Jo and Finnon Burks were arrested, signed a death warrant in July, but an appeal about the method of execution delayed the scheduled August 10 execution date. Elliott Chaze's long interview, circulated nationwide on August 4, rekindled public interest in Toni Jo, and for the next four months she remained in the limelight.

Cowboy Henry was reportedly brooding over his wife's fate. Robert Benoit, in his 1992 *American Press* retrospective, says that Cowboy made two attempts to escape prison and come to see Toni Jo. On August 19, 1942, Cowboy wrestled a pistol away from a guard and tried to escape, but he couldn't get out of the compound. Two hours later he was back in his cell.

On November 23, the Monday before Toni Jo was scheduled to die on Saturday, Cowboy escaped again. This time, Benoit says, he made it all the way to Beaumont before law officers captured him in a hotel room on November 25. He was transported immediately to the maximum security confinement of "the Walls" unit of the Huntsville penitentiary.

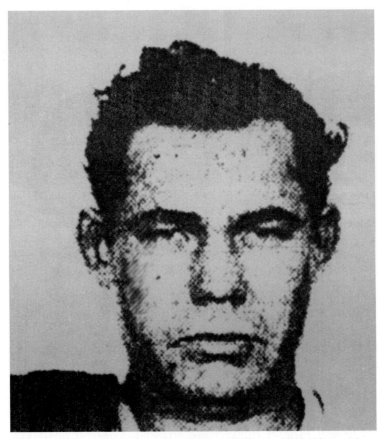

Cowboy Henry, at the time of his death in Dallas in 1945. (Copyright: Dallas Times-Herald. Computer enhancement by Leslie D. Schilling.)

On Friday, November 27, the day before she was executed, Toni Jo and Cowboy were allowed to talk one last time—for 10 minutes by telephone. Deputy Sheriff Henry Reid, Jr., explained the call as the response to Toni Jo's last request to see a relative. Toni Jo was calm, but Cowboy broke down and could say very little to her during the conversation.

The Lake Charles jailers, who overheard her end of the conversation, reported that she told her husband, "Honey, they couldn't do that," probably meaning that he had escaped hoping that jail officials would allow him to see her again. "The only thing to do is the right thing, and you know you shouldn't have done that."

Toni Jo told her husband to put his faith in God and during the remainder of his life to make every effort to live an upright and law-abiding life. "I'm glad I knew you as long as I did, honey," she said, "and I'm sorry that our relationship can't continue."

She spoke briefly about her execution, scheduled for noon the next day. "I know it has to come and I'm ready. Don't feel hard toward the authorities. It is their job."

Finally she told him: "Hurry up and get out of that zoot suit, and walk out the front door like a man, so your mother will be proud of you."

How would Toni Jo go out her own door, when the time came? People had speculated; most people who knew her well expected her to be strong. Fr. Richard describes her as fatalistic. She knew all along that she was going to be put to death.

The week before she was scheduled to die, Toni Jo did one last favor for Finnon Burks. She signed a notarized statement, through her attorney, in which she said: "I, Annie Beatrice Henry, fired the shot that killed J.C. Calloway. It is my hope that Finnon Burks will not have to suffer the death penalty." She had said in an interview, "I don't even think of harming Burks any more. He blamed everything on me, Burks did. But now we're both going to die. I wish he didn't have to go. His mother is alive and mine isn't. And the Bible says—an eye for an eye; it doesn't say two eyes for an eye."

A crowd had gathered around the courthouse in Lake Charles on Saturday morning, November 28, 1942. The newspaper account says 200 to 300 people. Fr. Richard remembers it as much larger, perhaps 2,000 to 3,000. When he went up to her cell on the second floor, Toni Jo was drinking coffee. She asked him if he wanted some, and poured him a cup. He was so nervous he couldn't lift it to his lips.

When the jailers came in to cut her hair, for the mask and electrodes, Toni Jo was upset. She said, "Look, I've been condemned to execution, not to mutilation." Fr. Richard had known how proud she was of her hair. He had stopped on the way to the courthouse that day and bought her a bright-colored handkerchief—red, white and green—for her to tie over her shaved head. She wore a plain black dress and black pumps.

The barber, Athan Coe, said when he left her cell: "Why, she's a pretty good fellow. She said hello and that she remembered me as being called on the jury at her trial." Coe had been on the jury panel for the second and third trials but had not served on either jury. He must have been a popular fellow himself: he was later invited back to be a witness at Finnon Burks's execution.

The night before, unable to sleep, Toni Jo had sat up all night. She wrote Cowboy a final letter. She refused a final meal. She gave her little black-and-white dog to jailer Gibbs Duhon, with the request that he give the dog to her niece in Shreveport. She told the jailer she was a little afraid. Everyone else found her remarkably calm.

The execution was scheduled for noon on Saturday. At 11:43 AM Deputy Sheriff Kinney Reid read Toni Jo the death warrant. She spent a last few minutes alone with Fr. Richard. Exactly at 12 PM, the big generators on the truck outside were turned on; at the same instant the bells of the nearby church began ringing.

At 12:05 PM, the generators humming louder below, Toni Jo left her cell, accompanied by Fr. Richard and Deputy Henry Reid, Jr., the sheriff's son. Fr. Richard remembers the newspaper photo taken that day and printed the day she was buried: Toni Jo holding onto his hand for support as they walked down the steps to the first floor of the jail, where the portable electric chair had been set up. He said he tried to step back into the crowd, but she asked him to step forward with her.

The electric chair had been brought down from Angola, the state penitentiary, Saturday morning. Warden D. D. Bazer was present, along with at least one convict trusty, the prison electrician, and the executioner, who in news accounts is unnamed but was known by all convicts and legal officials as Grady Jarratt. He performed all the electrocutions in Louisiana from 1941 to 1961, a total of 66 men and one woman. This is how the *American Press* described his final preparations:

> Quickly she came down the 22 steps to the first floor and marched straight to the chair that was wedged along with the master switch and other equipment in the eight-foot-wide first floor corridor.
>
> She had a smile on her face and she kept it there till the end. The executioner quickly set about the job of fastening the electrodes about her body. The brine soaked cap was placed on her head.
>
> "Goodbye Father," she said, looking up at Father Richard. "You'll be here, won't you?"
>
> "Yes, I'll be right here," the priest answered.
>
> A few seconds later, she looked at him again and smiled.
>
> Father Richard smiled back and said: "Keep smiling."
>
> She halfway joked with the executioner as he fastened buckles that clamped her arms and legs tight to the big oaken chair. Finally he had completed the job.
>
> "Do you have anything to say?" Deputy Sheriff Henry Reid asked her.
>
> "No, I haven't," she answered in a low, steady voice, still smiling.
>
> At that moment it looked like her calm composure might break. Her eyes began to water. But she looked at Father Richard and smiled.

"Goodbye, Toni Jo," the executioner said, as he applied the death charge, and she murmured an inaudible acknowledgment.

Toni Jo Henry, on the day of her electrocution, November 28, 1942, escorted down the jail steps by Father Wayne Richard and Deputy Sheriff Henry Reid, Jr. (Copyright: Lake Charles American Press. Computer enhancement by Leslie D. Schilling.)

The execution record indicates that the jolt of electricity was applied at exactly 12:12:30 PM. At 12:15 PM the same coroner who had examined Calloway's body, E. L. Clement, pronounced Toni Jo dead. The record lists seven official witnesses, one of whom, Clyde Manard, signed the record twice; two doctors; Grady Jarratt and Reverend Wayne Richard. Fr. Richard has always remembered the remark Jarratt directed at him, standing by the electric chair with Toni Jo sitting dead in it: "Well, Father, we did a good job." Fr. Richard could not even speak in reply.

"Toni Jo Pays Supreme Penalty," the headline of the *American Press* read that day. Fifty-two years later, Fr. Richard remembers the smell of burning flesh. When I asked him if the execution left him feeling depressed, he replied, "Absolutely. Even today I can still see her at the moment she was electrocuted. I could see the expression on her face."

When the execution was over, Fr. Richard drove from Lake Charles to Patterson, Louisiana, to visit his parents—just to get away for awhile, he says. Toni Jo was given the last rites of the Catholic Church and buried two days later "under a drooping camphor tree" along the edge of Graceland Cemetery in Lake Charles. Fr. Richard used to visit her grave. He was not aware of any family members who ever came to visit the grave.

Finnon Burks's date with Grady Jarratt came not quite four months later. With Toni Jo's notarized statement on his behalf, Burks had applied to the Louisiana Pardon Board for a commutation of his sentence to life imprisonment. In those days, and until the new Louisiana Constitution of 1974 took effect, the three members of the pardon board were the sentencing judge, the attorney general, and the lieutenant governor. Judge Pickrel voted for a commutation, but Burks lost his petition when the attorney general and lieutenant governor both voted no.

The last few weeks before Burks was executed, he had turned to God. His religious advisor, the Reverend Raymond McClung, baptized him the morning of his execution. "He made his peace with God," the Reverend McClung said later, "and I can't help but feel that he really meant it."

Burks wrote four letters—one to his mother and one each to his two sisters and a brother. He told his mother he was better off dead and that perhaps he would see his father in a short while. Burks apologized to the jailer, Gibbs Duhon. "I've given you lots of trouble, but I know you're as good a friend as I have."

Toni Jo had been considered a model prisoner. Finnon Burks was not. He had tried to escape three times. Once he had used hacksaw blades to saw through two bars on his cell. Another time he removed the casing from around a window in the corridor outside his cell. The third time he seized a gun and locked a jailer in the cell. The jailer told him the jailhouse was surrounded by officers who would kill him if he tried to leave, and Burks gave up.

Many people thought Burks was weak, that he would collapse and "cry like a baby," the newspaper account of the execution read. But it reported that he died calmly. He joked with officers up to the last minute and then walked smiling and calm to the electric chair. The last photo taken of Finnon Burks shows a smiling, handsome young man in a new navy suit and dark hat. The Reverend McClung is adjusting his tie. Burks looks for all the world like a soldier being welcomed back from duty overseas. Fifteen minutes later he was dead.

His last words were directed to the Reverend McClung: "The Lord Jesus Christ is my Savior," he whispered with a half smile on his face that was broken only by an intermittent twitching of his mouth. "I am ready to go."

His spirit might have been willing, but the body wasn't so sure. After one cycle of electricity, Burks's heart was still beating. After a second jolt, his heart continued beating for a few minutes longer. The execution record says that a jolt of electricity was applied at 12:13 PM on March 23, 1943, and Finnon Burks was pronounced dead at 12:19 PM. He was never as popular as Toni Jo Henry, never as charismatic, and whereas Toni Jo received hundreds of letters, on the day before Finnon Burks died he got exactly two—one from his sister and one from someone in Tulsa. But at the end, as the death row convicts say, "He went out like a man." Cope Routh, writing in the *American Press* that day, called it "the second installment on the debt due the state" for the Valentine's Day murder of Joseph Calloway, "in a bleak and deserted rice field near Lake Charles."

And what of Claude "Cowboy" Henry, whose imprisonment was the start of the chain of acts that would result in Calloway's death? Texas prison records show that despite the 50-year sentence, Cowboy was released on parole—technically called a "reprieve" in Texas at that time—on May 31, 1944. So he did heed the first part of Toni Jo's last advice—the part about getting out of that zoot suit and walking out the prison door like a man. On the second part, the part about putting his faith in God and living an upright and law-abiding life, he would unfortunately fall far short.

Cowboy's reprieve was revoked on July 13, but he was given another on April 18, 1945. Prison authorities reported that Cowboy had an incurable heart ailment, and that he might die at any time. They were right about dying at any time, but only indirectly about the heart part as the cause of death. Cowboy was shot to death in Dallas on July 15, 1945. Fr. Richard recalls hearing reports that Cowboy was trying to pull an armed robbery. Dallas police reports and local news reports tell a different story.

The *Times-Herald* reported the next day that Cowboy had died "in the typical gangster fashion that he knew so well." Cowboy, drunk and swearing, had approached S. W. Farrow as he sat inside a parked car with his wife and another man at 3:30 Sunday morning. Farrow knew Cowboy. When he got out to talk, Cowboy knocked him down several times, then hailed a cab and left the scene. A couple of blocks away, Cowboy ordered the cabdriver to turn around and take him back. "I'm not satisfied yet," he told the driver.

When Cowboy got out of the cab, Farrow opened fire. Three of the five shots he fired hit Cowboy, the fatal wound in the lung beneath his heart. Cowboy lay in the street for an hour before an ambulance arrived, and he died later in surgery at Parkland Hospital.

Dallas authorities were probably glad to be rid of Cowboy. He had been arrested dozens of times, in Illinois, California, and Texas, and was known to have beaten and robbed numerous men. While out of prison on his last reprieve, supposedly with the incurable heart ailment, he had eluded Dallas police in a high-speed pursuit, and he was reportedly drinking continuously and more pugnacious than ever. His own death by violence surprised no one. Prison authorities said he had never gotten over Toni Jo's death.

What would have happened to Toni Jo Henry if she had been tried today, for the same crime committed the same way? Would she still get the death penalty? "Absolutely not," Fr. Richard says. "Today she would never have gotten the death penalty." Fr. Richard believes that the trial would have been moved to another jurisdiction, less influenced by local publicity, and that more time would have elapsed before the trial. She would have been provided more experienced counsel. Most important, in the current scheme of guilt phase and penalty phase, if she had been convicted of first-degree murder and gone to the penalty phase, she would have been able to testify herself and have experts and family members testify about her early family life and her troubled adolescent life. He believes that a modern-day jury would be far more sympathetic toward Toni Jo, the criminal, rather than focusing exclusively on the crime against Joseph P. Calloway, the victim. Elements that seemed to make little difference in 1940—the several confessions she made, and her leading police to the undiscovered body—might be viewed as more significant evidence of remorse today.

But Toni Jo did not commit her crime in 1990's America, with its sophisticated defenses and heightened interest in family history and other mitigating evidence. She committed her crime in an era when blame was much more personal. Her crime was an ugly felony murder, highly publicized, that turned an entire town against her.

Toni Jo never said convincingly that she was sorry for what she had done. She never begged, and she never cried for forgiveness. Toni Jo's interviews strongly suggest that she believed what had happened was her own fault. She may have seen her death as atonement for her impulsive, desperate crime.

If Toni Jo had not been so impatient, if she had waited for her man rather than concocting her impetuous robbery scheme, all of them—Toni Jo, Cowboy, Finnon Burks, and the unfortunate Joseph Calloway—would have lived more obscure but surely longer lives. But Toni Jo was not the kind to wait it out. She had always gone at life head-on. Determined to free at any cost the man she loved, she set in motion the events that make up one of the enduring crime stories of Southwest Louisiana. In the end, it was her fate that seized all of them in its grasp: in Toni Jo Henry's closest circle, there were no survivors.

16

Struck by Lightning: Electrocutions for Rape in Louisiana in the 1940s and 1950s

BURK FOSTER

"These death sentences are cruel and unusual in the same way that being struck by lightning is cruel and unusual."

Justice Potter Stewart, *Furman v. Georgia* (1972)

From *The Angolite,* September/October 1996, Angola, La: Louisiana State Penitentiary.

For a brief time in the early 1970s Ehrlich Anthony Coker was a one-man crime wave rolling across Georgia. On December 5, 1971, at age 21, he raped and stabbed to death a young woman. The next year he kidnapped, raped, beat, and left for dead another young woman. For these crimes he received three life terms, two 20-year terms, and one 8-year term. The prison sentences were imposed consecutively, and the people of Georgia probably breathed a sigh of relief that this violent young man had been permanently incapacitated.

When they thought of Coker put safely away, they should have kept in mind Lady Caroline Lamb's description of Lord Byron: "Mad, bad, and dangerous to know." Within a year-and-a-half, Ehrlich Anthony Coker escaped from the Ware Correctional Institution outside Waycross, Georgia. He entered the home of Allen and Elnita Carver, tied up Allen, took his money and the keys to the family car. Then he took a knife, with which he threatened Mrs. Carver, who at 16 had given birth three weeks before: "You know what's going to happen to you if you try anything, don't you?"

Coker raped Mrs. Carver, stole the car, and took her with him. Police captured him before he did any further harm to the young mother. A Ware County jury convicted Coker of auto theft, armed robbery, kidnapping, escape, and rape. They gave him a lot more prison time, and, undoubtedly fed up with his viciousness by this time, they gave him the death penalty for rape. The jury found that Coker's crime contained two of the aggravating circumstances required for the imposition of the death sentence under Georgia law:

1. The offense was committed by a person with a prior capital felony conviction.

2. The offense was committed during the commission of another capital felony, in this case armed robbery.

The court sentenced Coker to death by electrocution. His central argument on appeal was that the death penalty for rape was cruel and unusual punishment under the Eighth Amendment. Race was not an issue, as it often was in other Georgia cases during this period: Coker was white, and his victims were also white. Appeals moved quickly through the state courts and then to the U.S. Supreme Court, which heard oral arguments on March 28, 1977.

The Supreme Court announced its decision on June 29, 1977 (*Coker v. Georgia,* 97 S.Ct. 2861 [1977]). As usual in the critical death penalty decisions of the 1970s, the justices' opinions were sharply divided. Justices White, Stewart, Blackmun, and Stevens "concluded that the sentence of death for the crime of rape is grossly disproportionate and excessive punishment and is therefore forbidden by the Eighth Amendment as cruel and unusual punishment." Justices Brennan and Marshall said that the death penalty is cruel and unusual punishment for any crime. Justice Powell said that the death penalty was inappropriate in this case, where an adult woman was raped without excessive brutality or serious, lasting injury, but it might be appropriate in other circumstances. Chief Justice Burger and Justice Rehnquist dissented, saying that Georgia had the power to impose the death penalty for rape if it wanted to. The Court's published decision reviews the evolving history of the death penalty for rape, noting that at the time Coker was convicted, only Georgia, North Carolina, and Louisiana continued to provide the death penalty for the rape of an adult woman.

The number of states authorizing the death penalty for rape had declined from 18 in 1925 to 16 at the time of *Furman v. Georgia* in 1972. Capital rape laws splintered after *Furman.* Several states did not classify rape as a capital offense post *Furman,* whereas others did so only when the rape was of a child, and some, like North Carolina and Louisiana, tried to make the death penalty mandatory, which caused their statutes to be invalidated on appeal. Only Georgia was left with a valid adult capital rape law, until *Coker,* providing for a discretionary proceeding similar to its capital murder proceeding: a jury finding of guilt for the capital offense, followed by a penalty phase weighing aggravating and mitigating circumstances.

The Supreme Court had sanctioned this proceeding in *Gregg v. Georgia,* 96 S.Ct. 2909 (1976) as it applied to capital murder, which showed the other states how to write death penalty laws that met uncertain Supreme Court standards. The opinion in *Coker,* coming a year later, further clarified the post-*Furman* ambiguities: capital punishment was not allowed for the rape of an adult who was not killed.

The language of the decision established the ideological foundation for a much broader criminal law precedent—that is, that the death penalty is not appropriate unless someone is killed. Thus, armed robbery, kidnapping, treason, piracy, train wrecking, and other formerly capital crimes were struck down by implication, establishing the rule that has prevailed for two decades: for a death sentence to be imposed, the defendant must be convicted of killing another person, and the jury must find that the aggravating circumstances of the crime and the criminal outweigh the mitigating circumstances.

Although the Supreme Court placed *Coker* in the context of evolving public and legislative attitudes about the crime of rape, noting that most state legislatures had not reenacted capital rape statutes post *Furman,* the decision can still be viewed as a bold break with tradition. Chief Justice

Burger, in his dissent, commented on the plurality view that since most state legislatures had not reenacted new capital rape statutes in the 1970s, support for the death penalty for rape must be waning:

> When considered in light of the experience since the turn of this century, where more than one third of American jurisdictions have consistently provided the death penalty for rape, the plurality's focus on the experience of the immediate past must be viewed as truly disingenuous. . . . Can it rationally be considered a relevant indicator of what our society deems 'cruel and unusual' to look solely to what legislatures have *refrained* from doing under conditions of great uncertainty arising from our less than lucid holdings on the Eighth Amendment?

In the decade before American executions dwindled to a halt in 1967, awaiting the high court decision that came out in the legally muddled *Furman* in 1972, the states and federal government were still executing people for rape, armed robbery, kidnapping, and treason. Indeed, the enduring death penalty case of the 1950s was that of Caryl Chessman, who was executed in California on May 2, 1960. Chessman was a convicted kidnapper, sex offender, and armed robber, but he was never convicted of killing anyone.

Even as the number of executions being carried out went into a sharp decline in the 1960s, the death penalty remained on the books for a wide variety of offenses. Hugo Bedau's *The Death Penalty in America* (1967) listed the death penalty crimes shown in Table 16.1.

As a practical matter, by the late 1960s the death penalty had nearly withered away for crimes other than murder and rape. From 1930 to 1967, over 3,300 persons were executed for homicide, 455 for rape, and only 70 (or less than 2% of the total) for all other non-homicidal offenses, including robbery, burglary, attempted murder, kidnapping, assault by a life-term prisoner, carnal knowledge, espionage, assault with intent to rape, and accessory to murder.

In this era, executions for rape were carried out exclusively in the southern states (including the border states of Oklahoma, Missouri and Delaware), and they were carried out predominately on black men convicted of raping white women. Of the 455 rapists executed, 405 (89%) were black.

Professor Marvin Wolfgang's research on the death penalty for rape, reported as "Racial Discrimination in the Death Sentence for Rape" in William Bowers's *Executions in America* (1974), showed that over one third of black defendants convicted of raping white victims received death sentences; in all other racial combinations of victim and defendant, only

TABLE 16.1

Death Penalty Crimes

Offense	Number of Capital Jurisdictions
Homicide	44
Kidnapping	34
Treason	21
Rape	19
Carnal knowledge	15
Robbery	10
Perjury in a capital case	10
Bombing	7
Assault by life-term inmate	5
Burglary	4
Arson	4
Train wrecking	2
Train robbery	2
Espionage	2

2% received death sentences. This 18-fold heightened likelihood of getting a death sentence had only one possible explanation, Wolfgang concluded after reviewing other possible explanations or linkages: "It is the racial factor of the relationship between the defendant and the victim that results in the penalty of death."

Among the 455 executed rapists were 14 men electrocuted in Louisiana from 1941 to 1957, almost one per year during this period. The basic information about these men and their crimes is presented in Table 16.2. Their capital cases were processed through Louisiana's legal system at a time when that system was undergoing transition in four important ways:

1. Electrocution would replace hanging as the means of carrying out the death penalty.

TABLE 16.2

Convicted Rapists Electrocuted in Louisiana: 1941–57

Defendant	Age at Defendant's Race/Gender/Crime	Victim's Race/Gender/Age	Parish	Crime Date	Execution Date
1. Willie Larkin	b/m/27	b/f/?	Madison	4-4-42	9-9-42
2. William Hamilton	b/m/18	w/f/9	Caddo	9-29-42	12-3-42
3. Anthony Wilson	b/m/27	w/f/?	Orleans	4-21-42	3-6-44
4. William Ayers	b/m/31	w/f/17	Winn	3-??-45	6-28-46
5. Jesse Perkins	b/m/39	w/f/?	E. Baton Rouge	6-21-46	7-18-47
6. Edward Spriggs	b/m/27	w/f/?	Iberville	4-5-48	6-25-48
7. L.C. Lloyd	b/m/31	w/f/?	Tangipahoa	4-23-47	3-11-49*
8. Edward Sanford	b/m/46	w/f/20	E. Baton Rouge	8-2-49	12-1-50
9. Edward Honeycutt	b/m/23	w/f/?	St. Landry	12-1-48	6-8-51
10. Paul Washington	b/m/22	w/f/?	Jefferson	3-16-48	7-11-52
11. Ocie Jugger	b/m/23	w/f/?	Jefferson	3-16-48	7-11-52
12. Walter Bentley	b/m/26	w/f/13	Orleans	11-19-50	9-6-52
13. John Michel	b/m/20	w/f/?	Orleans	2-10-53	5-31-57
14. Donald R. Edwards	b/m/29	w/f/45	Caddo	6-28-56	9-6-57

*Committed suicide in jail the day of his execution.

2. State authority would replace local authority in conducting the execution.

3. Lynching, as an informal, popular local practice, would die out as local and then state authorities asserted greater official control over the trial and punishment of capital offenders.

4. Executions would be removed from the public eye, to be carried out in private—acts done in the dead of night behind jail and prison walls, becoming first "by-invitation-only" events and later "official-business-only."

In the decades after the Civil War, the administration of the death penalty in Louisiana was left up to people in the parishes. If people were incensed enough about a particular offense and a particular offender, he (or occasionally she) was likely to be lynched without ever going to trial. If the offender got a death sentence at trial, the punishment was carried out by local authorities in public, usually through hanging on a gallows built on the courthouse square, until the execution was later made more private by moving it inside the parish courthouse, in a room specially designed with a trapdoor over a drop below.

The trappings of "progress" have often come late to Louisiana. The modern process of electrocuting offenders in a state prison under formal state authority, pioneered by the state of New York at the Auburn Prison in 1890, was not adopted by Louisiana until 1957. Only 11 men were executed at the Louisiana State Penitentiary at Angola over the next four years, ending in June 1961, when Louisiana's own moratorium on carrying out executions began. Louisiana would not execute another criminal until 1983.

Between the time of the Civil War and 1940, executions in Louisiana were considerably more informal. Capital crimes were tried at the parish level, and offenders were held in parish jails until they were hanged in the parish seat. Public hangings prevailed through the 1920s.

Before World War I it was probably more common for an offender to be lynched than to be executed by lawful authority. The NAACP's *Thirty Years of Lynching in the United States* counts 313 lynchings in Louisiana—49 whites and 264 blacks—in the period from 1889 to 1918. Frank Shay's *Judge Lynch: His First Hundred Years* (1938), counts lynchings over a longer period and comes up with a total of 421 through 1937. The average was 10 per year from the 1890s through World War I, but only 2 per year from 1918 through the Depression years.

The last Louisiana lynching for which a record can be found was in 1946. A black man, John Jones, who was accused of breaking into a white woman's house, was taken from the Minden jail by a mob and burned to death with a blowtorch after his hands were cut off. A second black man, Albert Harris, was beaten by the mob but not killed.

By the 1940s lynchings had all but died out in Louisiana, and electrocution had replaced hanging as the legal method of execution. Act 14 of the 1940 legislature provided that effective June 1, 1941, executions were to be carried out by electrocution. Over the next 20 years, 66 men and one woman, "Toni Jo" Henry, would be electrocuted in the state's portable electric chair—which was transported from parish to parish to do executions until 1957, when it found a permanent home in the Red Hats cellblock at Angola.

In looking at the cases of the 14 men electrocuted for rape, you can find something unique and different about each man and his crime, or the processing of his legal case, or the circumstances of his execution, but there is one overriding aspect of commonality: all were black men. Most were young; only two were older than 31 when they committed their crimes.

The first man electrocuted for rape in Louisiana, Willie Larkin, was the only one executed for raping a black woman. Larkin was a 27-year-old black man from Madison Parish. He was "charged with rape by several Negro women" according to the *Madison Journal* of September 4, 1942. The crime he was tried for was committed on April 4, 1942. Tried by a jury in Tallulah on May 11, 1942, Larkin was given a death sentence on July 13. But the district judge had sentenced him to hang, and hanging was no longer in use. Larkin's attorney objected to his client being electrocuted rather than hanged; however, the attorney general, Eugene Stanley, pointed out in a memorandum to Governor Sam H. Jones that the mode of inflicting capital punishment had been changed effective several months before the date of the crime, so no legal points substantiated the argument against electrocution.

Shortly after noon on Wednesday, September 9, 1942, just over five months after his crime, Larkin was electrocuted in the Madison Parish jail. His mother, who lived in Tallulah, had maintained until a day or two before his death that he would not die but that "dey would send him to war" instead. Larkin said before he died that he "had religion" and was satisfied. He had told his jailer in the days before his death: "A man gets what he works for."

The rapid and unimpeded processing of Larkin's case from crime to execution was typical of that day. The man who came after him, William Hamilton, was executed less than 10 weeks after the date of his alleged crime. The process, from September 29, 1942, to December 3, 1942, exhibited a speed that seems dazzling in comparison with today's glacier-like movement of death penalty cases.

Hamilton's crime was an ugly one for any era: he raped a nine-year-old white schoolgirl in a Shreveport park. The girl was returning from lunch when Hamilton stopped her in Highland Park. According to the original news accounts in the *Shreveport Times,* Hamilton pointed a gun at the girl and forced her to accompany him into the woods, where the rape occurred. He ran away afterward.

A city street department employee saw Hamilton leave the scene. When police went to Hamilton's home the next day, they found blood-soaked clothing. Hamilton confessed, three times. He said he had gone to the movies after the crime. At his trial on October 19, the evidence of guilt was compelling. The jury deliberated two and a half minutes before returning the death penalty for aggravated rape. Hamilton was sentenced to death on October 23, and six weeks later he was executed in the Caddo Parish Jail. Sixty-five days had passed from crime to grave. Louisiana carried out no executions for rape in 1943. The one black man who was executed in 1944, Anthony Wilson, went to his death proclaiming his innocence. Wilson was a seaman. He was convicted of attacking a 92-pound white woman walking home through the Carrollton section of New Orleans late on the night of April 21, 1942. He was convicted in district court on November 19; the jury, ignoring his insanity plea, returned a verdict in 40 minutes.

Wilson was sentenced on January 15, 1943, and executed in Orleans Parish Prison on March 6, 1944. His attorneys had sought a stay of execution, but were denied. The *Times-Picayune* of March 7 reported that Wilson confessed no religious faith. When the barber cut his hair at 10:00 AM, Wilson was singing the "St. Louis Blues." He was placed in the electric chair at 12:15 PM, given three shots of electricity, 2,500 volts each, and pronounced dead by the coroner at 12:25 PM.

William "Willie" Ayers was a 31-year-old farmhand when he raped a 17-year-old white girl near Winnfield, in Winn Parish, in March 1945. He escaped after the rape and was arrested a few weeks later working on a farm near Dixie in Caddo Parish. As his execution date of June 28, 1946, neared, attention was focused more on those who would operate the electric chair than on the one who would sit in it.

The electrocution of Willie Francis for murder in St. Martinville on May 3, 1946, was botched. The executioner said, "Goodbye, Willie," and threw the switch. Some current flowed, enough to give Willie a shock but not kill him. After another attempt, the executioner gave up. Willie Francis realized every condemned man's dream: he walked away from the chair. A year later, though, on May 9, 1947, after a heavy round of appeals and petitions for clemency, he was returned to the chair and successfully executed. He would go to heaven, Francis said, describing heaven as "a place where you have a white suit." (See Bob Hamm's articles on the Willie Francis case in the *Lafayette Daily Advertiser,* April 25 and 26, 1993, for a detailed account of this event.)

Another execution for murder was carried out without incident in Allen Parish later in May 1946, although the Francis snafu was still in the minds of the press and public as the time to execute Willie Ayers neared. The chair was installed in the Winn Parish Jail, and Ayers was led down to it just after noon on Friday. The executioner threw the switch and said just what he had said to Francis: "Goodbye, Willie." This time the machine worked perfectly. Willie Ayers, as far as anyone knows, got the same white suit Willie Francis aspired to.

The year 1947 would see eight men electrocuted in Louisiana, the most for any year under the modern process until another eight men were executed in 1987. Only one was executed for rape, Jesse Perkins, a 41-year-old Baton Rouge man. Perkins had served time at Angola for manslaughter. He was paroled in 1943 and returned to Baton Rouge.

Perkins was convicted of the aggravated rape of a young white woman in Bogan's pasture, a lover's lane area in Baton Rouge, on May 21, 1946. The woman and her male companion told police they were sitting on a blanket in the pasture when a "Negro crawled up on his hands and knees, pulled a knife on them, and threatened their lives. He then raped the woman and fled." The couple thought it unusual that their attacker was already bleeding from a neck wound.

Perkins was identified by police when he went to Our Lady of the Lake Hospital for treatment. The police investigation showed that Perkins had attacked another couple in Bogan's pasture earlier the same evening. That man, a city bus driver, had fought back and stabbed Perkins in the neck. Police found stolen property in Perkins' home that had been taken in yet another robbery in Bogan's pasture, from another bus driver, a month earlier. Police blamed Perkins for other robberies in the area in the weeks before he was caught.

Perkins maintained his innocence throughout his trial and confinement. He said the police had the wrong man. He complained in court that he had been beaten by the police, called a liar, promised light time, and "hit so many times he wished he was dead." Perkins said he had been cut when three men attempted to rob him as he walked home.

The rape victim, her companion, and the other man who had cut him earlier in the evening all positively identified Perkins as the attacker. The jury deliberated 18 minutes before convicting him of aggravated rape on November 8, 1946. The judge sentenced him to death on January 6, 1947.

Perkins was next to the oldest of the electrocuted rapists and almost surely the most social. He spent his last day visiting with several Baptist preachers, police officials; his attorney, Louis Berry; Sister Tharsilla, who had been bringing him cake in jail; his legal wife, Dorothy Perkins; his common-law wife, Bernice Martin; and his daughter, also named Dorothy. When his family members wept, according to the newspaper account, "he told them not to cry, that he 'had made his peace with his Maker' and was going to walk to the chair 'like a man.'" The *Baton Rouge Advocate* gave this account of Perkins's execution:

> As he was being strapped in the chair Jessie called to the three Negro preachers standing by him, "Be good! You'll meet me, Reverend, and when the roll be called, I'll meet it . . . Come shake hands with me, boys . . . Fine, feeling fine . . . Say, you tell all my friends to don't doubt me."
>
> Asked if he had anything to say, the Negro replied, "I'm not guilty . . . That's all . . . But I'm willing and ready to go."

The switch was thrown at 12:01:30. He survived the first jolt of electricity but not the second. About 50 persons witnessed the execution, and another 100 waited outside the Baton Rouge courthouse, which was closed for the execution.

Louis Berry, the black attorney who represented Jesse Perkins, also represented Edward Spriggs, who was executed the next year. Mr. Berry may not have had much to work with: the entire legal processing from crime to execution took 81 days, only 16 days longer than William Hamilton's record-setting pace of 1942.

Spriggs was arrested on Monday, April 5, 1948, in Plaquemine. He was charged with entering a home outside Plaquemine Monday morning, threatening a white woman with a knife, then raping her. The victim had the presence of mind, when the attacker was leaving the house, to grab a pistol and fire six shots at him, *The Iberville South* reported. All six shots missed.

Spriggs, who had a prior arrest for carnal knowledge of a black girl but no convictions, was arrested by Sheriff C. A. "Bobbie" Griffon, Jr., within four hours. He confessed to the crime, though he would later repudiate the confession. Local authorities took care to see that a black man served on the second grand jury that indicted Spriggs with aggravated rape, after his first indictment was quashed for violating the Fourteenth Amendment, and another served on the trial jury that convicted him—in a 22-minute deliberation. The local newspaper remarked how unusual this effort at minority representation was.

When the editor of the paper visited Spriggs in jail the day before his execution, Spriggs told him to come back in the afternoon, that he had a statement to make. The editor found Spriggs eating a piece of ice-cold watermelon the jailer had given him. Spriggs told the editor: "You can take this down. I committed the crime. Tell my friends I'm sorry. Don't they make the same mistake." Editor J. N. Rials's article said Spriggs repeated two or three times that his advice to other black men and to white ones as well was to stay on the right road, and don't "go wrong like I did."

Spriggs was executed the next day, June 25, 1948. His was the first execution in Iberville Parish since 1906. Spriggs left a widow and two children.

The execution of L. C. Lloyd, scheduled for March 11, 1949, in Amite, the parish seat of Tangipahoa Parish, indicates why authorities maintain a close "death watch" over condemned men in the final hours before their execution. Lloyd appears on lists of executed men as having been electrocuted, but in fact he broke his own neck in his jail cell seven hours before he was to be executed. The parish coroner reported that Lloyd wedged his head between the window sill and a bar and threw his body to one side with such force that his neck snapped. A black trusty heard the noise and called deputies.

Lloyd had been convicted on November 29, 1948, and sentenced to death on December 21, 1948, for the aggravated rape of an older white woman in Independence, Louisiana. On April 23, 1947, the woman was walking into town at dusk. When she passed a lumberyard, a man grabbed her and attacked her. The woman's son came along a short time later, looking for his mother, and found the black man still molesting his mother. The son hit the man on the head with a piece of lumber, and the attacker ran away.

Authorities began searching for Lloyd, who had an extensive arrest record for property crimes and had already served 11 years at the state penitentiary—a life sentence in those days—for a rape committed in Franklinton when he was 17. Lloyd undoubtedly knew what would happen to him this time. He escaped into Mississippi, was arrested for window peeping, escaped again, was arrested in Natchez for theft, and escaped another time. He was finally captured in Forrest City, Arkansas, 15 months after the crime, and returned to Tangipahoa Parish to stand trial. Court records indicate that after Lloyd's conviction, no appeal was made. His attorneys made no further effort to save his life.

Lloyd was not an easy person to maintain control of. After he was sentenced to death, he kept tearing up his jail cell, destroying equipment and fixtures. He was considered such a security risk that he was transferred to the Orleans Parish Prison until four days before his scheduled execution. Even after his return, security in the rural parish jail proved to be inadequate, allowing Lloyd to "cheat the electric chair," as the local newspaper reported.

Edward Sanford, who was electrocuted in Baton Rouge on December 1, 1950, also managed to escape the clutches of the law for a time. Sanford committed his aggravated rape in midsummer 1949. A young white girl parked with her boyfriend near the LSU quail farm on Perkins Road told police "a large Negro came up to their car, fired a shot into the windshield, then proceeded to rob them. He attacked her, she said, outside the car while he held a gun on her companion." The man told the couple he had killed five persons already. They offered him money, but he replied, "I want you."

Police suspected Sanford from the description the 20-year-old victim gave. He fled to New Orleans, where he was arrested in a shack by the industrial canal, on October 22, 1949. His trial started five weeks later, on November 29, 1949. Sanford's attorneys had asked for the trial to be moved out of Baton Rouge. One of them told the court, "A Negro charged with rape of a white woman has two and a half strikes against him before his trial begins."

When the defense suggested that Sanford had been coerced or tricked into confessing, Sheriff Clemmons testified that Sanford not only wanted to confess but wanted to plead guilty. In closing arguments, the black defense attorney had no recourse left but to ask for mercy: "I'm pleading for the life of an ignorant Negro." It took the jury 25 minutes to bring in a death verdict, and Sanford was formally sentenced to death on March 3, 1950. The *Baton Rouge Advocate* gave this account of his execution:

> A single, minute-long charge of electricity at 12:18 PM ended the life of the big, rawboned Negro, whose last words were, "I'm not guilty of this by myself."
>
> The last words addressed to him were, "Goodbye, Edward." They were spoken by the state's executioner as he, standing beside Sanford and wearing a big cowboy hat, jerked down the switch.

In the summer of the following year, the traveling executioner took his chair to the St. Landry Parish Jail in Opelousas to execute Edward Honeycutt, a black man from rural Farmerville who had been 23 years old when he committed his crime on December 1, 1948. Honeycutt was charged with raping a young St. Landry Parish farmwife with her two children, ages five and three, in the house. The crime took place on a farm road off U.S. Highway 190 outside Eunice.

The legal processing of the Honeycutt case followed a road about as rough as the one leading to the farm. Honeycutt was tried and given a death sentence in 1949. The Louisiana Supreme Court overturned the conviction because no blacks had served on the grand jury. He was reindicted and retried the next year.

Before he was brought to trial again, three white men removed him from the St. Landry Parish Jail and transported him to the Atchafalaya River. When they flipped a coin to see who would kill him—apparently unaware that lynching was no longer a social convention—Honeycutt jumped into the river and hung onto a limb until sheriff's deputies rescued him.

In the May 1950 second trial, the victim was identified and quoted by name. She was described as a "petite Eunice farmwife." She testified that when she responded to a knock on her front door, a black man pulled a gun on her. He forced his way inside and threatened to kill her and the two children.

Honeycutt was picked up in the area later in the afternoon and taken to the victim, who identified him: "He's the one." The defense claimed mistaken identity. One attorney said there "must be more than one 'tall, heavy-set Negro' around Eunice." A black farmwife and neighbor of the victim testified she saw Honeycutt enter the victim's home and later run into the woods behind the farmhouses.

Honeycutt was defended by three black attorneys—the indomitable Louis Berry and his colleagues V. B. Lacour and E. W. Jackson. One of these men is said to have pointed out that in Louisiana since 1907 no white man but 29 negroes had been condemned to death for rape. If his count was right, Honeycutt would make number 30. The jury was out 24 minutes. He was formally sentenced on June 2, 1950. After another appeal, this one unsuccessful, Honeycutt's execution was set for June 8, 1951. When he was interviewed by *Lafayette Daily Advertiser* city editor Vincent Marino the day before his execution, Honeycutt said, "I don't mind going to the chair, but it's something I didn't do." A few minutes later, he said, "I don't know. I can't think. My mind is all flubbergated, but I'm not afraid."

Honeycutt could neither read nor write. His parents had come to see him in jail only once or twice. He was pleased that his girlfriend had come to read to him through his cell door the day before he was to die.

He did not resist as he was strapped into the electric chair. Two shocks were administered, at 12:05 and 12:08. He was pronounced dead at 12:12:30 on June 8, 1951. Among the 100 spectators present in the jail to observe the execution were the victim and her husband.

Louisiana's only double electrocution for aggravated rape took place on July 11, 1952, in the Jefferson Parish Jail. The two men executed were Paul Washington and Ocie Jugger. Their crime had been committed more than four years earlier, in March 1948. Escapes and legal complications, based on Washington's claims of innocence and inadequate representation, resulted in the long delay, unusual in Louisiana for the era, before the pair were finally executed.

The crime for which Paul Washington and Ocie Jugger were executed was committed on March 15, 1948, in the Shrewsbury section of Jefferson Parish, off Highway 90 across the Orleans Parish line. A black man broke into the home of a married white woman, stole jewelry, and raped the woman.

Two days later, a man named Vincent North pawned a watch taken in the crime at a pawn shop on Rampart Street. When North was questioned by the police, he said the watch had been given him by a friend, Paul Washington. When Washington was questioned, he implicated Jugger. Both were jailed and charged with aggravated rape.

At their trial on November 20, 1948, both Jugger and Washington were found guilty and given death sentences. The sentence was not formally imposed until November 17, 1949. A month after sentencing, on the day his appeal was filed with the Louisiana Supreme Court, Jugger pried off a radiator grill and escaped the Jefferson Parish Jail through an air vent. He remained free for over two years, until he was stopped for a traffic violation in Houston in February 1952. He was returned to Jefferson Parish to await execution.

Washington's case had already been appealed to the Louisiana Supreme Court and the U.S. Supreme Court without success. The Louisiana pardon board, on April 2, 1952, declined to commute the pair's death sentences.

On April 15, Jugger gave a written statement to Alvin B. Jones, Washington's attorney, in which he assumed all guilt for the burglary and rape. Washington knew nothing of either crime; he was just waiting nearby while Jugger went inside the house, Jugger said. Washington had not testified to these facts at the trial, but he wished it be known that he was innocent of the crimes for which he was about to be executed.

The pardon board met again to consider the new evidence and on April 23 again rejected clemency for Washington, writing, "All of the facts and circumstances in the case still fail to justify clemency." A death warrant was signed for July 11, 1952. Washington and Jugger were executed in the Gretna jail on a Friday afternoon. The *New Orleans Times-Picayune* gave this account:

> First to enter the death room was Washington, a big, heavily built man. He watched impassively as the executioner strapped his arms and legs to the chair.
>
> As the executioner placed the black skull helmet on his head, Washington said: "I know my Lord is satisfied." He was masked. The executioner moved to the switch in the portable control box beside the chair.

"Goodbye, Paul," said the executioner. On the last word, he threw the switch. It was 12:09:30 PM.

Another round of current was necessary when Washington's heart fluttered. He was pronounced dead at 12:14 PM.

Jugger was brought into the room at 12:26 PM, accompanied by a Baptist minister. When he was asked if he had anything to say, he whispered, "God be with me—my soul is safe." Jugger turned to the jail superintendent and said, "I thank you for all the good treatment—may God be with all you men—that's all." Two charges were administered, and Jugger was pronounced dead at 12:31:30 PM.

On the day of Washington and Jugger's execution, the front page of the *Times-Picayune* was devoted to national political news: Dwight Eisenhower and Richard Nixon had been nominated for president and vice-president at the Republican national convention in Chicago. The account of the double electrocution, the only time the electric chair was ever used in Jefferson Parish, was buried on page 24.

Later in 1952 Walter Bentley was executed in Orleans Parish. Bentley was convicted of breaking into a house in the Lakeview area of New Orleans on November 19, 1950. When he found a 13-year-old white girl, a babysitter, sleeping on a couch, he woke her up, threatened her with a knife, and raped her.

Bentley held the teenager captive about two hours. She was finally able to scream for help. Neighbors came to the front door, and Bentley fled. He was captured on the lakefront about 3:30 AM. Police recognized him from the victim's description, which included a "Hitler-type mustache with a goatee."

More important for Bentley's capital trial in February 1951 were fingerprints he left on a filing cabinet in the home and the signed confession he gave police. He had a criminal record going back to 1938, when he was 14 years old. He had already served nine years at Angola for armed robbery. Bentley was found guilty on February 13, 1951, and sentenced to death on March 30, 1951.

Bentley's execution on September 26, 1952, was apparently unremarkable, except for the fact that he was reported to be the first person executed under the new state law setting the time of executions between midnight and 3:00 AM. Only a few official witnesses were present for the early Friday morning electrocution "in a room entirely cut off from view of all persons except those permitted by law." Bentley was pronounced dead at 12:13 AM.

Even as the cases of Honeycutt, Washington, Jugger, and Bentley were making their ways through the legal system, opposition to the death penalty for rape was building. Like the abrupt decline of lynching after the First World War, the imposition of death for nonfatal rape went into sharp decline after 1950.

One case in particular, not in Louisiana but in Virginia, focused widespread public and legal attention on the discriminatory application of the death penalty for rape. This was the case of the "Martinsville Seven"—seven black men who were electrocuted, four on February 2 and the other three on February 5, 1951, for the rape of a 32-year-old white woman in Martinsville, Virginia.

As Eric Rise has established in his research on the case (see "Race, Rape and Radicalism: The Case of the Martinsville Seven, 1949–1951," in *The Journal of Southern History,* August 1992, pages 461–490; or see the full-length account, *The Martinsville Seven and Southern Justice: Race, Crime and Capital Punishment in Virginia, 1949–1951,* Rise's Ph.D. dissertation from the University of Florida, 1992), the Virginia trial judge's insistence on following the procedural rules of a "fair trial" obliged the NAACP attorneys to broaden their attack on racism within the American legal system. What more obvious practice of racism within the criminal courts remained than the grossly disproportionate use of the death penalty against black men who had raped white women?

Walter Bentley was the last man executed for rape under local authority in Louisiana. Almost five years elapsed before the next black man would be executed for rape, and this execution would not take place in a parish jail. In 1956 the legislature changed the execution procedure to do away with the traveling electric chair. The Department of Institutions sought $250,000 to build a new death house at Angola. When the money could not be found, the warden had an office at the Red Hats disciplinary cellblock remodeled to hold the electric chair.

Joe Washington was electrocuted for murder in the Caddo Parish Jail on May 21, 1957, and then the traveling chair was taken off the road to its new home at the isolated camp behind the main prison at Angola. The dubious distinction of being the first man to die in the electric chair at Angola went to John Michel, convicted of aggravated rape out of Orleans Parish.

Michel, whose name is sometimes listed as John J. Michaels, was 20 years old when he raped a white woman in New Orleans on February 10, 1953. Newspaper accounts always refer to the crime as occurring during "Carnival season." He was convicted on May 28, 1953, and sentenced to death by electrocution on November 9, 1953. The Louisiana Supreme Court affirmed his conviction on December 5, 1955. Governor Earl Long signed Michel's death warrant, which fixed the execution date at May 31, 1957, between the hours of midnight and three AM.

The Red Hats building at Angola, where electrocutions were performed in the side building from 1959 to 1961. (Copyright: Burk Foster.)

Michel's execution went off with no problems. He was described as going to his death "calmly." Warden Maurice Sigler said Michel entered the death chamber at 12:10 AM, accompanied by two Catholic priests. Michel expressed his appreciation to those present for what they had done for him. The switch was thrown, and Michel was pronounced dead at 12:20 AM.

Three months later Donald Rufus Edwards became the last convicted rapist to die in Angola's electric chair. Edwards was an ex-convict who had done time at Angola for burglary. On June 28, 1956, he was prowling a Shreveport residential neighborhood looking for a home to burglarize. When he broke into a home on Monrovia Street, he found a 45-year-old white woman alone in the house, her husband and daughter out of town on a business trip. He held a knife to the woman and raped her, cutting her in the process. He then had the naked woman accompany him around the house, searching for valuables. He took several items, including a diamond wedding band. Then he raped the woman again and left the house.

Edwards was arrested later the same night. He had the victim's wedding ring in his pocket and other stolen items in his possession. His thumbprint was on a dresser drawer in the bedroom. He made a full confession to police within 12 hours after his arrest. The victim positively identified him as the attacker. His defense at trial in November? He did not do the crime: it must have been someone else.

The jury quickly brought in the death penalty verdict on November 16, 1956. On November 23, 1956, he was sentenced to be electrocuted. The Louisiana Supreme Court affirmed his conviction on April 1, 1957. No request for a rehearing was made. Governor Earl Long issued Edwards's death warrant on July 30.

The execution was set for September 6, 1957, 14 months after he committed the crime. Edwards was brought into the death chamber at 12:05 AM. Warden Sigler asked him if he had anything to say. According to the newspaper account of the execution, Edwards replied that "he was a Christian and that he did not rape the woman. He also expressed appreciation for his treatment at the prison." The event proceeded and Edwards was pronounced dead at 12:21 AM.

The execution of Donald Rufus Edwards, the last of Louisiana's 14 electrocuted rapists, did not mark an abrupt end to efforts to impose the death penalty for rape in Louisiana. On the day Edwards was electrocuted, acting governor Lether Frazar signed death warrants for two New Orleans men, Edgar Labat and Clifton Poret, who were on death row for the aggravated rape of a white woman in New Orleans on November 12, 1950. Their execution date was set for September 20, 1957, two weeks after the Edwards execution.

But Poret and Labat were never executed. The night before they were to be executed, their new attorneys got a federal judge to issue a stay. One stay led to another, and Poret and Labat, both of whom claimed to be completely innocent of this crime, became the Caryl Chessman of Louisiana. Their case remained in the federal courts until after Louisiana stopped executing people in 1961.

Poret and Labat remained on death row at Angola for several more years. Their names are listed among the 33 on death row as of August 8, 1966, 12 of whom were black men convicted of aggravated rape (Table 16.3).

TABLE 16.3

Inmate	Parish	Sentence Date
Wilbert Augustine	Orleans	6-7-60
Roosevelt Hughes	Orleans	3-19-63

TABLE 16.3 (CONTINUED)

Inmate	Parish	Sentence Date
Isaac Peart	Orleans	12-16-55
Eugene Scott	E. Baton Rouge	7-26-61
Emmett Henderson	Morehouse	11-10-61
Alton Poret	Orleans	3-23-53
Clarence Wilson	Tangipahoa	6-23-60
Andrew Scott	Livingston	9-11-60
Edgar Labat	Orleans	3-23-53
Earl Clark	Plaquemine	2-6-65
Bruce Barksdale	Orleans	3-16-64
Hezekiah Brown	Orleans	6-14-65

None of these men were ever executed. The last man executed in Louisiana, prior to the 22-year moratorium that ended in 1983 under the new post-*Gregg* statute, was Jessie James Ferguson. He was executed on June 9, 1961, for the rape and murder of Joyce Marie Thibodeaux, an 11-year-old Opelousas girl. Even without the murder, Ferguson would have been a prime candidate for the death penalty. His criminal record included six previous rape charges, including one for which he had served a 10½-year life sentence at Angola. The most likely reason Ferguson lived as long as he did was that he raped only black victims. At his execution, Ferguson is remembered for his last words: "Pray for me. Don't let it hurt."

After Ferguson, executions remained in limbo until the *Furman* decision in 1972 wiped death row clean. The 43 people on death row in Louisiana at the time had their sentences commuted to life imprisonment, and most of them were eventually released from prison at their parole or good-time release dates. In 1991 the state legislature changed Louisiana's method of capital punishment to lethal injection, so the 87 people—86 men and one woman—who were electrocuted in Louisiana from 1941 to 1991 make up a roster unlikely to be changed in the future. The 14 black men executed for capital rape in this era make up a doubly untimely bunch: both their crime and their manner of death have become extinct.

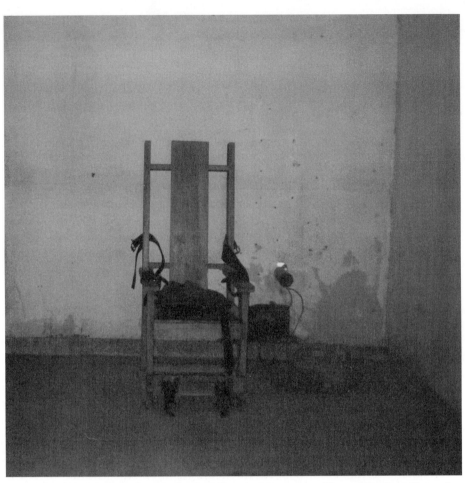

A replica of the electric chair in the Red Hats building today. (Copyright: Burk Foster.)

17

Unbalanced Justice

LANE NELSON

From *The Angolite*, March/April 1996, Angola, La: Louisiana State Penitentiary.

Antonio Gonzales James lived on death row for 14 years and survived 13 execution warrants. His 14th date with death stuck. He was 41 years old when led to the death chamber in shackles and executed minutes after midnight on March 1, 1996. While prosecutors and family members of the victim were glad to see an end to the 17-year-old case, attorneys and supporters for James called the execution a "miscarriage of justice."

Miscarriages of justice in death penalty cases were discussed in the 1993 U.S. Supreme Court case, *Herrera v. Collins.* "Clemency is deeply rooted in our Anglo-American tradition of law, and is the historic remedy for preventing miscarriages of justice where judicial process has been exhausted," wrote Chief Justice William Rehnquist. "Executive clemency has provided the fail-safe in our criminal justice system." Like the crime of murder, execution is irreversible; no mistake or future substantiated doubt can be corrected once the executioner pumps the poison into the condemned person. The "fail-safe" route of the clemency process should be available, said the Court, when there is real question as to innocence or fairness.

James was sentenced to death for the 1979 New Year's Day murder of 69-year-old Henry Silver. The killing occurred during an armed robbery. James and his partners, Levon "Smokey" Price and Edgar "Ironman" Taylor, were drug users who supported their habit through street stickups. According to James, the robbing trio operated on a rotation basis. One man would sit in the car, one would pull the pistol and rob the victim, and the other would back up the pistol man. They had only one pistol, which was passed from one to the other to pull the robberies.

As Silver stepped out of his car near the French Quarter, Price and James confronted him and a slight struggle ensued. Silver was shot once in the back of the head. Thirty-five dollars and some kidney pills were taken off his body. The two robbers made a clean escape.

Three weeks later Taylor and James entered a dry cleaning shop owned by 72-year-old Alvin Adams. Adams was shot through the eye and killed. The robbery netted $42. Again, there were no witnesses.

Three days after the Adams killing, James approached Robert Hooten while Hooten sat in his car on a side street in New Orleans. Price stayed in the background. James put the pistol to Hooten's head and demanded his money and watch. Hooten made a quick move, catching James off guard, and wrestled the pistol away. James ran, and Hooten shot him in the rear end. James was arrested later that evening at Charity Hospital, where he had sought medical attention for the gunshot wound.

Six months passed. The Silver and Adams murders went unsolved as James sat in jail waiting prosecution on the Hooten robbery. The gun

Hooten turned over to police sat in evidence storage. According to James, while in jail he was terrorized by nightmares and guilt over the deaths of Silver and Adams. Finally, he went to police and confessed. He identified Price and Taylor as the shooters in both killings and told detectives the murder weapon was in the possession of the police. Police ran the pistol through ballistics, then picked up Price and Taylor. But both men pointed to James as the shooter. They bargained with authorities and were promised sweet deals in exchange for their testimony.

James first went on trial for the Hooten robbery. He was convicted and sentenced to 99 years in prison. Two years later, with Taylor the key witness for the prosecution, James was tried and convicted for the Adams murder and received a life sentence without eligibility for parole. Taylor pled guilty to manslaughter for his involvement in the crime and served four and a half years in prison.

The state then took James to trial for the Silver murder. This time prosecutors used Price as their star witness. He testified that James had shot and killed Henry Silver. The jury believed him and gave James the death penalty. For his testimony, Price received a five-year suspended sentence. According to later evidence submitted to the courts and pardon board by James's appeal attorneys, both Taylor and Price were career criminals, long-time police informants, and liars.

In April 1995 James faced his 13th death date. He was denied clemency by the state pardon board and sent to the death cell to await execution. Four hours before the execution, the Louisiana Supreme Court surprisingly ordered a stay and sent the case back to the trial court for a hearing on new witnesses who said James's codefendants pulled the trigger.

That hearing took place in June 1995 before New Orleans District Judge James McKay III, the same judge who had set the prior 13 execution dates. James and his attorneys argued, as they did at a 1995 pardon hearing, that he did not kill anyone. They presented several sworn affidavits from people who said they had talked with Taylor and Price just after the 1979 arrests and that both men admitted to the killings. McKay, however, limited the scope of the hearing, did not give credence to James's witnesses—most of whom were felons or ex-felons—and denied a new trial.

Afterward, the Louisiana Supreme Court again declined to review James's appeal, and the 14th execution date was set. James's attorneys went to the federal district court, requesting an evidentiary hearing. Two days before the scheduled execution, federal judge Martin Feldman heard arguments from both sides. In a quickly written but lengthy opinion issued that same day, Feldman ruled against holding an evidentiary hearing and refused to halt the execution. "Mr. James had the gun," Feldman said.

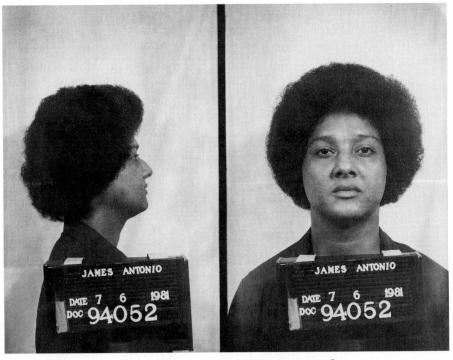

Antonio James as he came to death row. (Copyright: Louisiana State Penitentiary.)

"That is an unshakable fact. It has been an unshakable fact for the better part of 17 years."

Running against the clock and out of any real hope of having a court intervene, the "James gang" took their case to the pardon board for the second time. The hearing was held inside Angola's Training Academy conference room. Family members, friends, and supporters for James filled his section. Attorneys Denise LeBoeuf and Michael Fawer presented James's case a second time to pardon board members Larry Clark, John Grasso, Lynise Kennedy, Nettie Millican, and Chairman Cynthia Fayard. The board was not required to give James another hearing and reluctantly agreed to do so only after LeBoeuf promised not to rehash the extensive testimony presented at the first hearing. LeBoeuf said she would confine her presentation to evidence and witnesses not yet heard by the board.

Jack Peebles, a New Orleans assistant district attorney specializing in death penalty cases, and prosecutor Karen Arena represented the state. It was Arena's first capital clemency hearing. Fayard opened the hearing by commenting on the "intimidating effect" of the heavy media presence. She counted 10 videocams. Among them were crews from ABC's *PrimeTime Live,* the Discovery Channel, and several area TV stations. At one point LeBoeuf had to request that the mound of microphones on her table be moved back so she, James, and Fawer could have room to operate.

Fawer, a criminal defense attorney for 30 years, opened James's presentation. He focused on the procedural problems James faced after so many years of litigating and argued factual innocence—that affidavits and newly presented evidence cast serious doubt about who was the actual killer in both the Adams and Silver murders. "Levon Price admitted [he killed Silver] to six people between 1979 and 1995," Fawer said. "Each of those people has testified under oath in court without contradiction that Levon Price told them that. None of the 12 jurors who sat in that courtroom heard that testimony."

"What we want you to explain to us," Fayard asked Fawer, "is, because he is a participant in this crime, although he may not be the trigger man, would he still be eligible for the death penalty?"

"He would not be," answered Fawer. "Not death eligible. The law requires that you must have specific intent to receive the death penalty. And there's no evidence of specific intent to murder in this case." Peebles adamantly disagreed. "The defense is pointedly wrong to say if he wasn't the trigger man he didn't have the intent to kill. . . . If two people get together and have specific intent to rob a filling station, and eliminate the person at the filling station as a witness, it makes no difference who actually pulls the trigger. This is what the law says."

Peebles was right. Louisiana law provides that an active accomplice to capital murder is as guilty as the one who actually kills. Both defendants can be executed for the same murder. But if James was just a principal and Price was the shooter, then something is seriously wrong when the principal is executed and the killer walks free.

Board member Larry Clark raised the possibility of James being released in the future should the board reduce his death sentence to life imprisonment. "Mr. Clark, we won't be back," said LeBoeuf. "If we get a recommendation from you and you reduce the death sentence to life, we will not come back."

"We will put that in writing," added Fawer. "We will sign it. Antonio James, who is my client as well as my friend, will sign that. He's here saying 'I want to live.' And he understands that he deserves to be in prison."

The board did not seem impressed. LeBoeuf then took over the presentation and put on Phil Johnson, James's trial lawyer. Now a practicing attorney in California, Johnson explained he was the appointed lawyer for both of James's first-degree murder trials; first representing him in the

Adams murder, where the jury came back with a life sentence instead of death, then in the Silver murder. He admitted he did not put much effort in the second trial, figuring the outcome would be the same as the first—a life sentence. "I didn't know anything about how you put together a penalty phase," he admitted. "I had not done my homework."

LeBoeuf named several other people present who could testify Price told them he did the killing, not James. But, sensitive to the board's limits of tolerance, and realizing Fawer had used a significant amount of time in his dramatic oral argument, she decided to call only one more witness, Jean Thibodeaux, one of the jurors who sentenced James to death in 1982.

"If we had known more about the possibility of other witnesses, that's one thing that I think would have made a difference," said Thibodeaux. She adamantly stated she would not have voted for death had she known then what she knew now. Thibodeaux also admitted that over the past 15 years she had changed her view on capital punishment. "I still think I'm a real dedicated citizen who wants to support the legal system. . . . [But] I just don't know what makes us think we have the right to tie a man down and pump poison in his veins until he's dead."

Peebles opened the state's presentation by asking the board to consider that all the issues raised by James's attorneys were also presented to several courts and denied. He pointed to a colorful, well-designed chart next to his table that outlined the legal odyssey James had been through since his arrest in 1979. The chart depicted how James's case had gone through five different courts, 31 different reviews of various issues, 13 stays of executions, three evidentiary hearings, and two pardon hearings.

"Mr. James is willing to say whatever is necessary for him to say to get as little a sentence as he can," said Peebles. "I remind you he was convicted of the Hooten robbery, convicted of the first-degree murder of Alvin Adams. Then he was convicted of the Silver murder by a jury that, in the sentencing phase, decided death as the appropriate punishment." Peebles stressed that the witnesses who claimed Price and Taylor admitted being the shooters were all convicts or ex-convicts and could not be believed. Ironically, Peebles had no problem believing Price and Taylor, career criminals with lengthy police records.

"James's future is not in your hands. It was in the hands of the jury," continued Peebles. "Why should you inject yourselves into this situation when it has been fairly presented and decided upon? I'm here to tell you a different approach that you should consider. That is, the courts did their job. Once you are satisfied with that I don't think you will disrupt the judicial process by arbitrarily inserting an executive stoppage of what is a legitimate and legal procedure."

Peebles's strongly worded statement, that it was not the board's job to "interfere" once a case has been decided by the judicial system, is in direct conflict with the historical essence of the clemency process, adopted by this country from English common law. The reason for clemency is simple, reiterated by Rehnquist in the *Herrera* decision: "It is an unalterable fact that our judicial system, like the human beings who administer it, is fallible." Rehnquist went on to quote from the Blackstone *Commentaries,* a leading judicial authority. "[O]ne of the great advantages of monarchy, in general, above any other form of government; that there is a magistrate, who has it in his power to extend mercy, whenever he thinks it is deserved; holding a court of equity in his own breast; to soften the rigor of the general law, in such criminal cases as merit an exemption from punishment."

"Mr. James has changed. Isn't that great?" an emotional Betty Silver-LaCosta, niece of the murder victim, told the board. "But my uncle did not change. He's still rotting in his grave. He's been there for 16 years. We are not looking for revenge. We keep saying we want justice, so we can then say, Uncle Henry, rest in peace."

Alvin Adams, Jr., is the son of the dry cleaning shop owner who was killed. Although James received a life sentence for that crime, not death, Adams has continually been a vocal proponent for James's execution. He told the board at the first hearing that if the state could not afford the execution, he would write a check on the spot to cover the cost. When James received a stay four hours before last year's death date, Adams was bitter: "I want to see him dead," he told reporters inside the prison where he was on hand to witness the death. He promised to attend the 14th. "If they hold it in hell, I'll be there!"

With the passing of a year, Adams's demeanor changed. He spoke softly and briefly to members of the board. A thirst for revenge did not ring in his words. Perhaps the visit between Adams and James a week earlier helped him come to terms with the death of his father 17 years ago. At that visit James and Adams talked openly. But if facing James man to man was a healing balm to his soul, it did not change his mind about the execution. "I will not get any pleasure out of his death," Adams told the *Baton Rouge Advocate* the day before the hearing, "but it's time for Mr. James to ante up and face the music." At the hearing he told the board, "I am sorry for Mr. James' family, because I loved my father and I know his family loves him. But enough is enough." With that, the board went into a private session to arrive at their decision.

Twenty minutes later the board returned, and the vote was cast: 3-2 in favor of execution. Members voted the same way they had in 1995. Fayard, Grasso, and Clark voted to deny his request for a life sentence; Kennedy

Antonio James at his final pardon board hearing in 1996. (Copyright: Wilbert Rideau, The Angolite.)

and Millican voted to recommend it. The split vote went down the racial divide of board members. Fayard, Grasso and Clark are white; Kennedy and Millican are black.

"It has been 15 years, and we are sorry for that," Fayard told James. "We are sorry for what everyone has had to live through. . . . We have no sympathy for what you did, yet our hearts are filled with sympathy for you."

Fayard concluded the hearing. Security officers quickly surrounded James and took him out of the room and to the death house 100 yards away. His family and friends appeared shaken. Relatives of the victims, seated on the other side of the room, seemed relieved.

Earlier, while the hearing was underway, Governor Mike Foster was asked at a news conference about the James's case. Foster said that from what he had read about the case he felt no need to interfere, adding, "I would hate to be thinking about where I'd be going if I were him."

Louisiana's clemency system refused to stretch out the safety net to James. Since reinstatement of capital punishment in 1976, only two condemned prisoners have benefited through clemency action. One was Catherine "Kitty" Dodds, sentenced to death for arranging the murder of her husband, an ex-cop who allegedly abused her. After Dodds's death sentence was ordered commuted to life by the U.S. Supreme Court in 1977, her life sentence was later commuted to 30 years by Governor Edwin Edwards in 1986. Ronald Monroe had his death sentence commuted in 1989, after new evidence suggested the murder victim's common-law husband committed the 1978 crime. Then-governor Buddy Roemer felt the question of innocence in the case was enough to approve the pardon board recommendation of life in prison: "If there is any doubt in America, a man ought not be executed," Roemer said. "If there is any doubt, I cannot make a mistake on the side of execution."

The factual-innocence issue Fawer argued was not the heart of this case. It was the miscarriage of justice in the disparity between the punishment James suffered and what his codefendants had received. While there was real doubt as to who pulled the trigger on Silver and Adams, there has never been any doubt that all three men participated in the crimes. Justice is balanced when there is equity in sentencing. Antonio James was executed, and Edgar Taylor and Levon Price returned to the streets, perhaps to continue their criminal careers after the lucky break the legal system had given them. Was it equitable? Was it fair? Peebles thought so. The pardon board thought so. Governor Foster apparently thought so, too. So much for the "fail-safe" clemency process envisioned by the U.S. Supreme Court.

James spent his last day with 20 family members, including his son and two-year-old grandchild. They were required to leave James's side at 6:00 in the evening. Prison chaplain Father Joel Labauve and spiritual advisor Vangie Roberts stayed with him until the end. When it came, he was escorted to the death chamber flanked by security officers. Roberts walked beside him, her hand on his shoulder. James had no last statement to make, but, according to Warden Burl Cain, he talked freely with the medical team while they were inserting the intravenous tubes.

"We just took our time," Cain told reporters afterward. "We didn't want any mistakes." It took longer than usual, apparently because of the damage James's past drug use had done to his veins. He was strapped to the gurney for 15 minutes before medics found veins that would accept the poison.

James's last words, according to Cain, were to him. "Bless you," he said. Cain, who had befriended him during the last scheduled execution in 1995, held James's hand while he gave the signal for the poison to flow. He told James, "He's waiting for you, and hold on for the ride." Antonio Gonzales James was pronounced dead at 12:27 AM on March 1.

◆ FIRST, A FRIEND

Nicholas Trenticosta was Antonio James's lead attorney. When they met in 1984, he knew little law. He was simply a pen pal who visited James regularly. At the end of one visit, Trenticosta drove to LSU and signed up for law classes.

"Getting to know Tony and finding out more about his case," he explained, "I became angry. I didn't want him to be executed and I didn't know what else to do, so I became a lawyer."

Trenticosta graduated from law school in 1987 and then took over James's appeal. He has since been the lead attorney in several reversals and resentencing of death penalty cases and is one of the state's top death penalty attorneys. With James, Trenticosta not only lost a client to the executioner, but a friend who had changed his life forever.

◆ INTERVIEW WITH ANTONIO JAMES

His life coming quickly to an end, James requested an interview with *The Angolite.* It occurred two days before his execution—prisoner to prisoner, down to earth, and frank. James, accompanied by his close friend and spiritual advisor, Vangie Roberts, was in high spirits, until news that a federal court had denied him relief. His mood changed; he grew pensive. The following is excerpted from that interview.

> *How have you handled 12 years on death row, in a small cell 23 hours a day waiting to die?*

> I think I would be going through a tremendous amount of pressure had I not learned how to read and write. I quit school in the fifth grade. Reading has had a tremendous impact on my life, especially when I started using the dictionary, learning how to spell certain words. . . . Now I think a whole lot better than I used to. I can sit down and make certain decisions, not just fall into certain circumstances without thinking about it.

What was your childhood like?

My father worked on ships. Traveled around the world. He used to come home and drink a lot. He used to grab my mom and slap her. And I used to stand there and watch her cry like a baby. I used to try to run in between them and break them up. I was about eight, nine, ten years old trying to protect my mother. And when I did that, he would whip me. I mean just constantly whip me. He wouldn't stop. He would throw me out of the house. I was about nine, ten years old when he first put me out. I was sleeping in empty houses and old cars. I had to steal out of grocery stores and stuff like that. I had to go to those places that sell clothes, Goodwill stores, and steal clothes. I think that I suffered from a sense of some fear and rejection.

How does your dad feel about it all today?

He's doing the same thing he's always done, blaming somebody else. Blaming my mother and my brothers and sisters, that if it wouldn't have been for them I wouldn't be here right now. He remembers things that he did, but doesn't want to face them. I saw him last Sunday, and I could see the pain and suffering inside him. I told him: "Sooner or later you are going to have to try to live with it. You can continue to let it destroy you, or you can try to free yourself from it. Just let the truth be known. Just tell me why you did it?" Then I told him I loved him and forgave him.

You said you literally raised yourself on the streets. Did you have any friends, anyone like a teacher who took an interest in you?

No, nobody. I couldn't even turn to my sisters or brothers because they was afraid of my father. And I can never say that I had a good friend because they was all older than me and out there living the life of crime.

Have you ever had love in your life?

Not that I can recall. My momma.

Romantic love?

I don't think I ever really experienced what that really means. As far as having sex with a woman, yeah, but I ain't never experienced romantic love. Most of the girls I dealt with were young or old prostitutes in the French Quarter.

What about the crime, and your two codefendants?

Sometime I look at it like I was some dumb clown when I came forward and told these people about the murders. I knew I didn't have to do that because I let six months pass by. I mean, nobody ever got caught for the crimes. As far as I was concerned, no one was going to be arrested for it. [Price and Taylor] were both on the street and I was already in jail. I didn't have to do it. I mean, it would have been crazy for me to come forward and tell these people about two murders if I done it. I had enough common sense to know that.

But I think I had a conscience and that conscience was taking over, and I was having nightmares. The nightmares only got worse until I decided to confess that I was involved in two murders. That's when things started changing inside of me. But then in the process it got worse, too. I went to trial and got convicted and wound up getting the death penalty.

[James and Roberts find out the court turned him down.]

Your life is now in the hands of the clemency system. That's all you have left. Does that inspire hope or not?

I'm not concerned what someone is going to decide. I don't want to drain myself concentrating on that. Whatever happens is going to happen. I can only change my ideas and my conceptions. I can't change anyone else's no matter what I say. . . . Going through this same procedure over and over, and nothing positive has happened. It's like a scratched record. The truth is I wish I could just disappear right now.

You have the pardon board hearing tomorrow. You went through it once before, and they denied you. Do you expect anything more this time?

What can I possibly give to them? What can I possibly do that would change their minds? I just sense a spirit when I look at the pardon board members, that no matter what happens or what I say, they are going to ignore it. I can see their minds are made up. I don't think they're fully in control of their jobs. I think there's more behind it. And I can't control that. But God can, and I don't know if it's His will to do so.

Let's say you do get a life sentence through the clemency process. How would you spend the rest of your life in prison?

I think I would spend my life in a way that would be beneficial to me, and whatever effect that would take on, I don't know. I would try to use my experience in my life as an example for young kids. I think I can reach some kids, or even some grown ups who are still out there running wild. They might look at what I'm saying. They don't have to listen to me, or what I did, or what happened to me, but listen at the facts, the value of it.

Did you ever believe you would be executed?

No, never. Even though death to me is a frightening thing, especially when you are healthy and fully conscious and aware you have to die. How can you begin to prepare yourself mentally to accept to die? I think you need more to go on. So deep down inside me there is something that has always kept me alive and constantly tells me that somehow there's going be something that is going to keep me alive.

Is there a point of acceptance you must come to?

Acceptance in God. When you are fully committed and dedicated to God, then you know whatever is going to happen, God is going to provide.

Society wants you dead, for whatever purpose it sees your execution will serve. Is there anything you want to tell society?

If we continue to let the worst thing happen and continue to ignore and find excuses and reasons not to deal with fairness and honesty, then this system is going to be very much explosive, and it's going to destroy itself. That's what they are doing now, destroying each other. I'm glad in a sense I learned that. Even if it takes my life, it don't really matter. I lived long enough to understand, and to know what I'm dealing with and to know how I got caught up.

How would you like to be remembered?

As a person who has struggled hard with the experience I had on death row and the change that took on in my life, and to know that I experienced love and compassion and forgiveness from a friend (looks at Roberts), something I never thought I would have experienced, that people would care about me. That's why I don't feel all that bad, all stressed out. I mean, I don't have no type of fear, no anger or worry inside me. Whatever my destiny is, I can deal with it. My main concern is what is on the other side; what I look forward to. Whatever happens Thursday night at 12:01, or 20 years from now, that's not my main concern. My goal is what's on the other side. I have to believe it's better than this.

18

Tragedy

LANE NELSON

All things are connected
Like the blood
That unites us.
We did not weave
The web of life;
We are merely
A strand of it.
Whatever we do to the web
We do to ourselves.

Chief Seattle (1784–1866)

From *The Angolite,* March/April 1997, Angola, La: Louisiana State Penitentiary.

John Brown, 35, died by lethal injection on April 24, 1997, becoming the 24th person executed in Louisiana since capital punishment was reinstated in 1976. Brown was never lucky in life. His story is a tragedy, filled with out-of-control situations, love and sadness, victimization, and death.

The child was born in New Orleans on September 15, 1961. His proud mother cradled her new bundle of life as he squeaked and smiled and cried. When he opened his innocent, inquisitive eyes to the world he was brought into, he looked at a future with unlimited possibilities. The parents named their son John Ashley Brown, Jr.

According to his lawyers, Judy Martinez and Denise Puente, Johnny was three when his mother and father divorced after a physically and emotionally violent marriage. John Brown, Sr., moved to Florida and never saw his family again. The boy didn't want it that way, but that's the way it was—and his possibilities in life shrank.

Without support from her husband, Catherine Brown moved her family (Johnny, his 11-month older sister, Melissa, and his baby sister, Angel) to the poverty-stricken Florida Housing Project in New Orleans. A few years later Johnny entered kindergarten and continued through the elementary grades with enthusiasm. He was not the brightest child in class, and he did not wear the best clothes, but he may have been the most fun-loving, according to those who knew him.

Catherine worked hard to support her three children and, like many single-parent mothers, barely survived from paycheck to paycheck. But the Brown family didn't cringe at being poor. "We didn't have much money, but we had lots of love," John Brown told *The Angolite*. "My mom always told us that regardless of how little we had, we were supposed to share it between me and my sisters."

Catherine eventually moved her family into a modest two-bedroom shotgun house in Arabi, Louisiana, a less crime-ridden neighborhood not far from the Florida Projects. It was a happy time for the Brown family, a time of moving forward—a time that would not last. Shortly after the move, Catherine was in a near-fatal car accident. She suffered severe physical injuries and brain damage that required ongoing treatment. When it happened, John was at a summer camp for underprivileged children and did not find out about her condition until he returned home weeks later.

Catherine was no longer able to provide the supervision her children needed. Life in the Brown household took a sharp turn for the worse. The children were left to look after themselves. At age 11, it was more than John could handle. He stole his mother's medication and overdosed. His nine-year-old sister, Angel, found him unconscious and called an ambulance.

John was taken to New Orleans Charity Hospital, where he lay in a coma for three days. After the hospital, John stayed out late at night with his older sister, Melissa, to avoid confrontations with his mom. He loved his mom but did not know how to deal with the situation—a situation he had not asked for, nor brought about. His possibilities in life shrank further.

Three days after John's 12th birthday, a close relative lodged a formal complaint with juvenile authorities charging him with being ungovernable. A family court judge sentenced him to a juvenile prison, the Louisiana Training Institute (LTI) in Monroe. This would change his life forever.

More than 20 years later, Herman Acosta, the probation officer who drove Brown to LTI, remembered him as the youngest child he had ever transported to a juvenile prison. The case was more a matter of child neglect resulting from Catherine Brown's injuries than incorrigibility on Brown's part, Acosta testified at a 1993 post-conviction court hearing. Initially, he and other officials recommended that Brown be placed at "Hope Haven," a boys' home. But the treatment center was full, so the recommendations were changed to suggest a correctional setting. The judge agreed, and Brown, barely tall enough to look over the admitting desk at the juvenile prison, soon found himself among older, seasoned delinquents.

He had broken no law yet was confined to a criminal environment for being a "status offender," a juvenile whose sins consist of patterns of truancy, running away, disobeying parents, or alcohol consumption.

"The things I learned, like burglary, stealing cars, I learned when I was 12 in Monroe," Brown said. "Before I went to Monroe, I was a good kid going to school. I didn't know about stealing and drugs and all that stuff." His stay at LTI lasted eight months. Once he was released, school became the farthest thing from his mind. Instead, he wanted to try out the new things he'd learned from the older kids in prison. He stole a car and burglarized a house. He also started using drugs with his older sister, Melissa, and her friends. Twelve-year-old John Brown, Jr., a child born with unlimited possibilities, had switched tracks.

From the time he was 12 until the age of 17, he spent 26 months incarcerated in juvenile prisons. Every time he went in, he came out a little worse. "I was put into a different environment, a different element, and I had to adjust to where I was at," said Brown.

"It happened to me the same way," long-time Angola prisoner Jerry Head told *The Angolite*. "A judge sent me to LTI in 1964 for truancy when I was 11. It changed my life. I was a straight-A student in school before I was locked up, basically a bright kid. I didn't know anything about crime or drugs. But LTI taught me, just like it taught John. I'm a product of the system, and so was John." Head grew up in the same neighborhood as

Brown—the Ninth Ward—but was 10 years older. Now 44, he is a sixth offender serving 495 years for armed robbery. His crimes have been the same throughout his life: drugstore stickups.

Head explained what it was like to go to a juvenile prison at the age of 11. "I was scared, just like every kid is scared that first time," he said. "It's a whole new world. They take you out of a stable home—even though it's a one-parent home, it's stable—and they throw you into the system because you're poor and white, or poor and black. The juvenile judge looked at me like poor white trash standing in front him, and he tossed me to the system."

According to Head, imprisoning status offenders at the age he and Brown were creates a destructive cycle. "The cycle gets worse and worse, and you just get caught up in it. Most kids are impressionable at that age anyway, and you are around older kids who have been in the system and have taken on criminal ways. That's your environment, and you have to adapt to it. From there on it just changes your whole way of thinking. The system will eat you alive, and I'm sure it's worse today, with all the youngsters I've talked to who started off by going to reform school for minor offenses and are now in Angola."

He believes without a doubt that had the judge taken another option with him when he was 11, his life would have turned out differently. "I dreamed of what most kids dream of becoming, a lawyer, a doctor," he said. "Most kids at that age are doing good. When they get caught up in that system, they are actually doing good in school. And the situation they set you in—reform school—is not a mom and pop situation. But that's the state, that's the way it operates."

Once a kid is released from prison, he is marked for life, said Head. "Everyone knows where you just come from, which makes it so much harder. Your teachers, your friends, they look at you in a different light. You're the bad kid. You're the loser. And your life ain't even started yet." Head spent most of his teen years incarcerated. "Except for a few months here and a few months there, I was locked up all my teenage life."

It came too late for Head and Brown, but a 1977 report by the American Bar Association's National Juvenile Justice Standards Project called for an end to committing status offenders to juvenile prisons: "Juvenile acts of misbehavior," the report stated, "ungovernability or unruliness which do not violate the criminal law, should not constitute a ground for asserting juvenile court jurisdiction over the juvenile by committing them."

Studies have shown status offenders to be extremely impressionable, and when confined with hardened delinquents they become delinquent. Congress has responded by creating the federal Office of Juvenile Justice and Delinquency Prevention (OJJDP), which for the past 15 years has encouraged states to separate status offenders from criminal delinquents. There has been a concerted effort by juvenile justice systems to comply, but in most states (including Louisiana), status offenders are still subject to juvenile prison.

By the time John Brown was 17, he was knee-deep into drugs. He committed nonviolent acts to support addiction and was prosecuted as an adult for burglary and sentenced to jail. Released at the age of 19, he was arrested for another burglary three months later. This time he received two years at a state prison. There, for the first time, he met one of the street characters from his old neighborhood, Jerry Head, who now carried a hefty prison rep.

"I knew John's sister, Missy [Melissa], but didn't meet John until our time at Hunt Correctional Center (an adult prison near Baton Rouge)," said Head. "I was doing a 10-year sentence for a drugstore robbery. Johnny was doing a short sentence, a couple years, something like that. He was a nice kid, a real likable person. Just a young guy out of the neighborhood. He played on the prison football and baseball teams, and I think he got his GED." In fact, Brown was trying to pull his life together.

Then tragedy struck. Melissa went to Southern California. She was a beautiful, streetwise young woman and no one worried about her venturing to the Golden State alone. One day Brown was summoned to the prison chapel and told his sister had been murdered in Los Angeles. "It really messed Johnny up," said Head.

Shortly after Melissa's death, Brown discharged his prison sentence. He found employment as a maintenance worker at an apartment complex, his first job ever. He wanted a normal, law-abiding life, but struggled with the rage he held inside over the murder of his sister. Eventually, he turned back to drugs, heroin and cocaine. Nine months later he lost his job, and his drug use accelerated, which in turn prompted more daring actions to secure money for his drugs. He switched tracks again, from nonviolent to violent criminal.

In August 1984, armed with a pistol, Brown robbed four people on the Lakefront in New Orleans, shooting a man. "It looked like he was reaching behind his back for a gun. I panicked and shot him," Brown told *The Angolite.* The man lived. Brown got away.

Two weeks later, on a drug binge that involved cocaine, heroin, and Valium, he and a girlfriend, Anna Hardeman—the mother of his now-14-year-old son—spent the day drinking and drugging. Into the night they ran out of money and, according to the court briefs prepared by his lawyers, wanted more drugs, so they drove to the French Quarter to rob someone. That someone was Omer Laughlin, accompanied by his wife, Patricia.

Just before midnight, the Laughlins walked out of a restaurant toward their car parked a block away. Hardeman drove ahead of the unsuspecting couple, and Brown jumped from the passenger's side brandishing a knife. He pinned Laughlin to a nearby car and demanded his money. Laughlin resisted, Brown later explained, and he panicked. Patricia Laughlin turned and ran back to the restaurant, frightened and screaming. When she returned with others, she found her husband lying in the parking lot bleeding. Omer "Remo" Laughlin, an aerospace technician with a Ph.D. in engineering, a family man who had never committed a crime in his life, was dying from 13 stab wounds.

Patricia Laughlin gave a description of Brown and the car to New Orleans police on the scene and told them a woman with long dark hair had been driving. That description went over the police radio, and almost immediately a patrol car spotted what looked like the suspects entering a gas station. Police parked out of sight and observed Brown get out and wash himself with a hose on the side of the station while Hardeman filled the car with gas. When Brown walked back to the car, police arrested him. They noticed scrapes and bruises on Brown's forearms, indicating a struggle between him and Laughlin.

Brown was prosecuted on four counts of armed robbery and one count of attempted murder for the Lakefront crime. He received a 298-year sentence, which, with time off for good behavior, meant a discharge from prison in 2133. Then he went on trial for the first-degree murder of Omer Laughlin. It lasted all of 10 hours—from picking a jury to the guilty verdict to the jury's sentence of death. The 23-year-old Brown was shipped to Louisiana's death row in October 1985, where he would linger in a six-by-nine-foot cell for the next 12 years. For her part in the crime, Hardeman pleaded guilty to being an accessory to murder and received a five-year prison term.

In 1988 civil litigators Judy Martinez and Denise Puente were pulled into John Brown's life when the Louisiana Supreme Court appointed the prominent New Orleans law firm of Simon, Peragine, Smith, and Redfearn to handle Brown's appeals pro bono. The two lawyers had never handled a criminal case. For the first time in their lives they came face to face with a man sentenced to die. Determined from the start to afford Brown the best representation possible, they began by digging up as many personal history documents as they could find. Soon the pieces of John Ashley Brown's tragic life fell together, and with it came a close friendship with their client.

Martinez and Puente were puzzled. How could a jury sentence a man to death without knowing his life story? Surely, they thought, had the jury known about John Brown's childhood and heavy addiction to drugs, they

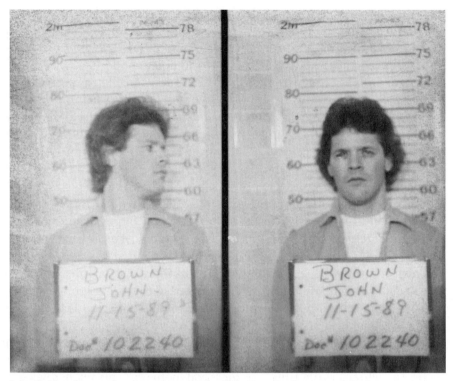

John Ashley Brown, Jr., as a young man arriving on death row at Angola. (Copyright: Louisiana State Penitentiary.)

would not have voted for the death penalty. They were confident that, presented with this information, a judge would reverse the sentence. The two efficient, hard-working attorneys believed in the system.

Years passed with nothing but frustrating denials in state courts. "I can't believe we've had to go this far with your case," Martinez told Brown after state court appeals were exhausted. They turned to federal courts for relief. It was bad timing. While Brown's case was at the first level of the federal court system in April 1996, President Bill Clinton signed into law the Effective Death Penalty Act (EDPA), designed to shorten the time between conviction and execution. It set stringent time limits on habeas petitions for state prisoners in federal court and limited the scope of review on those cases. Puente and Martinez figured the new law would not apply to Brown's case, since the case was already in federal court when EDPA was enacted. They figured wrong.

Once EDPA became law, the case sped up. A federal district court judge denied Brown a full review, and a three-judge panel in the appeals court refused to look at the case. With that denial came Brown's third execution date. The prior two dates were not considered critical because he had not fully litigated all his appeal issues. But with the new procedural rules of EDPA, those issues were now considered finalized. This third date was serious.

Meanwhile, the U.S. Supreme Court accepted a Wisconsin case, *Lindh v. Murphy,* that challenged the retroactive application of the EDPA, exactly the issue Brown now had. He and his lawyers breathed relief, believing a stay would come automatically until the high court resolved the retroactivity question. Seven days before the scheduled execution, his lawyers filed in the Supreme Court. "It's cutting it short," Brown told his girlfriend, Marilyn Baroni, a legal secretary.

Because of the impending execution, the pardon board set a hearing three days before the death date. John Brown, like two before him, Thomas Ward (executed May 16, 1995) and Antonio James (executed March 1, 1996), did not want the hearing. He saw the clemency process as "a bad joke. I don't see any sense in it," he said. "They aren't going to do anything for me or anyone else who has the death penalty." But, like Ward and James, Brown felt an obligation to the lawyers representing him, so he conceded to their wishes and to those of his family and friends. "What it is, is a chance for your family to speak and let them feel they're doing something for you," he explained to *The Angolite.* "I don't want to deny them that opportunity."

Brown's was the first death penalty case heard by Governor Mike Foster's newly appointed pardon board. Only four of the five members were present: Chairperson Sally McKissack, Julia Sims, Larry Clark, and the Reverend Paul Blange. Another board member, the Reverend C. J. Bell, was absent because of family health problems, said Blange.

Brown sat at a table with Martinez, Puente, and veteran appellate attorney Denise LeBoeuf. They had prepared a full packet of information for each board member that included a detailed outline of the hardships of Brown's life. About 10 people showed up, including his sister Angel, to show their moral support.

Martinez began the presentation:

Mr. Brown fully admits his part in this terrible crime, and for not one moment has he sought to blame anyone else. One day John Brown is going to face someone greater than all of us, and he is going to have to answer for that crime. But right now, you are the only four people who have ever been fully armed with enough knowledge of what made John be here today.

People in general, especially children, are defined by their environment, the way they are treated, the way they treat others, and the value they place on human life. John Brown grew up in a constant cycle of violence, in poverty, heavy drug use, in an environment that said people's lives didn't mean very much. It was an environment about as bad as it can be. Some people rise above that kind of environment and are able to break the cycle of violence and drugs, merely by their own sense of will and strength. Our client didn't, and in 1984 he responded about as badly as possible.

But since then, the story has been different. The death of Mr. Laughlin cannot change, but John Brown did. That doesn't lessen the need one bit for exacting and concluding justice, but it does show that in John's case the cycle of violence and despair has been broken. And you need to consider this morning whether the ultimate violence, the violence of execution carried out by our state, should now be imposed on this man. You need to consider whether John's 14-year-old son should be shown that his father's life is so worthless or such a threat to society that it needs to be discarded.

Martinez concluded by reminding the pardon board that the U.S. Supreme Court, in the 1993 case of Texas death row prisoner Leonel Herrera, pointed to gubernatorial clemency as a safety net, a "fail-safe" for cases like John Brown's. The mitigating circumstances of (1) a dysfunctional childhood and (2) a desperation to get more drugs as a motive rather than a plan to kill were not fully explained to the sentencing jury, she said.

Puente reiterated much of what Martinez said. She also spoke of a drug-free John Brown since his imprisonment, a changed man from the person who committed the crime over 13 years ago. She told of his love and protective attitude toward his mom, and his grief when she died five years ago, and about the love he held for his son.

Board member Blange asked Brown why he had become involved in crime and had continued in it for so long. "It was an easy way to get money," Brown said. "I used the money to get drugs." Brown then was asked why he deserved clemency: "I would like to ask y'all to spare my life so I can go on and help raise my little boy," he said in a soft voice, adding, "I'd like to say I regret what happened."

With that, Blange asked what Brown felt was an appropriate punishment for someone who commits murder and armed robbery. "I feel that a life sentence would be just," said Brown. "Once you take someone's life, you can't ever change that. Even though I made that mistake, and maybe I'm more personally involved with it, I realize that even though you regret it you can't take it back."

Assistant district attorney Val Solino opened the state's presentation by reminding the board that the case was more than 12 years old. "Every judge that has reviewed the claims in this case has utterly and categorically rejected every one of them," said Solino, who also claimed the jury did hear of Brown's hard life. "Mr. Brown's mother clearly testified to the sentencing jury. . . . His sister, Angel Brown, also testified very clearly to the sentencing jury that she and her brother started taking drugs at an early age." Solino failed to mention that Catherine Brown's testimony wandered and strayed. She interrupted herself several times. All attributable to an inability to concentrate resulting from brain damage, legal investigator Marie Campbell told *The Angolite*. And Angel, heavily addicted to drugs, appeared stoned while on the stand. What the jury heard from Brown's mother and sister was ineffective at best.

"This jury had competent and clear evidence of what Mr. Brown's chemical dependency history was. They were not an uninformed jury, and no court has concluded that they were," Solino continued. He then described the crime and told the board that John Brown was not intoxicated on drugs or alcohol that night. "His faculties were not impaired. He knew what he was doing. I suggest to you that he wanted to fill up his car with gas, and Mr. Laughlin paid for that with his life."

Laughlin's widow, Patricia, attended the hearing but declined to address the board. Her son, Steve Daffner, took her place. "We've heard about nuns who comforted a man on death row," he said, apparently referring to the movie *Dead Man Walking*. "Nobody called my mother, nobody comforted her. We heard about drug addictions and mental disorders. Murder, that's a mental disorder!"

Daffner spoke about the life of his stepfather. "Mr. Laughlin was a scholar, a gentleman, and educator," he said. "He was a patriot. He was an American and very proud of it. Remo was a person who had long-range goals and did the best of his ability to carry them out. Unfortunately, Mr. Brown cut short some of his obligations.

"One of the simple things Remo Laughlin wanted to do each morning was see the sun come up," continued Daffner. "He cracked his shade a few inches so when the sun rose in the morning he would see it. For $13\frac{1}{2}$ years a murderer has been allowed to see the sun rise from death row. Mr. Laughlin has not been afforded that opportunity."

Daffner's presentation was emotional, articulate, and very effective. He ended it by telling the board that he and his family were not looking forward to the execution. "We are not here today as a call for death," he said. "There will be no celebration when the event of Thursday occurs. It will be a time of mourning for me and my family. We will, however, take some comfort in the knowledge of the closure of this ugly chapter in our lives."

Board members then went into closed session. Fifteen minutes later they returned and announced their decision. "The vote is a unanimous decision to deny this application for clemency," said McKissack, who gave three reasons: serious nature of the offense, law enforcement and/or judicial objection, and insufficient self-improvement. Brown was immediately encircled by security guards and taken from the room in shackles. His sister, friends, and lawyers broke into tears, while the victim's family and prosecutors wore satisfied expressions.

Puente and Martinez were visibly shaken. They came to the hearing believing it was a viable avenue of relief for their client. That belief died in the force of reality. Brown had been right; he had expected nothing.

But the pardon board was not the end of the road. The U.S. Supreme Court had yet to decide whether to intervene and issue a stay.

Meanwhile, another prisoner on death row launched a quixotic attempt to save Brown's life and bring a halt to executions in Louisiana. Robert Tassin, sentenced to die for a drug-related killing, filed a temporary restraining order through the Department of Corrections in-house Administrative Remedy Procedure two and a half days before the scheduled execution. In his challenge, Tassin listed two claims:

1. The state was violating its own first-degree murder statute by intentionally and methodically putting others to death through execution; the connecting underlying aggravating factors were (a) the killing of more than one person and (b) the fact that the state was paying others to carry out the executions—in effect, committing "murder for hire."

2. The state and the Department of Corrections had violated state and federal laws that prohibit the purchase of controlled dangerous substances for the specific purpose to cause death to another human being.

He closed his written argument by pointing out that the first-degree murder statute and controlled dangerous substance statute listed no exceptions to allow anyone or any entity to commit the crimes listed. The prison's legal department refused his complaint the following day.

It was a desperate gesture. Tassin said he planned to take his complaint to state and federal courts. John Brown was moved to the death cell 16 hours before his date with death. Seven hours later the Supreme Court denied his application for a stay. "I don't understand it," said Martinez. "He has the same EDPA retroactivity issue as in the Wisconsin case that was just argued in the U.S. Supreme Court last Monday. Fairness and justice would dictate a stay of execution until the issue is decided."

His legal team worked frantically that afternoon and into the night petitioning state courts for intervention, but without success. Brown spent his last day visiting with friends and family members. At 6 PM his people were escorted out of the prison, leaving behind three spiritual advisors and Denise LeBoeuf. The five sat together and shared his last meal: boiled crawfish, salad, Neapolitan ice cream, apple pie, and a malt.

The clocked ticked. Angola warden Burl Cain periodically dropped by the death cell and tried to ease the tension by joking with Brown, who had always been indifferent toward security officers and prison administrators but showed respect when given respect. He and Cain had developed a brief but amicable relationship, owing primarily to the arrangements Cain made allowing Brown to visit with his son and a steady flow of visitors throughout the week leading up to the execution.

Brown asked Cain to let him know when the poison started flowing. According to the protocol of death, the condemned is strapped to the gurney, and waits in agonized anticipation until the warden, standing behind the gurney, eventually nods to the executioner. Cain agreed to the request.

In his last hour, Brown prayed and talked with his spiritual advisors . . . then the bell tolled. But Brown was not ready to go when they came for him, and it was not until 12:01 AM (about 10 minutes later than protocol requires) that he was escorted under heavy guard into the death chamber. Once inside the stark chamber—where 23 men had died before him—Brown stepped up to the microphone to give his last statement: "Let my baby sister know that I love her and thank the rest of my family for supporting me. I love you very much." Then he looked at LeBoeuf, who was there to witness his death, gave her a wink, blew her a kiss, hopped onto the gurney, and laid down for his flight into eternity. Minutes later, straps holding him tightly in place, he told Cain, "I'm ready to go now." Cain nodded to the executioner and, as agreed, said, "Okay, John, it's starting."

According to witnesses, when the lethal chemicals invaded his body John Brown uttered his final word, "Wow!" He shook violently for a minute, then lay still.

Brown was born healthy and vibrant, with all of life's options open to him. Circumstances diminished those options, drugs wrapped him in chains of desperation, and he was not strong enough to overcome the high hurdles he faced in life. He did not ask for it to be that way. No one wants to grow up to be a drug addict or a criminal. No one wants to die a violent death by execution.

It is a tragedy that Omer "Remo" Laughlin died before his time, bleeding to death in a lonely parking lot. It is a tragedy that John Brown died strapped to a gurney while strangers viewed his death through a plate glass. It is a tragedy that the friends and family of Omer Laughlin and of John Brown suffer the loss of their loved ones. What might have happened had Brown been placed in a treatment program or boys' home when he was 12 instead of a juvenile prison will forever be a mystery. But Omer "Remo" Laughlin would very likely have awakened April 24 to the sun shining on his face through the crack in his window shade, and Brown might have been off fishing with his son.

John Ashley Brown, Jr., was pronounced dead at 12:12 AM, April 24, 1997, at the age of 35—one year to the day after President Clinton signed the EDPA into law. Brown's body was taken out of Angola and cremated, his ashes spread in the New Orleans City Park.

◆ "JUST ME, YA DIG"

John Brown had never been in Angola's general prison population. He came straight to death row in 1985, to a small cell, where he sat for nearly 12 years before his execution. During that time hundreds of men entered Angola with life sentences. Some of their crimes were arguably more heinous than his. Why was he different? Why did he die while others live?

There are at least three reasons. First there was the district attorney who decided to go for the death penalty instead of a plea bargain to a life sentence. Then there was the jury that recommended the death penalty for Brown, while at the same time another jury in another section of the court-house recommended life for a man who had raped and murdered his young victim. Finally, there were the overworked and underpaid public defenders that sailed through Brown's 10-hour trial.

The Angolite asked New Orleans prosecutor Val Solino what made Brown's case deserving of death when almost all other prisoners in the jurisdiction of New Orleans received life for such outrageous crimes as multiple murder and raping and killing children. "The jury heard the evidence; the jury came back with a verdict," said Solino. "I don't have to justify that, and I won't."

"I understand this is for punishment, but I don't think it's right," John Brown told *The Angolite* seven days before his execution. "When I was in the parish [jail] they had guys in there with charges basically like mine, or worse—they were on the tier with me, and they got life sentences. I don't know. I guess by me messing up for so long they wanted to get rid of me. I was a third offender when I got arrested."

John A. Brown, Jr. with Lane Nelson, shortly before Brown was executed in 1997. (Copyright: Wilbert Rideau, The Angolite.)

A relaxed Brown talked candidly about his scheduled execution, and his life. "Life, it ain't never been fair. I'd like to find some [fairness], but I don't see it nowhere," he laughed, then grew serious. "Life has never been fair ever since I was little. My mom got in an accident and all that. My mom and dad got a divorce when I was three, and he took off. Life threw punches at me. I ended up with the responsibility of being the man in the family at a real young age. I had to be "the Man" for my two sisters."

At 13, fresh out of juvenile prison, he stole a car and got caught. Why did he want to steal a car when he was so small he had to use a telephone book to see over the dashboard? "To burglarize a house," he said. "The money wasn't a necessity. It's just I wanted the clothes and other things other kids had. You know, you're going to school and everyone is wearing good clothes and you come in wearing worn-out jeans and torn sweatshirts.

"I can write real good and I wanted to be an architect," he said. "I can write real small and I can draw fine lines." The dream of architectural design evaporated when he dropped out in the ninth grade. "Middle school had girls, but then I got into high school and all the girls disappeared," he said. "It was an all-boys school, and I didn't like that."

Romantic love eluded him during the short flings of freedom between incarceration. "It was whoever I was with at the time," he said. "I had a lot of female friends, and I'd be with one or the other now and then. No romantic long-term relationship. But since I've been here, I've got a good relationship right now."

He refers to Marilyn Baroni, a legal secretary in the law firm that represented him. The two had first met in a reform school when Brown was 16. Baroni was a secretary at the institution. It was friendship then. Twelve years later and working as a legal secretary, Baroni discovered that one of the pro bono cases the law firm had picked up was the death penalty case of John Ashley Brown. She immediately contacted him to see if this was the same energetic youngster she once knew. It was. A correspondence developed between the two and, eventually, love.

"Something like that," referring to his relationship with Baroni, "makes you more aware of other people's feelings," he said. "Relationships, friendships have been richer for me since I've been on death row, because this is the longest I've ever been without drugs. So I have a better focus on things." Since he finally found true love, Brown claimed it changed his thinking, bringing principles and values into his life. But now Louisiana was going to execute him. "It took all this time for me to get it together and now I'm going to be killed," said Brown. "Ain't that a bitch."

"I don't have a problem with *me* handling it," he said. "I *do* have a problem with the pain and hurt it's going to put on my family. They aren't responsible for any of this. But they are the ones who really have to suffer."

Brown said he lies in his cell thinking about execution, what it will be like. "I've read about the process they go through, and I don't like the part where they stop you from breathing," he said. "I'd just as soon skip over that. Really. You're already paralyzed, so what happens is, you're suffocating, and you're trying to get a breath. But the way they do it, they paralyze you so it won't look violent, but inside you're struggling. I think they should just skip over that part and stop the heart. If they're going to do it, let's get to it instead of wasting time on this extra step. I wonder about it. That's going to be a trip."

The hopelessness of his position was clear to Brown; he had no faith in the judicial system. "I know my lawyers did all they could, and I have a peace about that," Brown said. "So whatever happens now, that's on [the system]. I just want to make sure my family is going to be all right. If they are okay, then the state can do whatever it wants after that." He paused, then smiled. "I'm just real. Just me, ya dig?"

19

Sensory Anguish

LES MARTIN

Death Row is not only a challenge
To Life but also to Sanity.
The condemned must defend
Against a perpetual assault
On their emotions and senses
While politicians execute their strategies
With shrewd premeditation.
If any are to survive the homicidal campaign,
It is incumbent upon them to lobby
For the votes of jurors and judges
While coexisting with Fear, Uncertainty, and Dependency.

Life's flavor is decapitated by Isolation's guillotine,
Leaving only the senseless, meaningless body behind.
The metallic twang of rusty water
And the tastelessness of institutional food
Drown Vitality's happiness
In an ocean of bitterness.
Joy is soured by the burning acidity of Sadness
When Dignity and Liberty are strapped to the stake.

Legions of soundwaves bombard the ears,
Drumming away Peace's comfort.
Battalions of giant box fans
Roar their anger incessantly.
Squadrons of steel doors
Bang open and closed uninterrupted.
Phalanxes of television sets boom loudly
Over one another, the fans, the doors.
Prisoners of war scream their frustration over all.
Noise's cacophony torments the brain
And murders Concentration's stability.

The musty odor of sweat and moldy mops
Pervades the tiers
And causes Yearning's want for *anything* pleasant.
A perfumed letter
Or the smell of fresh-mown grass
Intensifies Ache's longing for nature.
Industrial cleaners eradicate the fragrances
That make Life meaningful,

Sterilizing Dream and Hope with antiseptic Death.
In time one craves a scent of Madness,
Which offers relief
From the stench of Suffering and Frustration.

Felt acutely is Retribution's knife,
Which punctures the skin
To extract blood payments
For transgressions—real and imagined.
Harsh Concrete and Steel
Punish the bodies of their caged victims,
Baking them in Summer's ovens,
Freezing them in Winter's ice box,
Bruising them year round in Torture's cubical chamber.

To appease Vengeance,
A Woman's compassionate touch
Is sacrificed to coarse male egos.
Love is asphyxiated by Hate's strangling grip,
Which wrings debt owed
From the Undead souls hanging on the rack.
Pain is a constant presence,
Making Himself felt at every touch.

Loneliness and Depression rise
To watch friends carried away
By surreptitious huntsmen
Trained to slaughter wild beasts.
The butchers glance furtively at those remaining,
Endeavoring to justify their actions
While sneaking around in Shame's company.
Light is extinguished when the electricity dies.
Witnesses move with Stealth and Darkness
To examine the meat left on the block
And leave with food that never sates Appetite:
Loss brings Starvation to all.

Astronomical is the sensory anguish
Experienced on Death's emotional teeter totter.
Oscillating between Hope and Despair,
Who alternately visit

In forms of family, friends, and attorneys,
Until able to stand the roller coaster ride no more,
One is eventually pulled into the black hole of Numbness.
We struggle to escape Gravity's vacillating hold,
But few succeed.

In the end
A meteor shower of lead
Introduces Life to Extinction,
Just when most are on the verge
Of coping with Anxiety's infinity.
Fear, Uncertainty, and Despondency
Have retired from an empty office.

Leslie D. Martin, on death row at Angola in 1999. (Copyright: Wilbert
Rideau, The Angolite.)

A tier of cells on death row at Angola. (Copyright: Wilbert Rideau, The Angolite.)

20

Truce

Lawson Strickland

How admirable, he who thinks not, "Life is fleeting," when he sees the lightening!

Basho

The man in the cell next to me, whom I call "neighbor" to conjure the irony of a more suburban scene, laughs incessantly. Huge deep guffaws, snickers, and whoops punctuated by energetic curses and other self-motivational cheers. He laughs and sucks in shuddering breaths with each pause before another fit.

He laughs to ease the pain of hate for his loneliness, misery, and frustration. No one has spoken a word to him, and I wait with uneasy anticipation to hear a sob, a contraction of the throat, something to give me satisfaction. For the self-pity he grates across my nerves; for months' worth of days' hourly aggravations.

It is only early, the sun still weakly low in the eastern sky. Yet I feel weary and worn and frayed at edges which no sleep may knit. Not with night's restless turning and body uncooled by sweat. Each day I arise a bit more unravelled—the loom a bit more broken. If only hope, my last commodity to barter with despair, may hold the threads together a moment more. If only all doors were open.

I stand to make my bunk, what I wish to be a bed, with plastic mattress under threadbare sheets, supported by sturdy legs. And a concrete floor, four concrete walls, toilet, and table is all for the home where twenty-three hours each day I spend. Home to the conscious dead.

The most prominent object in my cell is a window centered within the back wall. It is all steel and hardness, mesh alienation and welded barred separation; two glass panes to crank open only so far. I bide my time there, yet even now. From morning's rise to evening's sunset.

I long to feel across the skin freeness of breezes fresh with nature's scent, of new-cut grass and honeysuckle and pine. To spy upon warblers and sparrows and jays plucking along rows of razored fence line, oblivious to the kept. The canaries free, loved by the caged cat.

This is sustenance living at its best, each emotion too dangerous to be left unchecked. Living a subtle balance between wishful prayer and wretchedness in despair. Left with only the illusion of nonchalant disinterest to feign, hope the greatest sin.

My neighbor will sleep through the day. He confesses existence here is easier in that way. The nights are shorter and cooler, more forgiving to lose the self within. One dreams less in the light amid the cursing, clanging, endless tortuous twisting of the screeching, blowing, and banging din.

Days such as these are stacked to construct the altar of execution, with years to hone the finer edges of hate. We count them either up or down with a determined resolution, to that once and final date.

I fail to anticipate my day, whether it be near or farther yet, but it lurks some days in close among the shadows or just beyond my horizon's crest. It neither reveals itself as an enemy, nor as a friend offering hints of release. Ever the unknown entity, it waits with patience's peace. That day to surely come promises only with a flickered gleam in the eye, the taking of all before the leaving again. Both the sins and the condemned to die.

Only today there are decisions still to be made, with issues of which I am not privy. My attorney will call for me to be chained and trudged to a phone by security. It is rare for us to speak for any length of time. Each of us tired of questions that cannot or will not be answered. We are left only to amuse each other with superficial banter.

What books have I read? How is my mother? How might be you? He's sad to say there is still no news, though it's been one year, close to two. Or, the court has turned me down, it has been two weeks since. He thinks I'd be interested to know that, while I can only wince.

Maybe things are looking up. There's always the option of a life sentence. In that may I somehow find solace? He swears in my place he would. Does he even think he could pretend at my position? I doubt he truly could.

He is a good man, though. One of conscience, an advocate for all we hold dear. He promises to be up to see me, and I chuckle that I will be here. He regrets that it may be some time, with all the other clients and cases which arise. And in the end all is said, but that which is left between the lines. For me even now, after so many years of this long uncomfortable game, those unspoken words are ever clear, which neither time nor place shall change.

Shadows will move relentlessly, stretching across the cellblock floor. The hands on the clock spin. While I sit and write and read and muse, the day will make room for more, coming to an end. They mean nothing to me now, pages on a paper calendar that yellow and fade away.

I am in my own middle passage, a voyage far from all I've known. Trapped and stuffed in among society's misery, tucked away and set adrift. I'm detached, antagonized, brutalized, morally astray. A stunted soul without room to grow.

I draw within under a siege mentality, ignoring the people around me. Breathing shallowly to avoid the polluted air, mentally sandbagged into my own reality. One which only I may know, that cannot be cut or yanked or beaten out of me physically. I search my memory for ages long gone, times when I laughed, cried, and had the courage to care. I write those scraps and fleeting images in little books I keep hidden, for when the memories are no longer there.

Death does not leap at you from a table or a chair. It begins years in advance, creeping up to steal your humanity, your individuality, your notions of what is right and wrong and fair. When the time does come, as

I've watched those who have gone before, the truth is in the lost light extinguished in the eyes. The blank vacant stare.

How do you meet those eyes again and again and never whisper into the night, *Una salus victus nullam seprare salutem?** When the sound of hard-soled boots marching in step towards death pulls part of yourself with them? How do you overcome the going? When the threat of execution, of retribution, loses its ability to exact a payment and becomes nothing less than mercy? Victim and victimizer alike, closure is issued out to more than one soul on those nights. Burn candles for both.

I'll be in the window watching the night, alone with myself. Cool breezes of freedom pushing their way in to me, carrying hints of softening dew. It is senseless to fight, to yearn, to dream for what will never be true. You either go crazy or sign a truce with destiny and resign. A pact to keep hope in check in return for having nothing to lose.

My neighbor is arising, stirring with the other night prowlers, all who have avoided the face of another day. I pity and love them in a way, understanding the relief they seek to find. But I cannot join them, cannot partake in their aggravations, the fights and pestering they heap upon each other to lesson the sting of their mind.

Lawson Strickland on death row at Angola in 1999. (Copyright: Wilbert Rideau, The Angolite.)

---

*"The one hope of the doomed is not to hope for safety" (Virgil, *The Aeneid*).

I can only turn myself away, turn my bed down, turn myself off and resist the temptation to kneel and pray.

Somewhere, monotonously, the sun is moving, planets turning in kind. Bringing forward toward me again all the things I cannot leave behind.

Over and over and over and . . . day after day after day.

A death row exercise yard at Angola. (Copyright: Burk Foster.)

21

A Killer Year

LANE NELSON

From *The Angolite,* January/February 1998, Angola, La: Louisiana State Penitentiary.

Twenty-five years ago the U.S. Supreme Court ruled the death penalty, as then practiced, unconstitutional. That decision, *Furman v. Georgia,* emptied America's death rows. Four years later the Court approved reformed capital punishment statutes and procedures in Georgia, Florida, and Texas. Other states followed suit, sweeping the cobwebs out of their death rows or building new ones and filling them up. With Gary Gilmore's wish to die in Utah in 1977, executions were back on line.

In the post-*Furman* era of capital punishment, 432 executed human beings later (as of December 31, 1997), America's death penalty remains arbitrary and unfair, according to attorney Steven B. Bright, director of the Southern Center for Human Rights in Atlanta, Georgia. In 1997 Bright released a 22-page report describing seven specific and longstanding areas of abuse with the death penalty: race, poverty, arbitrariness, innocence, mental retardation, mental illness, and children. With each subject, Bright pointed out grave judicial inadequacies that call for an immediate end to capital punishment. The American Bar Association agreed and for the first time publicly announced its support for a moratorium on executions. "Today, administration of the death penalty, far from being fair and consistent, is instead a haphazard maze of unfair practices with no internal consistency."

Texas put to death Mexican national Irineo Tristan Montoya in June 1997 amid a roar of protest from Mexican citizens and officials. His body, driven over the border and into Mexico, was met with cheers and salutes from 300 Mexican citizens who paid tribute to their slain countryman and shouted curses at the United States and Texas. Montoya was executed for the 1986 murder of John Killheffer, who had given Montoya and another hitchhiker a ride just north of the Mexican-American border. Montoya supporters said police refused to inform him of his right to an attorney or his right to contact the Mexican embassy for legal help. He also signed a four-page confession written in English, a language, said a Mexican official, Montoya did not read, write, or speak.

Montoya's execution was one of 74 carried out in 17 states in 1997 (see Table 21.1), the most since 1955, when 76 were put to death. For the 3,316 men and 49 women lingering in death row cells across the country, things probably will not get better anytime soon. "The execution train is still speeding down the track, and it's very hard to stop, or even slow down," Richard Dieter told Associated Press at the end of 1997. Dieter, director of the Death Penalty Information Center in Washington, DC, said the Effective Death Penalty Act (EDPA), signed into law in April 1996 to speed executions, is starting to take effect.

That effect was previewed in Texas last year. On the heels of EDPA, Texas passed its own state law limiting appeals in capital cases. Because

TABLE 21.1

Executions in All States: 1997

Date	Condemned	State	Date	Condemned	State
1/8/97	Paul Ruiz	AR	6/17/97	Eddie Johnson	TX
1/8/97	Earl Von Denton	AR	6/18/97	Ireneo Montoya	TX
1/8/97	Kirt Wainwright	AR	6/25/97	William Woratzeck	AZ
1/10/97	Billy Waldop	AL	7/1/97	Harold McQueen	KY
1/23/97	Randy Greenawalt	AZ	7/2/97	Flint Hunt	MD
1/22/97	Eric Schneider	MO	7/17/97	Roy Smith	VA
2/6/97	Michael Carl George	VA	7/23/97	Joseph O'Dell	VA
2/10/97	Richard Brimage, Jr.	TX	7/29/97	Robert West, Jr.	TX
2/26/97	Coleman Wayne Gray	VA	8/6/97	Ralph Feltrop	MO
3/12/97	John Barfield	TX	8/6/97	Eugene Perry	AR
3/25/97	Pedro Medina	FL	8/13/97	Donald Reese	MO
4/2/97	David Herman	TX	8/19/97	Carleton Pope	VA
4/3/97	David Spence	TX	8/20/97	Andrew Six	MO
4/14/97	Billy Joe Woods	TX	9/9/97	James Davis	TX
4/21/97	Benjamin Boyle	TX	9/17/97	Mario Murphy	VA
4/24/97	John Brown	LA	9/22/97	Jessel Turner	TX
4/26/97	Kenneth Gentry	TX	9/24/97	Samuel McDonald, Jr.	MO
4/29/97	Ernest Baldree	TX	9/25/97	Benjamin Stone	TX
5/2/97	Walter Hill	AL	9/30/97	John Cockrum	TX
5/7/97	Terry Washington	TX	10/1/97	Dwight Adanandus	TX
5/7/97	Scott Carpenter	OK	10/2/97	Ricky Lee Green	TX
5/13/97	Anthony Westley	TX	10/13/97	Gary Lee Davis	CO
5/15/97	Harry Moore	OR	10/22/97	Alan Bannister	MO
5/16/97	Clifton Belyeu	TX	10/28/97	Kenneth Ransom	TX
5/19/97	Richard Drinkard	TX	11/4/97	Aua Lauti	TX

Continued

TABLE 21.1 — (CONTINUED)

Executions in All States: 1997—cont'd

Date	Condemned	State	Date	Condemned	State
5/20/97	Clarence Lackey	TX	11/6/97	Aaron Fuller	TX
5/21/97	Bruce Callins	TX	11/7/97	Earl Matthews, Jr.	SC
5/22/97	Larry White	TX	11/13/97	Dawud Majid Mu'min	VA
5/28/97	Robert Madden	TX	11/19/97	Durly Eddmonds	IL
6/2/97	Patrick Rogers	TX	11/19/97	Walter Stewart	IL
6/3/97	Kenneth Harris	TX	11/19/97	Michael Sharp	TX
6/4/97	Davis Losada	TX	11/20/97	Gary Burris	IN
6/4/97	Dorsie Johnson	TX	11/21/97	Charlie Livingston	TX
6/6/97	Henry Hays	AL	12/2/97	Robert Williams	NE
6/11/97	Earl Behringer	TX	12/9/97	Michael Lockhart	TX
6/12/97	Michael Elkins	SC	12/9/97	Michael Satcher	VA
6/16/97	David Stoker	TX	12/11/97	Thomas Beaver	VA

Source: Tonya McClary, *Death Row U.S.A.*, NAACP Legal Defense and Education Fund, Inc., 1998.

defense lawyers contested the new law, Texas, the leader in executions for years, executed only three people in 1996, two of whom were "volunteers," inmates who abandoned their appeals for the sake of a speedy death. After Texas courts upheld the speedy-execution statute, the state got back into the groove and made up for lost time, executing 37 in 1997.

Seventeen states were responsible for the 74 executions that occurred in 1997 (see Table 21.2), compared with 19 states for the 45 executions of 1996. Of those executed in 1997, all were male. There were 41 whites, 26 blacks, 4 Latinos, 2 Native Americans, and 1 Asian. Their crimes accounted for a total of 95 victims—50 males and 45 females.

Virginia trailed a distant second to Texas in the body count for 1997, with 9 executions versus Texas's 37. One was Joseph O'Dell, who represented himself at trial against charges of rape and murder in 1985. Despite pleas from an array of supporters, including Pope John Paul II, Mother

TABLE 21.2

Execution States: 1997

	No. Executions
Texas	37
Virginia	9
Missouri	6
Arkansas	4
Alabama	3
Arizona	2
Illinois	2
S. Carolina	2
Colorado	1
Florida	1
Indiana	1
Kentucky	1
Louisiana	1
Maryland	1
Nebraska	1
Oklahoma	1
Oregon	1
Total:	74

Source: Death Penalty Information Center, Washington, DC.

Teresa, and the Italian government, Virginia governor George F. Allen refused to intervene, and O'Dell, 54, was executed by lethal injection in July.

After the execution, the victim's sister told news media, "We're all very fragile at this point. It's like the Italians hate us. They in essence have said to my family, 'You are worthless. Helen's life didn't matter.'" Hours before his execution, O'Dell married Lori Uris, a Boston University law student who had worked on his case. In his last statement, he said this was "the happiest day of my life because I got married to my wife." There was no honeymoon.

Arkansas kicked off 1997 with a triple execution, the second there in three years. Two of the men—Arkansas's longest-serving death row inmates—were convicted for the 1977 murder of a town marshal and park ranger. The other man was executed for the murder of a convenience store clerk in 1988. The three were lined up for execution according to their prison number, the lowest going first. Prison officials explained the benefit of mass executions: cheaper for the state, and less emotional trauma for staff.

Kirt Wainwright, the last in line, certainly did not see it that way. According to journalist Christopher Hitchens ("Scenes From An Execution," *Vanity Fair,* January 1998), Wainwright received a last-minute stay by U.S. Supreme Court Justice Clarence Thomas so the Court could decide a legal claim raised by Wainwright's attorneys. While the justices deliberated, Wainwright remained strapped to the lethal injection gurney, with the needle in his arm. An hour later the Court gave Arkansas the green light, and the poison was released into Wainwright's body.

Colorado wiped the dust from its death chamber after a 30-year hiatus. Gary Lee Davis, 53, and his wife were convicted of the 1986 kidnap-rape-murder of a 33-year-old mother of two. Davis's wife received life in prison. "Colorado . . . fired a shot heard around the state that gave fair warning," said the victim's father after the execution. "[I]f you deliberately take a life of one of us, you will pay the penalty, and the penalty is death."

Kentucky unlocked its chamber door to carry out its first execution in 35 years. Harold McQueen, convicted along with his brother-in-law, Keith Burnell, of a robbery and murder, got stuck with a court-appointed trial attorney who received only $1,000 for the defense. Burnell, on the other hand, secured a high-priced attorney for his trial. In July, McQueen was strapped into the electric chair and burned into eternity, while Burnell was out on parole.

In so many words, Florida approved of burning at the stake. Pedro Medina caught fire during his March execution. Witnesses said foot-long flames streaked from Medina's head as the electric chair malfunctioned, and windows had to be opened to rid the chamber of flesh-burning stench. It was the second time in seven years that Florida's 74-year-old electric chair torched a man, having done so to Jesse Tafero in 1990. Like the Tafero incident, the Medina "malfunction" prompted immediate court hearings to decide if death by Florida's electric chair was cruel and unusual punishment. And for the second time, the state supreme court decided, no problem, prison officials could keep "Old Sparky" sparking. Governor

Lawton Chiles praised the court ruling, saying it was "appropriate and well-reasoned." He then assured Floridians that he would set execution dates on two more death row prisoners as soon as possible.

A suggestion by the Supreme Court to switch from the electric chair to lethal injection did not go over well with Florida's Republican-led legislators. "[Lethal injection] appears to be a medical procedure," said Senate majority leader Locke Burt. "A painless death is not punishment," agreed Florida's attorney general, Bob Butterworth. Just days after Medina was fried, Butterworth warned at a press conference, "People who wish to commit murder, they better not do it in the state of Florida because we have a problem with our electric chair."

Because of the legal challenge, Medina was the only person executed by Florida last year, making him the 225th man roasted in Old Sparky since 1923, when it was built by prisoners at the Florida State Prison.

Convicted murderer Terry Washington probably did not fully appreciate his punishment as Texas strapped him to the gurney, stuck a needle in his arm, and killed him. Washington was mentally retarded. The jury who sentenced him to death was not told his IQ was between 58 and 69, giving him the mental capacity of an eight-year-old child. Appeal courts did not think it was important the jury was not told.

Scott Dawn Carpenter was 19 when he walked into a bait shop near Lake Eufaula, Oklahoma, in 1994. He left the store with a full tank of gas, snacks in his pockets, and 56-year-old A. J. Kelly dead in a back room. Carpenter was quickly arrested, tried, convicted, and sentenced to death. He waived his appeals and was executed in May, at the age of 22, becoming the youngest person executed in the post-*Furman* era of capital punishment. "I don't think he understands the difference between life and death," said Carl Kelly, the victim's son. "If he gave any value to life, he wouldn't be so ready to give his up." The *Dallas Morning News* reported Kelly had mixed emotions over the execution.

Louisiana may be on its way to establishing a pattern of killing one person a year. John Ashley Brown, Jr., 35, was executed last April, the third execution in as many years. He killed a man during a street robbery gone bad. In comparison to other homicides, Brown's was actually less heinous than those of hundreds of prisoners now serving life sentences in Angola. The victim fought, and a drugged-out Brown stabbed him. Brown, 22 when the crime happened, had been raised in juvenile prisons since the age of 12.

Brown's post-midnight execution will be the last in Louisiana—not the last execution, but the last at that time. State legislators passed a law in 1997 that requires executions to occur between 6:00 PM and 11:59 PM (providing a six-hour window instead of the previous three-hour window from 12:01 to

3:00 AM). Many, including the bill's author, state senator James David Cain (D-Dry Creek), see the time change as less stressful and easier for prison staff. But Corrections Secretary Richard Stalder told the *Baton Rouge Advocate* that the change was designed more as "an accommodation to the victims' relatives and other witnesses" than staff convenience. The time-change bill also includes allowing two relatives of the murder victim to watch the execution. In the past, prison officials had the discretion to invite relatives of the victims into the witness room. That policy is now law.

Louisiana joined a growing list of states, including Texas, Virginia, and Arizona, that have moved their execution time from the traditional pre-dawn hour. The lawyer representing the condemned man who prompted the time change in Arizona last year does not think it matters much. "About the only difference," he said, "with 5:00 PM is, once the flurry [of appeals] is over, the restaurants are still open." His client was executed.

In 1981 KKK leader Henry Hayes and another white man kidnapped Michael Donald, 19, whom they beat, stabbed, and strung up to a tree. Hayes paid for his crime last year, becoming the first white in Alabama executed for killing a black since 1913. According to the NAACP, only 5 of the 432 executions since 1977 have been for white-on-black killings.

Massachusetts—the state that in 1970 attempted to declare the Vietnam War unconstitutional and outlaw its citizens from serving in it—made a lunge in 1997 to reinstate the death penalty. Public fervor for vengeance rumbled through the state following a media-hyped child murder by two suspected pedophiles. A death penalty bill was introduced at the annual legislative session. When the bill passed the senate and acting governor A. Paul Cellucci publicly pronounced his blessing, it appeared a shoe-in.

Then came another child-killing trial, the controversial and internationally publicized one of British au pair Louise Woodward, who was found guilty of second-degree murder just days before the death penalty bill went up for approval in the state house of representatives. Representative John Slattery changed his vote because of the Woodward conviction. "If I can't be certain that I'm getting the right guy, I have a very big problem with the death penalty," Slattery told members of the state house. "Almost all my constituents think that [Woodward] was wrongly convicted. It presupposes the question . . . that mistakes can happen." With Slattery's switch, the death penalty bill died in an 80-80 tie. Massachusetts, which held its last execution in 1947, remains one of 12 states with no death penalty.

Texas very likely executed an innocent man last year, reported *New York Times* columnist Bob Herbert. David Wayne Spence and three other men were convicted of the 1982 murders of three teenagers. It was a brutal crime, involving rape and torture, and received national attention as the "Lake Waco Murders."

Whereas Spence received death, two codefendants, under threat of execution, pleaded guilty in exchange for life sentences. The fourth man received the death sentence but was acquitted of all charges at a second trial. No physical evidence linked any of the men to the crime. Moreover, solid alibis put them elsewhere than at the scene of the crime, and Spence's car, which was suggested by the state as having been used to move the bodies, was torn apart and analyzed by the FBI, yet no trace evidence from the victims was found. Spence was convicted on the testimony of jailhouse informants who were offered a variety of favors for their testimony—leniency for the felony charges they faced and "special" visiting in the jail that allowed them to have sex with their wives and girlfriends.

"It's real easy to get an inmate, somebody who's already in jail for committing a felony, to do just about anything you want him to do," said former district attorney Felipe Reyna. "I was never in favor of that. If I didn't have independent testimony, good solid evidence, I wouldn't go to the grand jury." Reyna was the district attorney over the case when the crime happened. Today he says he would not have prosecuted Spence or the others.

Before the murder investigation was finished, Reyna lost his DA chair to Vic Feazell. Truman Simons, a narcotics cop and close friend of Feazell, promised the new DA, "[Y]ou assign me that case and I can solve it in a week." The lead investigator in the case at the time, homicide detective Ramon Salinas, was removed and Simons put in charge. "My opinion is that David Spence was innocent," said Salinas. "Nothing from the investigation ever led us to any evidence that he was involved."

With Salinas moved out of the way, Simons went to work, sniffing out jailhouse informants with a handful of favors. A Simons's informant later admitted, "We all fabricated our accounts of Spence confessing in order to try to get a break from the state on our cases." The informant's repentance came too late for Spence, who claimed innocence to his last dying breath.

In *Herrera v. Collins,* a 1993 Texas death penalty decision, the U.S. Supreme Court ruled that innocence is not a constitutional claim federal courts have to review, proclaiming the clemency system to be the "safety net" for such cases. That has not worked out. "The commutation process in [Texas] is in essence nonexistent," defense attorney David Botsford told CNN's Larry King in January 1998. "Look at 1997. There were 16 requests for commutation to the board, and not one of the 18 members of the Board of Pardon and Parole recommended any for commutation."

Three years after the *Herrera* decision, Congress shut down 20 "death penalty resource centers," federally funded law offices staffed with dedicated appellate counsel. With the centers gone, many death-sentenced prisoners are left either with no attorney representation or with underpaid state-appointed lawyers unskilled in the legal complexity of capital appeals. In California, which has a death row population of 477, the *San Francisco Chronicle* reports that 156 of the condemned are without lawyers to appeal their cases.

The same year Congress closed the centers, President Bill Clinton signed into law the EDPA, limiting the appeals for death-sentenced prisoners and making it even tougher to receive a full federal court review. A year and a half later, Clinton found himself facing serious allegations of sexual harassment, abuse of power, and obstruction of justice. The president then whistled a different tune than on the day he signed EDPA. In an interview on *Newshour* (PBS, January 21, 1998), he told Jim Lehrer, "It's easy to get charged with something, but it's almost impossible to prove your innocence." David Wayne Spence could have told him that.

◆ LAST REQUEST

It is the stereotypical execution: A man faces a firing squad, blindfolded. His last request is for a cigarette. The warden lights one, sticks it in the condemned man's mouth, and allows him a few puffs of relaxation. Such a harmless and easily accommodated request. Times have changed.

After spending 18 years in a small cell on Texas's death row, Larry Wayne White was executed in 1997. His last-meal request was simple enough, liver and onions with cottage cheese. After the meal he requested a single last cigarette. He was denied. The Texas prison system is under a no-smoking policy, evidently without exception—even at a dying man's last request.

Postscript: From Gilmore's execution in 1977 to January 1, 1999, 500 people have been executed in the United States, three of whom have been women. The death row population as of January 1999 was 3,549—and growing.

22

Far-Off Places

LANE NELSON

From *The Angolite*, March/April 1994, Angola, La: Louisiana State Penitentiary.

"If at first you don't succeed, try again," is the message the Russian government sent as it executed Andrei Chikatilo, the country's worst serial killer. The 57-year-old former teacher was shot in the back of the head—execution "Russian style"—after being convicted of the murder and mutilation of 52 women and children. According to a Russian news agency, Chikatilo was arrested as a key suspect in 1984 but later released because of inconclusive blood and hair samples. Russian authorities claim Chikatilo continued his murderous rampage until he confessed in 1990.

Chikatilo's final arrest and conviction came a little late for another man authorities admit to have mistakenly executed a few years back for the same crimes.

The Iranian Parliament has proposed expansion of the death sentence to include producers and distributors of pornographic videos. Although harsh sentences are nothing new to this Islamic country, some in-nation experts do not believe executing solicitors of pornographic films will have any major deterrent effect. They claim the enterprising drug trafficking that continues to infiltrate their religion-dominated country in spite of its death-for-dealers policy demonstrates the point.

Iran's supreme religious leader, Ayatollah Ali Khamenei, is unpersuaded by the experts' analogy. In blaming the Western world for promoting an unhealthy influence on his people, Khamenei considers death the appropriate punishment for porn dealers. "Our enemies are encouraging young people to turn away from Islamic beliefs. We have to launch a cultural campaign in confrontation," he said.

Peru is pushing to extend its death penalty to include terrorists. If successful, it will become the first Latin American country to renounce the "San Jose Agreement" (SJA). This 1969 agreement is a commitment made to the American Convention on Human Rights. Fifteen Latin American Countries signed the SJA in 1969, promising not to expand their death penalties beyond what they already were. At the time, Peru's constitution allowed for execution only in cases of wartime treason.

Peru's decision to break away from the SJA was prompted by the 1992 arrest of Abimael Guzman-Reynoso, founder of the revolutionary organization Shining Path. The guerilla is reportedly responsible for the deaths of 30,000 Peruvians over a 13-year span. Peru's President Alberto K. Fujimori, who came into power in 1992, told Latin American leaders last summer that he would have no problem with personally "sending Reynoso to hell."

Under Fujimori's reign, Peru has fallen to near dictatorial control. Suspected terrorists are tried by military tribunals, in which defendants, generally denied meaningful access to skilled lawyers, are often not allowed to confront the evidence against them. Judges and prosecutors wear masks and use voice-distorting machines to avoid recognition. In 1993 these military courts sentenced nearly 600 people to prison for terrorism. "There is a serious lack of due process in the judicial system in Peru, and it is still troubled with corruption," commented a Western official. "We have real problems with the judicial process and the faceless judges, and that makes us concerned about how they will apply the death penalty."

After Ferdinand Marcos and his martial law capsized six years ago, the new Philippines government drew up a fresh constitution, one that prohibited capital punishment. Five and a half years later, and despite strong opposition from the Catholic Church and outnumbered congressmen, the death penalty is back. The insurgence of crime in this economically weak and politically corrupt country gave recently elected president Fidel Ramos the needed edge to garner support for the capital punishment law.

The new law went into effect on December 13, 1993. It covers 13 crimes, including murder, kidnapping, drug trafficking and theft of public money. Ramos, a longtime proponent of capital punishment, has no qualms about executing public officials found guilty of theft. "[It is] a clear warning to others who continue to view public office as an opportunity for private profit," he said.

But no corrupt public official, or anyone else, is likely to be executed soon. According to a prison official, the country's only electric chair was struck by lightning 12 years ago and has been out of order ever since. No matter. The Philippines government stipulated in the new death penalty law that the gas chamber and not electrocution will be the legal means of execution. But there is no gas chamber to be found in the country, and no money in this year's budget to buy one. Corrupt public officials are now stealing not only to get rich but also to stay alive.

British-ruled Caribbean countries are speeding up death penalty appeals in an effort to hang the condemned as quickly as possible. The frenzy comes in the wake of a landmark decision handed down by the Judiciary Committee of the Privy Council—the highest judiciary authority over British Commonwealth territories. Their decision involves two prisoners sentenced to death 14 years ago. The Privy Council ruled that spending so much time on death row amounted to unnecessary "agony of mind" and represented "inhumane punishment," ordering the prisoners' sentences commuted to life in prison. The council strongly suggested that anybody on death row for more than five years should be given a life sentence.

In Jamaica, one of more than eight countries falling under the Privy Council's authority, the ruling affects approximately 80 death row prisoners who have served more than five years. Another 89 have served less than five years, 25 of them more than four years. The Jamaican government has targeted these 25, pulling out all stops to expedite their appeals and execute them before they reach the five-year time limit—making one man's blessing another man's curse.

Condemned prisoners who have served more than five years on the row will receive the blessing of life. But for those who have served less than five years, and now watch the calendar like an AIDS patient counting his T-cells, a curse is bestowed. They fall prey to a speedy and shaky appeals process that will more than likely result in swift death.

23

One Man's View

JAMES C. MCCLOSKEY

From *The Angolite,* September/October 1995, Angola, La: Lousiana State Penitentiary.

What has it come to in this great nation of ours when the entire state and federal judiciary silently stood aside, as did the governor, and allowed Texas earlier this year to execute Jessie Jacobs, a man whose prosecutor even admitted was innocent of the shooting for which he was put to death? You think I exaggerate? Not so. You see, after Mr. Jacobs's conviction for the deadly shooting, the state of Texas conceded that it was Mr. Jacobs's sister, not Mr. Jacobs, who shot the woman. Although Mr. Jacobs forcibly took the female victim to his sister's house so that the two women could settle a dispute, Mr. Jacobs's own prosecutor later told the sister's jury that he now agreed that Mr. Jacobs had no idea the sister had a weapon or that she intended to use it; that Mr. Jacobs stood by in total surprise when she shot the woman to death.

And for that, our esteemed machinery of justice puts a man to death? How hard-boiled and desensitized a society have we become when our courts with hardly a blink of the eye behave in such a callous fashion? Jacobs's death must be laid at the feet of all those members of the judiciary—right up to the U.S. Supreme Court—for not stepping in and righting this wrong, and thereby saving an innocent life.

James C. McCloskey. (Copyright: James C. McCloskey.)

Particularly disturbing is the statement of the federal appeals court in New Orleans that, "it is not for us to say" when considering the possibility that Mr. Jacobs's jury had made a mistake in convicting him. I If not they, then who? The U.S. Supreme Court? Sadly, its majority, too, does not believe that it has the responsibility for reviewing new evidence that has emerged indicating that someone who has been convicted and sentenced to death could very well be innocent. Writing for the majority in 1993, Chief Justice Rehnquist held in the *Herrera* case that a state prisoner, facing execution for a murder he claims not to have done, is not ordinarily entitled to federal court review based on new evidence. He said, "Because of the very disruptive effect that entertaining claims of actual innocence would have on the need for finality in capital cases . . . the threshold showing for such an assumed right would necessarily be extraordinarily high." Referring to the rule that claims of innocence in and of themselves are not grounds for federal review, he also said, "This rule is grounded in the principle that federal habeas courts sit to insure that individuals are not imprisoned in violation of the Constitution, not to correct errors of fact."

Justice Scalia concurred in *Herrera* stating, "There is no basis in text, tradition, or even in contemporary service for finding in the Constitution a right to demand judicial consideration of newly discovered evidence of innocence brought forward after conviction." Nastily, he then mocked those whose "consciences are shocked" by this opinion. Surely most Americans who have some sense of fairness are indeed shocked at this absurdity. In another death penalty case this year (Kyles), Justice Scalia, in a dissenting opinion, stated, "The reality is that responsibility for factual accuracy in capital cases, as in other cases, rests elsewhere."

Again, we might ask, "Where?" Justice Rehnquist in *Herrera* (a case in which the defendant was, by the way, executed in 1993) passes the buck to gubernatorial executive clemency as the "historic remedy for preventing miscarriages of justice where judicial process has been exhausted." In today's political climate, it is virtually impossible to find a governor or a state board of pardons (appointed by the governor) through which an innocent person must pass on the way to the governor, who has the courage to grant clemency to an unjustly convicted "murderer" on death row. Clemency petitions are either dead on arrival or in a terminal state once they land on the governor's desk. A camel trying to pass through the eye of a needle has better odds.

Politicians of all stripes bow before the altar of "tough on crime" rhetoric as a sure-fire means to boost their electability. In their feeding frenzy for votes, candidates for office outdo each other in vowing to the electorate how tough they will be on criminals once they assume office by either "burying 'em" or "burning 'em." This pandering to the electorate has no ameliorating effect whatsoever on reducing crime. In fact, it is a distraction from tackling the hard solutions to crime. Thus, it is a profound disservice to the American public and its well-being.

Justice Rehnquist reinforces his point that clemency is the ticket for freedom for the innocent on death row by noting, "History is replete with examples of wrongfully convicted persons who have been pardoned in the wake of newly discovered evidence establishing their innocence." "History" may be; but not now or in the foreseeable future will pardons issue from governors' mansions—not when we have, in Supreme Court Justice Stevens's words, "a political climate in which judges who covet higher office—or who really wish to remain judges—must constantly profess their fealty to the death penalty." The same holds true for governors.

So where can innocent persons consigned to death go to prove their innocence, and thereby secure life and liberty, if the federal courts and governor's mansion are effectively foreclosed to them? To state courts? Please consider this fact of law: In 17 different states an innocently condemned inmate cannot present any new evidence that demonstrates his innocence if that new evidence emerges more than 60 days after his conviction. Eighteen other states insist it must be developed within one to three years of conviction. Only nine states have no time limits. Fortunately, New Jersey is one of those nine states. You talk about having the deck stacked against you! When I first began working to free the innocent across the nation, I could not believe that state laws actually exist that seal off presentation of new evidence with such severe time constraints. Nonetheless, it is so.

Once wrongly convicted and sentenced to death, a defendant is treated as a leper. No one wants to touch him or her. Those in authority seem to be more interested in finality, expediency, speed, and administrative streamlining than in truth, justice, and fairness. What should be more important to a judge or an elected or appointed executive than saving an innocent life? Federal judge Lee Sarokin wondered aloud to a Harvard Law School audience in 1993, "Can [we] really respond to a person facing execution that he already had his chance to be heard, and thus nothing new may be presented, no matter when discovered or how persuasive? If we are engaged in balancing the state's need for finality in capital cases against the possibility of wrongfully executing someone, there should be no contest as to what tips the scales of justice." It is not often that we hear a federal judge speaking publicly from his soul about a possible injustice done to an individual. Such judges appear to be in the distinct minority. When I encounter one, as I do every now and then, my heart truly leaps with joy.

It just seems to me that in the United States' contemporary society of law and order, the bureaucratic mind-set has completely overpowered and subdued the prophetic voice, which is more and more a voice in the wilderness, as it demands justice and new life for the hapless individual who has had the misfortune of tumbling into the justice system's grinding machinery of death. As he surveyed and reflected on his own society's systems of laws and justice some 2,500 years ago, the great prophet Isaiah lamented that, "Justice is turned back, and righteousness stands afar off for truth has fallen in the public squares . . . the Lord saw it, and it displeased him that there was no justice. He saw and wondered that there was no one to intervene."

If I may be permitted another scriptural analogy, I cannot help but immediately think of Pontius Pilate and how his actions so closely parallel how the imprisoned innocent are treated today by our own criminal justice system. Pilate, a governor, after first trying to pass the judgment of Jesus off onto Herod, three times told the people and the religious rulers that he was going to release Jesus because he found him innocent of all charges, especially of any deserving death. However, the voices of the people clamoring for crucifixion prevailed. Pilate, washing his hands before the crowd, told them, "I am innocent of this man's blood; see to it yourselves." So the federal and state courts, albeit on a more subtle level, deal with those unjustly convicted of capital crimes. They say to these petitioners, "It is not for us to say," and "The responsibility rests elsewhere."

As we all know, executing the innocent is an irrevocable act. Although none of us want that to happen, it can occur more often than we think. Even Chief Justice Rehnquist admits that, "History is replete with examples of wrongfully convicted persons . . . ." He is right. Consider the following: A 1993 House Judiciary Committee report documents 48 cases since 1973 where a convicted person was released from death row because of innocence. As of March 1995, that number is now up to a staggering 54.

During that same period of time, 226 were executed. This means that during the last 20 years, for every five death row inmates executed, one has been released and exonerated. That points to a rather cracked system, one prone to serious and frequent mistakes. This being the case, it seems to me that the judicial watchwords should be caution and openness rather than speed and foreclosure. The U.S. Supreme Court sees it differently. It is cutting off access to the federal courts for those proclaiming their innocence. It is strongly urging "finality" of capital cases; and yet when "finality" is achieved in death cases, it is discovered that almost 20 percent are innocent.

And that is not to say that all those 226 who were executed were guilty. Mr. Jacobs was innocent. I know of at least two others who were innocent because I personally reinvestigated both cases from top to bottom and developed considerable new evidence demonstrating their innocence. One was Jimmy Wingo in Louisiana and the other was Roger Coleman in Virginia.

Wingo's 1983 trial lasted one day. His lawyer was more interested in "hitting" on Jimmy's attractive sister than going to bat and swinging for Jimmy in the courtroom. On the eve of his 1987 execution, Centurion Ministries brought forward the two state witnesses against him, both of whom confessed to lying at his trial due to intense police intimidation and threats of long imprisonment. Neither the Louisiana Board of Pardons (whose chairman later pled guilty to selling pardons to convicts) nor Governor Edwin Edwards (who during his term at that time was twice tried on federal charges) wanted to hear this. My personal presentation of Jimmy's innocence to the board and to the governor's top executive aide on the day before and the day of the execution fell on deaf ears. Jimmy was electrocuted on June 16, 1987.

Then, five years later, the exact same thing happened again when Roger Coleman was electrocuted outside Richmond, Virginia, on May 20, 1992. Neither of Roger's young, court-appointed trial attorneys had defended anyone in a felony prior to their ill-prepared and spiritless defense of Roger in 1982. Grundy is a town of 1,700 people tucked in the southwestern corner of Virginia, only 12 miles from where the McCoys and the Hatfields went at it in nearby Kentucky. Some of the citizenry had unfurled a sign next to the courthouse on the eve of trial that read, "Time for another hanging in Grundy." This 22-year-old Appalachian coal miner's fate was sealed before the trial began.

A four-year exhaustive reinvestigation of both the murder and Roger's conviction, conducted by Centurion Ministries, yielded a wealth of new evidence which pointed to two brothers, who were the victim's backyard neighbors, as the real killers. The investigation also amply demonstrated how the police and prosecutors had lied and cheated as they ran right over Roger's rookie lawyers in their zeal to convict Roger and calm the community. The entire state and federal judiciary, however, refused to review this new evidence using as an excuse the fact that Roger's prior attorneys had submitted a notice of appeal one day late years before, earlier in the appellate process. Therefore, the courts said, they were procedurally barred from accepting Roger's case for review.

We then proceeded to Governor Douglas Wilder for a stay of execution so that his office could examine our executive clemency petition. We did not have a chance. Roger's prosecutor was the brother of an extremely wealthy coal baron in Buchanan County (Grundy is the county seat). These two brothers also had an uncle who was a state legislator. The entire family were strong financial and political supporters of Governor Wilder. Even though Roger's face graced the cover of a sympathetic *Time* magazine four days before his execution under the headline, "This Man Might Be Innocent. This Man Is Due To Die," it was not enough. Internal and secretive political machinations proved too powerful to save an innocent man.

There is not a week that goes by that I am not haunted by the terribly unjust deaths of these two indigent men. Up until only minutes before they were led away to their gruesome deaths, I sat with both men, only ten yards away from their respective electric chair chambers. Both men met their fate with equal equanimity, quiet gracefulness, and calm courage. Both men, as they sat strapped in the electric chair shaved from head to foot, with seconds to go before the switch was turned on, proclaimed not only their innocence but their love for humanity. Some people teach us how to live. Jimmy Wingo and Roger Coleman taught me how to die.

I do not need Justice Rehnquist to remind or inform me that "history is replete with wrongful convictions. . . ." Ever since I founded Centurion Ministries 15 years ago, I live and work and breathe unjust convictions of murder every day. Working hand in hand with savvy and tirelessly dedicated attorneys, we at C.M. have been able to free and exonerate 16 men and women from life or death sentences since 1983. We hear from and constantly assess the claims of innocence from thousands of others. Many, many of them have merit, but we will not be able to get to them because of limited capacity. I could write a book on the sad subject of the convicted innocent but can only devote a few paragraphs here in this commentary.

Convicting the innocent occurs with alarming frequency in most county courthouses, large or small, rural or urban, throughout the country. In my view they are as abundant as pigeons in the park. As an example, I am reminded of the study published in the New York University's 1991 *Review of Law and Social Change* wherein 59 instances of wrongful New York state homicide convictions from 1965-1988 were identified and documented. And how about the recent spate of DNA-based exonerations of men wrongfully convicted of rape? There have been close to 20 since 1991 (two have been C.M. cases). These men were convicted based on the well-intentioned but completely erroneous identification by the victims who convincingly told their juries that, "I'll never forget that face. He's the man." Well, he wasn't the man. It was someone else. FBI statistics show the same thing. One third of the 2,500 rape suspects the FBI is asked by local police agencies to do DNA testing on are exonerated. These men are suspects based primarily on eyewitness testimony. To be wrong 33 percent of the time is scary.

Eyewitness evidence is notoriously unreliable in any kind of case or situation. It is constantly used in capital cases. To have weight, it must be corroborated by other substantial evidence. England is way ahead of the U.S. on this score. Five years ago, concern about eyewitness reliability prompted England to ban trials where the only evidence against a suspect is an eyewitness.

The criminal justice system misfires against innocent homicide defendants for many other reasons as well. One of them is the frequency of either unskillful, lazy, unprepared, and/or ill-compensated defense lawyering. Coleman and Wingo are but two ill-fated examples. Ninety-five percent of the current (September 1995) 3,000 or so death row inmates are indigent and had court-appointed lawyers at trial. Often these attorneys are overwhelmed and inexperienced. Always, no matter how well-intentioned and serious they might be in wanting to put up a diligent defense, the funds and resources available to these court-appointed lawyers are scarce and woefully inadequate. Whenever the prosecution brings to the courtroom its plethora of expert witnesses and police investigators, because of lack of funds the indigent defendant cannot afford his own investigators and experts. Thus, he cannot rebut the state's case nor develop the evidence that could possibly exonerate him. This tilts the scales of justice heavily in favor of the prosecutor. It is vastly unfair. It is also a primary reason why innocent but indigent capital murder defendants fall helplessly into prison for the crimes of others.

The pervasiveness of perjury is another cause of unjust convictions. Ed Rendell, a former DA of Philadelphia and now the mayor, once said that "in almost any factual hearing in trial, someone is committing perjury. . . ." If a judge or jury mistakenly believes a lying witness, as can and does easily happen, then a perversion of justice is once more upon us.

Prosecutorial use of nefarious criminals as their star witnesses is also rather commonplace and leads to false convictions. These can take the form of career criminals looking to get out of their own serious troubles or real perpetrators and accomplices who will falsely incriminate an innocent person in exchange for generous sentencing leniency such as non-custodial sentences. I see this so often it sickens me, especially when the real killer is the one who dispatches the innocent to death row as the chief witness for the prosecution.

Inept or corrupt forensic criminalists for the state too often see the results of their examination of physical evidence through the lens of advocacy for the police agencies who employ them rather than through the lens of scientific objective analysis. In 1993 an independent team of serologists discovered that from 1979 until 1989 the head serologist of the West Virginia State Police had "lied about, made up, or manipulated evidence" in at least 36 cases. Also in 1993, several New York State Police officers admitted fabricating false fingerprint evidence in over 25 different cases.

Another common trait of wrongful convictions is the prosecutor's habit of suppressing or withholding evidence which he is obliged to provide to the defendant in the interests of justice and fairness. Clarence Darrow was right when he said, "A courtroom is not a place where truth and innocence inevitably triumph; it is only an arena where contending lawyers fight not for justice but to win." Many times this hidden information is not only "favorable" to the defendant but would clear him or her.

In the Kerry Max Cook, Tyler, Texas, capital murder case that this author has been working on since 1990, the original DA forced his own fingerprint police specialist to falsely testify that Mr. Cook's prints found at the victim's house were 10–12 hours old. This, of course, coincided with the time of death. As any latent print specialist will tell you, it is scientifically impossible to "age" a print. Mr. Cook still sits innocently on Texas's death row, as he has for the last 18 years.

And in the Gordon Marsh case near Baltimore, Maryland, the state failed to tell the defendant that its main witness against him was in jail when she said she saw him running from the murder scene. One has to wonder what the primary objective of a prosecutor is. Is it to convict, regardless of the factual truth, or is it to pursue justice?

The prosecution is the "house" in the criminal justice system's game of poker. The cards are his, and he deals them. He decides whom and what to charge for crimes, and if there will be a trial, or whether a plea is acceptable. He dominates. Unfortunately, his power is virtually unchecked because he is practically immune from punishment for offenses, no matter how flagrant or miscreant. From the defense's vantage point, prosecutorial misbehavior occurs with disturbing frequency. And when the "house" cheats, the innocent lose.

Lamentably, we see prosecutors throughout the nation continually violating the standards set for them by the U.S. Supreme Court in 1935, when it said that "the prosecutor's interest in a criminal prosecution is not that it shall win a case, but that justice shall be done. . . . He is in a peculiar and very definite sense the servant of the law, the twofold arm of which is that guilt shall not escape or innocence suffer. . . . While he may strike hard blows, he is not at liberty to strike foul ones. It is as much his duty to refrain from improper methods calculated to produce a wrongful conviction as it is to use every legitimate means to bring about a just one."

Racism and community pressure also sow seeds of false capital convictions. The case of Clarence Brandley, freed from 10 years of false imprisonment on Texas's death row, exhibited both of these factors. Clarence was the black supervisor of three white janitors at Conroe High School, 50 miles north of Houston. Clarence was arrested in late August 1980, four days after a white female student was found raped and murdered in the school's auditorium loft. School was to begin in a week. The school was flooded with telephone calls by panicked parents who refused to send their children to school until the murderer was caught. As a local police officer said shortly after the murder to a white janitor standing near Brandley, "He's the nigger, so he's elected." His arrest calmed the community, and school started on schedule. Once the Texas Ranger arrested Clarence, his investigation began in earnest. The ranger then spent 500 hours building the case against Brandley in the ensuing months.

Clarence was finally exonerated and declared innocent by a retired state judge who was brought in from West Texas to preside over the evidentiary hearing and examine the new evidence. Two of the janitors came forward and told how they had lied about Clarence at the original trial because of pressure to do so by the Texas Ranger. One of the two janitors first came forward, with Centurion Ministries' encouragement, eight days before Clarence was to be executed. Since his release in 1990, Clarence has been a church minister in Houston.

When all of us come to a capital case in one capacity or another and enter the bar of justice, we bring with us our passions and prejudices, our ambitions and desire for recognition and rewards, our flawed egos which allow us to be manipulated, our fears and insecurities about being alone or different from the group, and our capacity to deceive and be deceived. Consequently, we see others and they see us through a prism that distorts our vision, making it difficult to separate fact from fiction. We think we are right, but we can be wrong. If we are wrong, we hate to admit it. Pride and arrogance can seep in and puff us up. These human frailties common to us all can produce mistaken interpretations that result in wrongful convictions, both in capital and noncapital cases. Consequently, many of us will agree with Lafayette, who, said to the French Chamber of Deputies in 1830, "I should ask for the abolition of the punishment of death until I have the infallibility of human judgment demonstrated to me."

Most of those who are in favor of capital punishment concede that it is not a deterrent to murder. Philadelphia is rapidly gaining a reputation for being "the capital of capital punishment" (July 16, 1995, *New York Times Magazine* cover story). Its current DA, Lynne Abraham, is a zealot in pursuing the death penalty in cases when she can, probably more than any other prosecutor in the United States. Even she admits the death penalty is not a deterrent. Consider Philadelphia's homicide rate after Pennsylvania reinstituted the death penalty in 1978. From 1984 through 1990, when capital punishment had been in full swing for a number of years, it dramatically and consistently increased:

Year	No. Homicides in Philadelphia
1984	263
1985	275
1986	346
1987	355
1988	402
1989	501
1990	525

In the same *New York Times Magazine* article, Manhattan DA Morgenthau pointed out that in 1994 Manhattan reported 320 homicides, 21% fewer than Philadelphia. This is significant in that both counties have virtually the same size population, yet at that time New York did not have the death penalty while Pennsylvania did.

Besides that, murder is not a rational act done by rational people who carefully think through the consequences of their actions. Those who murder are usually either consumed by hate or anger or are in a warped emotional state. They are demented, pathological people who, at the time they kill, do so with utter disregard for human life. Many are either high on drugs or in desperate need for more drugs. Killers are by and large antisocial people, who do not respond to such behavioral disincentives not to kill as the threat of the death penalty. Acceptance of normal societal values is alien to their natures. For us to think that we can deter such people from killing through the warning of capital punishment seems to this author in itself irrational.

How about a more prosaic rationale for the death penalty: money? DA Morgenthau also made it clear in an Op Ed piece in the *New York Times* (August 13, 1995) that since the death penalty does not deter murder, "the millions of dollars expended on it would be better spent on solutions—from prisons to drug treatment programs—that do." He went so far in another article to declare that capital punishment hinders the fight against crime. Yet the death penalty is far more costly than life imprisonment.

A definitive study on this subject by two professors of public policy at Duke University was released in 1993. They studied the costs of every death penalty case (77 of them) in North Carolina in 1991 and 1992. This study concluded that the extra cost to the state of each execution actually carried out was $2.16 million. This means that it cost approximately $3 million to try, convict, sentence, litigate, house, and then finally execute a person, while it cost slightly over $1 million to secure and carry out a life imprisonment sentence.

According to my calculations based on this data, since there are now almost 3,000 people living on death row throughout the U.S., and if each is executed, it will cost the U.S. $9 billion to accomplish this Herculean task. Since life imprisonment for these 3,000 would cost $3 billion, the extra cost to the nation is $6 billion. In my view this is an absurd and complete waste of billions and billions of dollars which certainly could be used to combat crime in a far more effective and productive manner.

The death penalty exists in 38 states. The local county district attorney has sole discretion on when to apply or seek its use. Thus, its application against the total number of homicides that occur in a county can be surprisingly sparing and selective, depending on the particular view of the local prosecutor. Consequently, its use as applied to very similar murders in different counties in the same state can be inconsistent and even contradictory.

In 1994 Pittsburgh's career prosecutor, Robert Colville, declared only eight of 104 murders to be death penalty eligible while Philadelphia, the national leader, did the same in 159 out of 404 homicides. Mr. Colville told the *New York Times Magazine* that, "I never had a lot of thought that the ultimate revenge was necessary. The death penalty can't cure everything." Dallas' DA sought death only twice in 1994. Even Houston's long-term prosecutor, Johnny Holmes, who is well-known nationally as a strong death penalty advocate, sought death in only 10 percent of his county's eligible 1994 homicides. Gil Garcetti asked for death in 18 of Los Angeles's 2,000 murders last year. He only got it in six cases. In the last five years New Orleans juries issued death verdicts only twice. Chicago's Cook County obtained only seven death sentences in 1994.

With the advent of the death penalty in New York state earlier this year, the Bronx DA, Robert Johnson, has said that he will never seek the death penalty because of his belief in the "intense respect for the value and sanctity of human life." For all the hullabaloo over the death penalty across the nation, I think the above statistics, as they reveal how few murders in high-crime urban cities either qualify for the death penalty or involve the seeking of death, will shock most advocates of the death penalty. Given its relatively low use and its disproportionately high and exorbitant cost, my question is why even use it at all?

I agree with the 1972 U.S. Supreme Court who, in striking down the death penalty, characterized its application as "arbitrary and capricious" as well as "harsh and freakish. . . ." Its use is also racially biased against blacks. Historically, this has been the case; and in applying the death penalty to a rapidly expanding base of federal crimes, it still flagrantly discriminates against blacks.

From 1930 through 1980, 3,862 people were executed in the United States. Of these, 54 percent were black. Included in this number 455 men were executed for rape, 90 percent of whom were black. During this period of time, blacks represented about 10 percent of the total population.

The situation somewhat improved from 1977, the year after the Supreme Court upheld the constitutionality of revised state capital-punishment laws, through 1993. According to a U.S. Department of Justice 1994 report, 4,259 people entered death row during this period of time. Forty percent were black and 58 percent were white. Of the 226 people actually executed during these same 17 years, 39 percent were black and 53 percent were white. The black percentage of the total American population during these years was about 12 percent.

In 1991, for the first time in 50 years, a white man was executed for killing a black person. There are scores of examples in the reverse where a black person was executed for murdering a white. The implication of the way in which the death penalty has been administered in this nation is the not-so-subliminal message that a black person's life has less value attached to it than does the life of a white person. That is the way I read it, anyhow.

If you think that somehow we are becoming more sophisticated and therefore less discriminating in the way we administer the death penalty, look at what's happening in the federal system. There has not been a federal execution since the Rosenbergs in 1953. Since the expansion of the modern federal death penalty laws and procedures in 1988, the federal government has initiated approximately 50 death-case prosecutions. In order for a U.S. attorney to do so, the procedures insist that he receive authorization by the U.S. attorney general. Of the 50 capital prosecutions to date, 85 percent of the defendants are minorities. Here we go again!

If the death penalty is so disproportionately costly and discriminatory against the poor and people of color, and if it is indisputable that it is not a deterrent and that innocent people get executed, then why do we do it and why is it so popular in the United States? Because it makes us "feel good" when we can unleash our anger and satisfy our deep seated need and desire for revenge. DA Abraham of Philadelphia says it gives to citizenry a "feeling of control." DA Morgenthau rebukes capital punishment by characterizing it as "violence in the name of vengeance." I believe that's why the public overwhelmingly sanctions it. Somehow it viscerally assuages not only our lust for vengeance but our outrage and helplessness at the unprecedented levels of bloodshed and violent crime throughout America.

Recently, a prominent resident of Princeton, whom I know only casually, stopped me on the street to declare that he believes in the death penalty because "even the Bible says an eye for an eye and a tooth for a tooth is how society should strike back at violence." That's true, the Old Testament does say this. However, as a Christian I believe in the ultimate authority of the words of Jesus Christ as presented in the Gospels of the New Testament.

In the Sermon on the Mount, as recorded in Matthew, Jesus says, "You have heard that it was said 'an eye for an eye and a tooth for a tooth.' But I say unto you . . . ." He then goes on and tells the people that, "If any one strikes you on one cheek turn the other to him" and "to love your enemies." Also the great Apostle Paul in his letter to the Romans urges them to "repay no one evil for evil" and to "never avenge yourselves but leave it to the wrath of God for it is written, 'Vengeance is mine, I will repay,' says the Lord." Vengeance, as personified in capital punishment, in my view, is in direct opposition to the spirit of Christ.

Grounded as I am in these spiritual values, I find the death penalty to be morally repugnant. I do not believe the state should be in the killing business. It sends the wrong message. It tells society that if you kill at the bottom of society, we will kill at the top of society. As a result, the killing never stops and peace will not come to the land.

One last point I would like to make. Practically speaking, the death penalty simply does not work. Think of all the energy and anguish and hard work expended by national and state legislatures, judges, prosecutors, police, juries, and attorneys, as well as the billions of dollars spent by the states and counties on behalf of capital punishment! Now consider this. According to a Department of Justice 1994 report, 42 percent of all death-row inmates between 1973 and 1993 were removed from death row primarily due to conviction/sentence reversals and commutations. This means that almost half of the convictions that resulted in the death penalty had serious constitutional flaws. Imagine the waste of money and resources in producing what turns out to be counterfeit death sentences in almost one out of every two instances.

As a result of the foregoing, I have thrown my lot in with former U.S. Supreme Court Justices Harry Blackmun and Lewis Powell, both of whom voted for the death penalty during their U.S. Supreme Court tenure. Just before retirement, in a 1994 dissent, Justice Blackmun wrote, "From this day forward, I no longer shall tinker with the machinery of death. . . . I feel morally and intellectually obligated to concede that the death penalty experiment has failed." Justice Powell told his biographer in 1994 that, "I have come to think that capital punishment should be abolished" because "it brings discredit to the whole system." Thus, both of these men wrestled long and hard with capital punishment, and came to see the complete futility of its usefulness.

All the nations of western continental Europe have abolished capital punishment, as have Canada (1976) and Great Britain (1971). In my view, it is the mark of a higher civilization when a country finally chooses to eradicate forever from its heart and soul the damnable practice of killing for vengeance. Eventually capital punishment will fall from its own weight. Future American generations will wonder in amazement how and why we continued capital punishment for as long as we did.

Postscript: The first National Conference on Wrongful Convictions and the Death Penalty was held at the Northwestern University Law School in November 1998. Conference organizers identified 73 men and two women freed from death row since 1976 because they were innocent.

24

A Lawyer's Opinion: Kind and Usual Punishment

David E. Marcantel

From *The Angolite*, September/October 1997, Angola, La: Louisiana State Penitentiary.

In the French colony of Louisiana in 1757, Governor Kerlerec described with pride the standards of justice under his government. The matter involved two Frenchmen who were accused of murder. He wrote:

> Their trial was conducted very properly and, by the assembled War Council, the said Baudreau and Bazille were condemned to have their bones broken while alive, to die on the wheel, and to have their bodies cut into quarters and thrown on the garbage heap, which was carried out three hours after sentence was rendered, before the assembled troops.

My ancestor, Francois Marcantel, who was at the time a French soldier in Louisiana, was perhaps among the troops who witnessed these horrible executions.

A contemporary observer, Jean Bossu, believing Baudreau was not guilty, wrote the following commentary:

> When one reflects on the fate of the unfortunate Baudreau, one well feels that he must have been judged incorrectly and by military men who were ignorant of civil and criminal laws, since he could not have deserved the cruel punishment which they made him suffer. If politics requires that, for public safety, one does not leave a crime unpunished, justice asks, in favor of humanity, that the judge fear more to punish too much than to not punish enough, following this axiom: it is better to let ten guilty men go free than to punish an innocent man.

We the inhabitants of Louisiana at the dawn of the twenty-first century would like to think that we have changed for the better. We read the description of the execution of these two Frenchmen more than two centuries ago with horror. But since that sad day in 1757, more than a thousand Louisianians have been executed by the different powers that have governed this region of the American Deep South. Today there are more people awaiting execution in Louisiana than ever before.

In what sense has humanity progressed? Has the death penalty been abolished in Louisiana? No. Do we today fear to execute an innocent person? Not at all. According to the polls, 75% of Americans are in favor of the death penalty even while acknowleding that there are inevitably some innocent people executed. The attitude is, "Too bad for them."

Instead of abolishing the death penalty, humanity busies itself with finding means that are more and more "humane," that is to say, *efficient*, to kill people. From the capital punishment of the cross, we have advanced to burning Joan of Arc at the stake, to death on the wheel, then hanging, then the guillotine, the electric chair, the gas chamber, to arrive today at lethal injection. We have replaced physical suffering of the condemned by psychological suffering that lasts, not hours, but 10 years, 15 years, 20 years, and extends the punishment to the whole family of the condemned person, to his or her lawyers, friends, and spiritual counselors.

Article 5 of the Universal Declaration of Human Rights stipulates, "No one shall be subjected to torture, nor punishment of treatment which is cruel, inhumane or degrading." The most "humane" death penalty imaginable violates this article.

In Louisiana and in America in general, violence is everywhere. Firearms are easy to obtain and, if one lacks a pistol, a knife will do as well. In the United States there are 25,000 murders per year.

The Constitution of the United States forbids cruel and unusual punishment. Since the Supreme Court has declared that the death penalty is not unconstitutional, it logically follows that it is a kind and usual punishment.

But with 25,000 murderers per year, everyone cannot benefit from this kind punishment. It would cost too much to kill so many people. So there has to be a selection process. In the United States, how do prosecutors decide between the murderers for whom they will ask the death penalty and the murderers to whom they will offer a plea bargain for a prison sentence? That depends on things that are completely capricious—an election for a prosecutor on the horizon, for example.

Let us say that for campaign reasons, the prosecutor decides that to ask for the death of someone. But whom? First, the person that the state seeks to execute will probably be poor, ignorant, and very often black. If the accused person is also retarded or mentally ill, so much the better for the state.

Let us examine the operation of that curious institution, the death penalty, by studying the case of Antonio James, a black man executed by the state of Louisiana on March 1, 1996. For Antonio, the long march toward death began in January 1979, when he decided, with a friend, to rob a white man in New Orleans. The white man was killed. The codefendant, a convicted felon, testified for the prosecution that Antonio fired the fatal shot. Antonio denied it, saying that it was done by the codefendant. The codefendant did not even receive any prison time. Antonio was condemned to death.

In the American system, a conviction such as this marks the beginning of years of appeals to the state courts at all levels, to the federal courts, and finally to the U.S. Supreme Court. Certain lawyers were ordered by the Court to save the life of Antonio. At the same time, the lawyers of the state, much better financed, sought to kill him. Americans have the impression that they have a legal system where the two sides are on equal footing. In reality, the game is rigged in advance in favor of death.

The day and the hour of the execution of Antonio were set and postponed 13 times. Each time Antonio would see the days fly by, see the approach of his execution, spend sleepless nights. Once the order to postpone the execution arrived only three and a half hours before the moment fixed for his death.

Antonio spent 13 years on death row. From time to time, he visited with his family, consulted with his lawyers, prayed with his spiritual advisor. He matured. He changed. Finally, the person confined in the tiny cell on death row was not the same person who could have performed an armed robbery or killed a person. After 17 years, the state can no longer kill the criminal, the monster. He is no longer there.

In Louisiana, when all the appeals are finished and all have failed, one can ask for a pardon from the pardon board. There, it is not a question of lack of guilt, but a plea for mercy. At the time, the board was composed of five people, two blacks and three whites. On February 28, Antonio, his family, and his lawyers presented his request before them. The board listened attentively, deliberateed for five minutes, and refused the request. In the four years that the board had served, it had never voted to pardon anyone in a capital case. As usual, the two blacks voted for life, and the three whites voted for death.

Here, the events took a surrealistic turn. The *danse macabre,* the dance of death, began. The execution was set for March 1 at one minute after midnight. On February 29, at noon, the prison hosted a gathering for the condemned man and his family in the death house. Assembled in the visiting room were the aged mother of the condemned, his son, his brothers and sisters, nieces and nephews. Some of them were young children. They talked about things in the past or the weather. They did not talk about the fact that the guest of honor would be killed by the state in a few hours. They took family photos, many photos—Antonio with his mother, with his son, with his brothers and sisters, surrounded by his nieces and nephews. Ah, happy memories!

Once the last family visit was finished, the family had to leave and wait outside the prison gates. There they found themselves beside supporters of the death penalty. Normally there are confrontations between the family of the condemned man and the spectators who are there to celebrate the death of a criminal.

Hours passed. It was time for an old tradition in the United States, the last meal for the condemned man. According to custom, the condemned man can order his favorite gastronomic delicacies. Being a Louisianian,

Antonio selected fried oysters and crab gumbo. He enjoyed the meal in the company of several people, among them the warden of the prison, the person who, in a few hours, would give the order to kill him. The warden seemed to like Antonio. It was not he who wished Antonio's death. Everyone was just following the law. No one was responsible for what would be done to Antonio. It was just God's will being carried out, said the warden.

More hours passed. The condemned man dressed for his execution. He put on a diaper. At the moment of his death, he would need it. We think of everything.

The execution would take place at one minute after midnight. There were two red telephones attached to the wall of the execution chamber. The governor of the state could call at the last minute and pardon the condemned man. So there was still hope. . . . but not much—these calls rarely come.

Just before midnight, the people attach Antonio to a table, and we insert the tubes through which we will inject the poison. The condemned man never resists. They say that there is no physical pain for the condemned man. Perhaps not, but there is spiritual and psychological pain that spreads out over the family of Antonio, over his spiritual counselor who has prayed with him for 11 years, over his lawyers who see the result of 17 years of effort, and over all right-thinking people who consider the death penalty as one more murder, this time committed by the state.

March 1, 1996, begins with the execution of Antonio James. Prison life returns to a normal rhythm. There are still 62 people on death row in Louisiana and more than 3,000 on death rows across the United States. Antonio is no longer here, but death does not lack partners. The *danse macabre* will begin again, and we are all invited.

Since the goal of this whole procedure is not to stop crime but to create suffering, we see that our modern death penalty is clearly more efficient than it was in the French colony of Louisiana in 1757. Today the sentence and the suffering last much longer and touch many more people.

The death penalty is not new. Jesus was executed. Two thousand years have passed. The death penalty still exists. But from time to time, we are supposed to ask ourselves, "What *would* Jesus say about our society and its "humane" death penalty?"

In fact, what *will* Jesus say?

Postscript: David Marcantel, a partner in the Jennings, Louisiana, firm of Marcantel, Marcantel, Wall, and Pfeiffer, has practiced civil law for more than 20 years. He has been involved with criminal law for only the past six years, taking cases through the public defender's office. "I have never

Attorney David E. Marcantel. (Copyright: David E. Marcantel.)

represented a person in a capital murder trial," Marcantel said, "but I have represented people who could have been charged with a capital offense. It is up to the DA to ask for death or offer a plea bargain for a lesser offense. That really showed me how capricious this law is."

Inspired by the 1996 Discovery Channel documentary, "Final Judgment: The Execution of Antonio James," Marcantel submitted a speech about capital punishment in Louisiana to the annual international speech competition held in Caen, France, at the Peace Memorial Museum. Lawyers from around the world submit speeches on topics of human rights violations, from which ten are chosen and their authors invited to deliver them personally at the competition. Marcantel was selected as a finalist, and he traveled to France to compete.

"I was the only one from the United States, and the only one who spoke on the death penalty," he said.

Two panels judge the speeches. One is composed of lawyers, legal journalists, representatives of human rights organizations, and presided over by France's chief jurist. The other is composed of persons chosen from the audience.

"I was trying to make an emotional impression on the French audience in the very few minutes that I had to talk to them," Marcantel said, adding that he gave the speech in French. "I tried to personalize the death penalty, not bore the audience with statistics or legal arguments. I must have succeeded because one of the judges said that my speech had the effect of a blow to the stomach." Both panels voted him the winner.

"I am indebted to Wilbert Rideau and the group that made the documentary, 'Final Judgment,'" he said. "If I had not seen it, I would not have won the contest." He returned to Caen as a member of the official panel of judges for the 1998 competition.

25

Any Last Words?

LANE NELSON AND BURK FOSTER

Revised from *The Angolite,* July/August 1995, Angola, La: Lousiana State Penitentiary.

Have you given any thought to what you would say if you were asked to make a final statement before death? Most of us will never be in a position to make a rational, complete last statement that others will remember us by. If we leave any last words, it is an epitath our survivors choose for our tombstone.

For almost all of humanity, death is unpredictable and not a time for speechmaking. Death comes for us when we are old, and sick, and incapacitated physically and mentally, or it comes with the suddenness of a stroke or heart attack. Or it comes unnaturally with the unanticipated accident or homicidal attack. What were their last thoughts, we might wonder? What message would they leave us?

About the only two categories of persons about to die who are in a position to tell us exactly what is on their mind are those persons commiting suicide and those whom the state has decided to kill. When a person commits suicide, we look for a note of explanation. Sometimes a note is found, sometimes not. Sometimes it makes sense, as when a person rationally ticks off all the aspects of his life that have gone wrong, leaving him no other choice; often it does not, when the suicide's problems seem to be more in his own mind, or no worse than those of the people reading the note. Was this *it,* you wonder?

The suicide chooses to end his life, but his act is typically spontaneous, a response to specific circumstances within a state of despair, and often surprising. The deaths of persons executed by the state are very different. As Albert Camus has discussed so precisely in "Reflections on the Guillotine," capital punishment is the moral equivalent of the most premeditated of murders—a killing in which the victim is given a date upon which a horrible death will be deliberately inflicted upon him, and then confined at the mercy of the state, under the most restrictive conditions, until that date arrives.

The person being executed by the state would not otherwise be considered a "dying man." He is typically a young, healthy man in good physical shape. He is not suicidal, or he would already have killed himself. Even the "volunteers" for execution do not kill themselves; they merely stop fighting the state's efforts to expedite the process. In their "assisted" suicides, the state plays the role of Dr. Jack Kevorkian, a.k.a. "Dr. Death."

What is the mental state of persons awaiting execution? Robert Johnson, in *Death Work,* and others have described the feelings of anxiety, powerlessness, fear, doubt, boredom, and despair that prevail on death row. Given their completely dependent status, the degree of security they live under, the isolated, sanitized nature of their confinement, and the absence of stimulation in their lives, what else would you expect from this very special group of prison inmates?

What is truly surprising to people who interact regularly with death row inmates is how tenaciously these people—whom outsiders categorize as "animals"—cling to their humanity. Spend a day with them, on or off the row, and you see how hard they struggle to remain normal. Many of them succeed much better on death row than they ever did in the free world.

When their execution date finally comes, they watch the hourglass of time, the minutes trickling down like sand until only a few grains remain. How do they want to be remembered from that traditional last statement they will be allowed to make? Will they try to impart words of wisdom to loved ones, will they make one last proclamation of innocence, will they protest in bitterness, will they express remorse, will they be abject or defiant? Some may ramble on for minutes (there are inmates whose last statements have been forcibly stopped), while others simply stare in stony silence, refusing one last time to play "the man's" game.

What do they say, given this last precious opportunity? Think about it. What would *you* say, if you knew that five minutes from now, lethal chemicals would be injected into your bloodstream and your voice would be forever silenced? What final message would you leave behind? Here is what some executed persons, from long ago up until the present, chose to say with their last words:

"That is false. I have always served my king loyally and sought to add to his domains." Vasco Nunez de Balboa, the discoverer of the Pacific Ocean, before he was beheaded as a traitor, based on bogus evidence, in 1519.

"The executioner is, I believe, very expert, and my neck is very slender. O God, have pity on my soul. O God, have pity on my soul." Anne Boleyn, second wife of Henry VIII, as she was about to be beheaded for alleged adultery in 1536.

"This is a sharp medicine, but it is a physician for all diseases." Sir Walter Raleigh, as he touched the blade of the axe with which he would be beheaded for treason on October 29, 1618.

"This is a very fickle and faithless generation." Captain William Kidd, sea captain and pirate, before his hanging in England in 1701. He had been promised a pardon if he surrendered.

"I did not think they would put a young gentleman to death for such a trifle." Jean François le Fevre, Chevalier de la Barre, about to be executed for having mutilated a crucifix in France in 1766. He was 19.

"Farewell, my children, forever; I am going to be with your father." Marie Antoinette, queen of France, at her execution on October 16, 1793.

"Be sure you show my head to the mob. It will be a long time ere they see its like." Georges Jacques Danton, leader of the French Revolution, to his own executioner as he faced the guillotine on April 5, 1794.

"Nothing succeeds with me. Even here I meet with disappointment." Michael Bestuzhev-Ryumin, Russian democratic revolutionary condemned to death for plotting against Emperor Nicholas I in 1825, when the first rope broke at his hanging.

"I hope you will not keep me waiting any longer than necessary." John Brown, the abolitionist, as he was about to be hanged on December 2, 1859, for leading the raid on Harpers Ferry.

"Don't draw it too tight. I can't breathe. . . Long live Anarchy. . . This is the happiest moment of my life." Adlof Fischer, an instigator of the Haymarket Square riot in Chicago, at his hanging in 1886.

My Dream
I dreamt I was in Heaven
Among the Angels fair;
I'd never seen none so handsome
That twine in golden hair.
They looked so neat and sang so swell
And played the Golden Harp.
I was about to pick an angel out
And take her to my heart;
But the moment I began to plea,
I thought of you, my love.
There was none I'd seen so beautiful
On earth or Heaven above.
Good bye, my dear wife and Mother
Also my sister.

Rufus Buck, a young outlaw of Oklahoma Territory, wrote this poem, in which the spelling and punctuation have been corrected, on the back of a picture of his mother the day before he was hanged in Fort Smith, Arkansas, on July 1, 1896. Buck, who was mixed black and Creek Indian, led a gang on a two-week rampage of murder, rape, and robbery in 1895.

"Oh, Father, forgive them, for they know not what they do! Father, forgive me—oh, Father, forgive me! Father, forgive them, Father, oh Father, forgive them!" Ruth Snyder, sitting in the electric chair at Sing Sing, January 12, 1927, about to be electrocuted for murdering her husband.

"Beautiful world." Charlie Birger, looking out from the gallows before he was hanged, April 19, 1928, in Benton, Illinois.

"Yes, hurry it up, you Hoosier bastard! I could hang a dozen men while you're fooling around." Carl Panzram, who claimed to have killed at least 23 people and committed hundreds of homosexual rapes, robberies, and burglaries all over the world, when asked by the hangman at Leavenworth if he had anything to say, September 5, 1930. In the letter to the Society for the Abolition of Capital Punishment, dated May 23, 1930, Panzram had written, "The only thanks you or your kind will ever get from me for your efforts on my behalf is that I wish you all had one neck and that I had my hands on it."

"It's kind of funny—dying. I think I know what it will be like. I'll be standing there, and all of a sudden everything will be black, then there'll be a light again. There's got to be a light again—there's got to be." Arthur Gooch, the night before he was hanged in the Oklahoma State Penitentiary on June 19, 1936, the first person executed for kidnapping under the Lindbergh Law.

"I don't want to have to look at people." Barbara Graham, asking for a blindfold before entering California's gas chamber on June 3, 1955.

"Hell no! No one ever did anything for me. Why in the hell should I do anything for anyone else?" Charles Starkweather, when asked before his electrocution on June 25, 1959, if he wanted to donate his eyes to the Lions Club eye bank.

"Take it easy . . . It's all right . . . Tell Rosalie goodbye. . . ." Caryl Chessman, the "Red Light Bandit," as the cyanide pellets dropped in California's gas chamber, May 2, 1960. Chessman was executed for kidnapping, not murder.

"I'd kill your mother, your father, or your daughter. I love to kill. So you'll be doing society one of the best jobs you ever did." James D. French, to his executioner, as French was about to be electrocuted in Oklahoma for strangling his cellmate while serving a life sentence for murder, August 10, 1966.

"Let's do it!" Gary Gilmore, Utah, January 17, 1977, before he was executed by firing squad in Utah, resuming executions in the United States after a 10-year layoff.

"This is just one more step down the road of life that I've been heading all my life. Let's go." Jesse Bishop, as he stepped into the gas chamber in Nevada, October 22, 1978.

"Well, the Lord is going to get another one." John Eldon Smith, Georgia, December 15, 1983.

"My final words are—I am innocent." James Dupree Henry, Florida, September 20, 1984.

"I'm ready for the rocket to take off." Ramon Hernandez, January 30, 1987, as he jumped onto the lethal injection gurney in Texas.

"I love you." Sean Flanagan, Nevada, June 23, 1989. Remarks directed to the prosecutor.

"You can be a king or a street sweeper, but everybody dances with the Grim Reaper." Robert Alton Harris, California, April 12, 1992.

"I'm going home, babe. . . . The rest of you can kiss my ass." James Allen Red Dog, Delaware, March 3, 1993.

"I am an African warrior, born to breathe, born to die." Carl Kelly, Texas, August 20, 1993.

"Adios." John Thanos, Maryland, May 16, 1994.

"I'm human! I'm human!" David Lawson, North Carolina, June 15, 1994, screamed while strapped in the gas chamber, fruitlessly fighting the deadly fumes.

"I have news for you. There's not going to be an execution. This is premeditated murder." Jessie DeWayne Jacobs, Texas, January 4, 1995.

"Governor Tucker, look over your shoulder; justice is coming. I wouldn't trade places with you or any of your cronies. Hell has victories. I am at peace." Richard Wayne Snell, Arkansas, January 19, 1995.

"I love you, Mom. Goodbye. Goodbye, Mom." Jeffery Dean Motley, Texas, February 7, 1995.

"I think it's best for me to just say nothing at all." Karl Hammond, Texas, June 21, 1995.

"I hope you can go on with your lives and we can put an end to this." Kenneth Harris, Texas, June 3, 1997, addressing Vicki Haack, the sister of the woman he was condemned for raping and murdering, from the lethal injection table.

"Don't let it hurt me; pray for me." Jesse James Ferguson, executed June 9, 1961, for the rape and murder of an 11-year-old Opelousas girl. He was last man executed in Louisiana until 1983.

Twenty-five men have been executed in Louisiana in the 15 years since capital punishment resumed in 1983. Here are the final statements of each of these men.

Robert Wayne Williams was executed on December 14, 1983, for killing 67-year-old Willie Kelly, a security guard at a Baton Rouge supermarket during a robbery on January 5, 1979. Williams maintained that the shotgun he was using in the robbery discharged accidentally, striking Kelly in the face. Williams's last words were, "I told the truth about what happened. I would like it to be a remembrance for Louisiana and the whole country that would be a deterrence against capital punishment and show that capital punishment is no good and never has been good. I would like all the people who have fought capital punishment to keep on fighting—not just for me but for everybody."

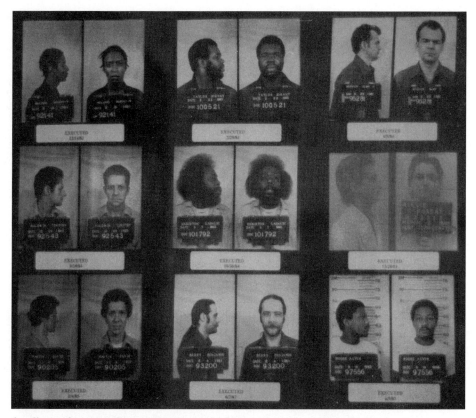

A gallery of prison photos showing the 25 men executed at Angola from 1983 to 1999. (Copyright: Chris De Lay.)

Johnny Taylor, Jr., was executed on February 29, 1984, for stabbing to death David Vogler, Jr., on February 8, 1980, when stealing a car. Vogler was attempting to sell his wife's car, left in a Kenner parking lot with a "For Sale" sign in the window. Taylor called to arrange a meeting with Vogler in the parking lot. Vogler's body was found in the trunk of his own car the next day. Taylor was found driving Mrs. Vogler's car in Alabama four months later. Taylor's last words were, "I've done a lot of wrong, caused a lot of hurt. I guess this is the price I pay for it. I found God in Christ. I made a commitment with him. I'm ready to see this through. There are those out there who need help. I wish in some way you could all contribute to helping them. Living has been hard for me and it's time for me to die, for whatever reason. . . . I hope you will not leave with the sense this is going to deter crime. That's it, let's go."

A gallery of prison photos showing the 25 men executed at Angola from 1983 to 1999. (Copyright: Chris De Lay.)

Elmo Patrick Sonnier was executed on April 5, 1984. Sonnier was convicted, along with his brother, Eddie, in the murders of teenagers Loretta Bourque and David LeBlanc in a field in Iberia Parish on November 5, 1977. Both Sonnier brothers also raped Bourque. Eddie Sonnier was also given a death sentence for the crimes, but his sentence was commuted to life by the Louisiana Supreme Court, which ruled that he did not commit the killings. Although Eddie Sonnier later claimed that he had done the murders, the courts and the governor let Pat Sonnier's death sentence stand. Pat Sonnier was one of the two death row inmates featured in the book version of Sister Helen Prejean's *Dead Man Walking*. Sonnier's last words, addressed to Lloyd LeBlanc, the father of one victim, and to Sister Helen Prejean, were, "Mr. LeBlanc, I can understand the way you feel. I have no hatred in my heart, and as I leave this world, I ask God to forgive what . . . I have done.

I ask you to have forgiveness" [at which Mr. LeBlanc nodded and said, "Yes"]. "I love you" [directed to Sister Helen].

Timothy George Baldwin was executed on September 10, 1984, for beating to death an 85-year-old blind woman, Mary James Peters, during the robbery of her West Monroe home on April 4, 1978. Peters, who was a former neighbor of Baldwin's and the godmother of his youngest child, was beaten with a skillet, a stool, a small television set, and a telephone. Baldwin, who maintained his innocence, gave this final statement: "I've always tried to be a good sport when I've lost at something, and I see no reason not to leave this world with the same policy. After all, it was a hell of a battle. I therefore congratulate all those who have tried so hard to murder me. I definitely have to give them credit, as it takes a very special kind of person to murder an innocent man and still be able to live with themselves."

Earnest Knighton, Jr., was executed on October 30, 1984, for shooting to death Ralph Shell, a Bossier City service station proprietor, during an attempted robbery on March 17, 1981. Knighton's last words were, "I am sorry, more sorry than I can say Mr. Shell is dead and that I'm responsible. I feel sorry for Mrs. Shell and all of Mr. Shell's family and friends. I feel sorry for my mother, my family, and everyone else who will grieve for me. I have asked God to forgive me. . . . I have to say that what you are doing is wrong. If I thought my death would bring back Mr. Shell or would save someone else from a murder, I would volunteer, but I know it won't. You don't teach respect for life by killing. I urge you not to kill anyone else. I ask God to forgive you for killing me. I now ask God in the name of Jesus to receive my spirit."

Robert Lee Willie was executed on December 28, 1984, for the rape and murder of Faith Hathaway which occurred in an area south of Franklinton on May 28, 1980. Hathaway was raped by both Willie and his codefendant, Joseph J. Vaccaro, and then stabbed to death; each man said the other did it. Willie was convicted of other violent crimes, including kidnapping and rape, and said that he had committed other murders as well. He was also featured in Sister Helen Prejean's *Dead Man Walking*. Willie's last words were addressed to the parents of the Faith Hathaway, Vernon and Elizabeth Harvey, who became known as Louisiana's most ardent supporters of the death penalty: "I would just like to say, Mr. and Mrs. Harvey, that I hope you get some relief from my death. Killing people is wrong. That's why you've put me to death. It makes no difference whether it's citizens, countries, or governments, killing is wrong." When the hood was placed over his head, Willie asked that it be removed, and he winked at Sister Helen, who was present as his spiritual advisor. Then the hood was replaced.

David Dene Martin was executed on January 4, 1985, for a quadruple murder committed on August 14, 1977. The victims, Bobby Todd, Terry Hebert, Anne Tierney, and Sandra Brake, were shot to death in Todd's mobile home near Houma. Martin's wife had told him she was having an affair with Todd; the other three victims were strangers who just happened to be present when Martin burst in and began shooting. Martin, who was an active Seventh-Day Adventist and an even more active drug addict, made no final statement at his execution. But at a pardon board clemency hearing the afternoon before his death, Martin had said, "To take someone's life is out of character for me. It is not David Martin. I am devastated at what I have done, but I can't remember it. My life has been dedicated to saving lives, helping people, not destroying people. I know I wouldn't willfully take another person's life. Something bad went down. But it wasn't David Martin. I wasn't right. I don't know. I don't know. That's all."

Benjamin Berry was executed on June 7, 1987, for the fatal shooting of Robert Cochran, an off-duty Jefferson Parish sheriff's deputy working as a bank guard, during a bank robbery attempt on January 30, 1978. Berry made no final statement.

Alvin R. Moore was executed on June 9, 1987, for raping, robbing, and stabbing to death Jo Ann Wilson, a former neighbor, at her Bossier City home on July 9, 1980. Moore made no final statement to the public; his attorney said his last words to him were, "They can kill my body, but not my soul."

Jimmy L. Glass was executed on June 12, 1987, for shooting to death Newton and Erline Brown while burglarizing their Dixie Inn home on Christmas Day, 1982. Glass and Jimmy Wingo had escaped from the Webster Parish Jail the day before. Glass claimed that Wingo forced him at gunpoint to kill the Browns. Glass's last words were, "I'd rather be fishing."

Jimmy Wingo was executed four days later, on June 16, 1987. Although Wingo and Glass had escaped from jail together, Wingo's story was that he was not even present when Glass killed the Browns. Wingo's final statement was, "I am an innocent man. You are murdering me this day. I do still love you all in Christ. God bless you all."

Willie Celestine was executed on July 20, 1987, for raping and strangling 81-year-old Marcelianne Richard in her Lafayette home on September 13, 1981. He had also been convicted of raping two other elderly women in the same neighborhood. Celestine's final statement was, "I'd just like to tell the Richard family that I'm very, very sorry. I hope in their hearts they can forgive."

Willie Watson was executed on July 24, 1987, for the kidnapping, rape, and murder of Kathy Newman, a Tulane University medical student, in St. Charles Parish on April 5, 1981. When asked if he had any last words, Watson calmly shook his head, "No." Sitting in the electric chair, Watson mouthed the words, "I love you," to his spiritual adviser, Sister Leigh Scardina, through the witness room window.

John E. Brogdon was executed on July 30, 1987. Brogdon and his codefendant Bruce Perritt were convicted of raping, beating, and stabbing to death 11-year-old Barbara Jo Brown behind a levee near Luling on October 7, 1981. Perritt received a life sentence when the jury deadlocked in the penalty phase. Brogdon made no formal final statement. As he turned to seat himself in the electric chair, his last words were, "God bless y'all."

Sterling J. Rault, Jr., was executed on August 24, 1987, for raping, stabbing, shooting, and burning the body of Jane Ellen Francioni, a 21-year-old secretary who worked in the same gas company where he worked as an accountant, on March 1, 1981, in New Orleans. Rault had given several varying, bizarre confessions to the crime. Rault's final statement was, "I would like the public to know that they are killing an innocent man at this time. I pray that God will forgive all those involved in this matter. I, personally, do not hold any animosity towards anyone, though. This country professes to be 'One nation under God,' but the death penalty goes against the word of God. Jesus Christ died on the cross in order that all people would have mercy and we need to start giving that mercy to our fellow man. Into the arms of love of God I now go. I love you all. May God bless you all."

Wayne Robert Felde was executed on March 15, 1988, for shooting Shreveport police officer Thomas Glenn Tompkins on October 20, 1978. Felde was a Vietnam veteran and prison escapee from Maryland who had been arrested on a drunkenness complaint. Shreveport police had tried to get a cabdriver to take Felde home, but the cabbie refused. When police searched

Felde, they missed a loaded gun in his waistband. In the back of the police car, Felde pulled the gun and began shooting aimlessly. One of the five rounds fired ricocheted off a spring in the passenger seat and struck Tompkins in the right leg, severing an artery. Tompkins bled to death. Felde was critically wounded by police shotgun blasts when he was captured minutes later.

At trial, Felde's defense was based on post-traumatic stress syndrome occurring as a result of his military service in Vietnam. When the jury returned a verdict of guilty to first-degree murder, Felde took the stand to ask the jury to sentence him to death. His final words were, "You can kill the messenger, but you can't kill the message."

Leslie Lowenfield was executed on April 13, 1988. Lowenfield killed five people—his former girlfriend, Jefferson Parish Sheriff's Deputy Sheila Thomas, her four-year-old daughter, Shantel Osborne, the girl's father, Carl Osborne, and Thomas's mother and stepfather, Myrtle and Owen Griffin—in Marrero on August 30, 1982. The jury gave him three consecutive death sentences and two manslaughter sentences. Lowenfield claimed to be in Florida at the time of the killings. His final statement included remarks directed at two attorneys, Wayne Walker and John Craft, who had worked on his trial and appeal. Lowenfield's last words were, "I hope you all feel satisfied. Don't give up on me although my life will be over tonight, because the one responsible is out there. There is no reason to hold anything against me and the rest who would lie. When I'm gone, the body will be gone, but the spirit will live on. Mr. Walker and John Craft, your job was more important than my life. I hope you feel satisfied. Thank all of you all. Peace!"

Edward R. Byrne, Jr., was executed June 14, 1988, for the murder of Roberta Johnson, a Bossier City service station cashier, during an August 14, 1984, robbery. Byrne had previously dated Johnson. He beat her on the head and upper body with a ballpeen hammer, then robbed her of $7,000. Byrne made no final public statement. He told the pardon board, the day before his execution, "I don't know exactly what it is that I can say to y'all. I was planning to rob this woman all along. It was all set up. There were no flaws that I could see. I just attempted to knock her unconscious. It didn't work. She didn't become unconscious. I just kept hitting her until she did."

Dalton Prejean was executed on May 18, 1990, for shooting Louisiana State Police Trooper Donald Cleveland outside Lafayette on July 2, 1977. Prejean, who was 17 at the time, had already served juvenile time for killing a Lafayette cabdriver at age 14. Prejean's final statement, addressed to his supporters and the family of Trooper Cleveland, was, "Nothing is going to be accomplished. I have peace with myself. I'd like to thank all of those who supported me all these years. I'd also like to thank my loved ones for being strong. . . . My son will be a better person for not letting something like this bring down his life. . . . Keep strong, keep pushing, keep praying. They said it wasn't for the revenge, but it's hard for me to see, to understand. I hope they're happy. So I forfeit my life. I give my love to all. God bless."

Andrew Lee Jones was executed on July 22, 1991 for the kidnapping, raping, and strangling of Tumekica Michelle Jackson, his former girlfriend's 11-year-old daughter, in Baton Rouge on February 18, 1984. Jones was the last man electrocuted in Louisiana before the state switched to lethal injection. Jones made no final public statement at his execution. Speaking at a pardon board hearing three days before he was executed, he said, "There's a possible chance I did it, a possible chance I didn't do it. If I had not been drunk, nothing like that would have happened. I'm like anybody else. . . I don't want to die or anything like that."

Robert Wayne Sawyer was executed on March 5, 1993 for the rape, beating, burning, and mutilation of babysitter Frances Arwood in Gretna on September 28, 1979. Sawyer's codefendant, Charles Lane, received a life sentence. Sawyer was the first man lethally injected in Louisiana. Sawyer's final statement was, "I would like to tell young kids who might read this, that drinking and hanging with the wrong people will get you where I am sitting right here and I hope that nobody else ever has to go through what I have gone through, especially young kids. I'm sorry for any hurt and pain they say I caused. I have no hard feelings toward anyone. I just want my sister, my brother-in-law, my son, all of my family and friends to know that I love them and I'll be waiting on them in heaven."

Thomas L. Ward was executed on May 16, 1995 for killing Wilbert John Spencer, his wife's stepfather, in New Orleans on June 23, 1983. He also shot Lydia Spencer, his wife's mother. Ward's trial featured testimony that he had sexually abused many children, including the woman who later married him and his own 10-year-old daughter. Ward declined to make a formal statement in the room before he was executed, but he dictated these last words to his attorney: "I am leaving the world at peace with myself and with the Almighty. I feel remorse for the things that I did. I hope that young people today will learn that violence is not an answer. I hope the legal system learns that lesson, too. The death penalty is not a solution."

Antonio G. James was executed on March 1, 1996, for the robbery and murder of Henry Silver on January 1, 1979, in New Orleans. James had also been sentenced to life for the January 23, 1979, murder of Alvan Adams during another robbery and to 99 years for still another armed robbery. His case was documented in the ABC News program "Judgment at Midnight." When James was brought into the execution chamber, he declined a final statement, saying, "I don't want to say anything." Warden Burl Cain, who was holding James's left hand when James was put to death, said James's final words to him were, "Bless you."

John A. Brown, Jr., was executed on April 24, 1997, for the stabbing death of Omer Laughlin in a robbery attempt outside a New Orleans restaurant on September 7, 1984. Brown's final statement was, "Let my baby sister know I love her and the rest of my family, for supporting me. I love you very much. I'm ready to go now." As he felt the lethal drugs enter his system, Brown's last word was, "Wow!"

Dobie Gillis Williams was executed on January 8, 1999, for stabbing to death Sonja Knippers in her home in Many on July 9, 1984. Williams was on a prison furlough from a burglary sentence when he broke into the home. He maintained his innocence to the end. His last words were, "I just want to say, I don't have any hard feelings against anybody. God bless ya'll. God bless."

You have had a few minutes to think. Quickly, the witnesses are waiting. Any last words?

Contributors

Victor L. Streib is dean and professor of law at the Ohio Northern University College of Law. He is also an attorney working exclusively on death penalty cases. His scholarly publications, particularly those on the death penalty for juveniles and for women, have established him as a leading death penalty authority, and he has testified on such issues before committees of the U.S. Congress and of seven state legislatures. As an attorney, he has represented death-sentenced juvenile offenders before the U.S. Supreme Court and several state supreme courts, as well as having served as an expert witness. His media appearances include *60 Minutes, Larry King Live, All Things Considered, Time, Newsweek, The Wall Street Journal,* and the *New York Times.*

Craig J. Forsyth is professor of sociology at the University of Louisiana–Lafayette, where he has been on the faculty for 16 years. A former merchant seaman, he received his B.A. and M.A. from the University of New Orleans and his Ph.D. from Louisiana State University. A nationally known scholar in topics related to criminology and deviant behavior, Dr. Forsyth was recognized as a Distinguished Research Professor at UL-Lafayette in 1991. Dr. Forsyth is editor of the journal *Deviant Behavior.* In the past decade, he has worked as a mitigation expert in capital murder cases across Louisiana.

Watt Espy is America's foremost death penalty historian. A former salesman and librarian, he is the founder of the Capital Punishment Research Project, headquartered in Headland, Alabama. He has documented almost 20,000 legal executions in America since colonial times.

Leslie Martin is an inmate on death row at the Louisiana State Penitentiary at Angola. He is 32 years old and is from DeQuincy, Louisiana. He was convicted of a first-degree murder that was committed in Calcasieu Parish, Louisiana, in 1991.

Lawson Strickland is also an inmate on death row at Angola. He was sentenced to death in 1993 for a robbery and murder that took place in Leesville, Louisiana, in 1992. Strickland is from Leesville and was an escapee from the Vernon Parish Prison at the time the crime was committed.

James C. McCloskey is the founder of Centurion Ministries in Princeton, New Jersey, an organization that works to free defendants wrongfully imprisoned. After a career as a businessman and management consultant, Mr. McCloskey graduated from Princeton Theological Seminary and became an ordained minister. His organization now investigates possible wrongful capital convictions across the United States. Since 1983 his work has resulted in the exoneration of 21 men and women, and early parole for 6 others.

David E. Marcantel practices both civil and criminal law in Jennings, Louisiana. He has been in private practice for more than 20 years and more recently has represented indigent felony defendants as counsel appointed through the parish indigent defender's office.

Lane Nelson is a first offender who has served more than 18 years on a life sentence for second-degree murder. He is originally from California. Nelson is confined at the Louisiana State Penitentiary at Angola, where he writes for the prison magazine, *The Angolite.* In his free time he pursues college correspondence courses, freelance writing, and participates in the prison hospice program as a volunteer caregiver.

Burk Foster is associate professor of criminal justice at the University of Louisiana–Lafayette, where he has been a faculty member for 26 years. Originally from Oklahoma, he is a former police officer and U.S. Air Force security police officer. He is recognized as an expert witness in state and federal courts, and he has testified as an expert on the subjects of imprisonment and clemency in death penalty cases in Louisiana. He is a contributing editor of *The Angolite* magazine and a member of the Louisiana State Penitentiary Museum Foundation board of directors.

Bibliography

Chapter 1: Why Death Is Different: Capital Punishment in the Legal System

BROWNLEE, SHANNON, DAN MCGRAW, AND JASON VEST. "The Place for Vengeance." *U.S. News and World Report,* June 16, 1997, pp. 25–32.

COKER V. GEORGIA, 433 U.S. 584, 97 S.Ct. 2861, 53 L.Ed. 2d 982 (1977).

DAVIS, MICHAEL D., AND HUNTER R. CLARK. *Thurgood Marshall: Warrior at the Bar, Rebel on the Bench.* New York: Citadel Press, 1994.

EGELKO, BOB. "Death Row Only for Poor People, Experts Conclude." *Baton Rouge Advocate,* September 6, 1994.

FORD V. WAINWRIGHT, 477 U.S. 399, 106 S.Ct. 2595, 91 L.Ed. 2d 335 (1986).

FOSTER, BURK, AND CRAIG J. FORSYTH. "Meanest of All." *The Angolite,* July/August 1994, pp. 26–31.

FURMAN V. GEORGIA, 408 U.S. 238, 92 S.Ct. 2726, 33 L.Ed. 2d 346 (1972).

GREGG V. GEORGIA, 428 U.S. 153, 96 S.Ct. 2909, 49 L.Ed. 2d 859 (1976).

LEWIN, TAMAR. "Who Decides Who Will Die? Even Within States, It Varies." *New York Times,* February 23, 1995, p. A1+.

LOCKETT V. OHIO, 438 U.S. 586, 98 S.Ct. 2954, 57 L.Ed. 2d 973 (1978).

PAYNE V. TENNESSEE, 501 U.S. 808, 111 S.Ct. 2597, 115 L.Ed. 2d 720 (1991).

SNELL, TRACY L. "Capital Punishment 1996." U.S. Department of Justice, Bureau of Justice Statistics Bulletin. Washington, DC: U.S. Government Printing Office, 1997.

WOODSON V. NORTH CAROLINA, 428 U.S. 280, 96 S.Ct. 2978, 49 L.Ed. 2d 944 (1976).

Chapter 12: A Practice in Search of an Ethic: The Death Penalty in the Contemporary South

COHEN, DOV. "Law, Social Policy, and Violence: The Impact of Regional Cultures." *Journal of Personality and Social Psychology* LXX, 1996, pp. 961–978.

DENNIS, DOUGLAS. "Victimhood." *The Angolite,* May/June 1995, pp. 4–5.

ELLSWORTH, PHOEBE C., AND SAMUEL L. GROSS. "Hardening of the Attitudes: Americans' Views on the Death Penalty." *Journal of Social Issues* L, 1994, pp. 19–52.

FOSTER, BURK. "Executed Rapists." *The Angolite,* September/October 1996, pp. 36–47.

FOSTER, BURK, AND MICHAEL NEUSTROM. "Ups and Downs of Murder: A 20-Year Study of State Homicide Rates." *The Angolite,* March/April 1996, pp. 28–35.

HACKNEY, SHELDON. "Southern Violence." *American Historical Review* LXXIV, 1969, pp. 906–925.

HOFFMAN, FREDERICK L. "Murder and the Death Penalty." *Current History,* June 1928, pp. 408–410.

KINDER, D. R., AND D. O. SEARS. "Prejudice and Politics: Symbolic Racism Versus Racial Threats to the Good Life." *Journal of Personality and Social Psychology* XL, 1981, pp. 414–431.

KROLL, MICHAEL. "Chattahoochee Judicial District: Buckle of the Death Belt." Death Penalty Information Center, 1991.

"MOVING BACKWARD." *The Nation,* May 1, 1929, p. 524.

SNELL, TRACY L. "Capital Punishment 1997." U.S. Department of Justice, Bureau of Justice Statistics Bulletin. Washington, D.C.: U.S. Government Printing Office, 1998.

Chapter 14: The Executed Warden

CHIPMAN, N. P. *The Tragedy of Andersonville.* Blair-Murdock Co., 1911.

DENNEY, ROBERT. *Civil War Prisons and Escapes: A Day-by-Day Chronicle.* Sterling, 1995.

FUTCH, OVID L. *History of Andersonville Prison.* Gainesville, FL: University Press of Florida, 1968.

RANSOM, JOHN L. *John Ransom's Andersonville Diary: Life Inside the Civil War's Most Infamous Prison.* Berkley Publishing Group, 1994.

SEGARS, J. H. *Andersonville: The Southern Perspective* (Journal of Confederate History Series, V. 13). Southern Heritage Press, 1995.

Chapter 16: Struck by Lightning: Electrocutions for Rape in Louisiana in the 1940s and 1950s.

BOWERS, WILLIAM J. *Executions in America.* Lexington, MA: D. C. Heath and Co., 1974.

NATIONAL ASSOCIATION FOR THE ADVANCEMENT OF COLORED PEOPLE. *Thirty Years of Lynching in the United States.* New York: Negro Universities Press, 1969.

NEWTON, MICHAEL, AND JUDY ANN NEWTON. *Racial and Religious Violence in America: A Chronology.* New York: Garland Publishing Co., 1991.

RISE, ERIC W. "Race, Rape, and Radicalism: The Case of the Martinsville Seven, 1949–1951." *Journal of Southern History* LVIII (3) August 1992, pp. 461–490.

SELLIN, THORSTEN. *Capital Punishment.* New York: Harper and Row, 1967.

SHAY, FRANK. *Judge Lynch: His First Hundred Years.* New York: Ives Washburn, Inc., 1938.

WOLFGANG, MARVIN E. "Racial Discrimination in the Death Sentence for Rape." In Bowers, *Executions in America.* Lexington, MA: D. C. Heath and Co., 1974.

Index